SNAKEPIT 2009
BY BEN SNAKEPIT

DISTRIBUTED IN THE BOOK TRADE BY TONY SHENTON
SHENTON4SALES@AOL.COM

FIRST EDITION, 2000 COPIES

ISBN 978-0-9826595-0-2
ISSN 2153-4128

BIRDCAGE BOTTOM BOOKS

WWW.BIRDCAGEBOTTOMBOOKS.COM
INFO@BIRDCAGEBOTTOMBOOKS.COM

CONTACT BEN SNAKEPIT AT:
P.O. BOX 4944 ATX 78765
OR BENSNAKEPIT@GMAIL.COM

SNAKEPIT IS, WAS, AND EVER SHALL BE
INTENDED TO BE READ ON THE TOILET.

PRINTED IN CANADA

HELLO AGAIN, FRIENDS!

WELL IF 2008 SEEMED LIKE I WAS GETTING OLD AND SELLING OUT, WAIT TIL YOU READ THIS ONE! THE WORLD IS A VERY DIFFERENT PLACE THAN IT WAS IN 2000, WHEN I STARTED DRAWING SNAKE PIT. BACK THEN, THE INTERNET WAS STILL JUST FOR NERDS, AND ONLY A HANDFUL OF PEOPLE WERE DOING D.I.Y. DAILY DIARY COMICS. SKIP AHEAD TEN YEARS, AND EVERYONE AND THEIR MOTHER HAS A MYSPACE AND A FACEBOOK AND A TWITTER AND A BLOGSPOT, AND THE IDEA OF RECORDING AND SHARING WHAT I DID EVERY DAY IN THREE PANELS DOESN'T SEEM LIKE SUCH A GOOD IDEA ANYMORE. OF COURSE, I'M A VERY DIFFERENT PERSON THAN I WAS BACK THEN AS WELL. I'M OLDER, FATTER, LAZIER, AND I GIVE LESS OF A SHIT ABOUT EVERYTHING. I THINK IT HAPPENS TO EVERYONE, ON SOME LEVEL. YOU'LL PROBABLY READ A FEW HINTS IN THIS BOOK ALLUDING TO A FINITE END FOR SNAKEPIT. THIS MAY OR MAY NOT HAPPEN, BUT THERE'S NO NEED TO DWELL ON THE FUTURE. AS THE OLD SAYING GOES, "IF YOU WORRY ABOUT WHAT MIGHT BE, AND WONDER WHAT MIGHT HAVE BEEN, YOU WILL IGNORE WHAT IS." WITH THAT IN MIND, I PRESENT TO YOU *YET ANOTHER* YEAR OF KINDA BORING COMICS.

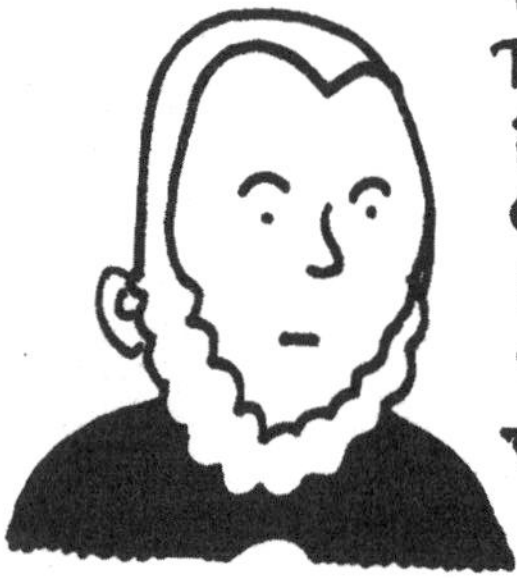

"ENJOY."

♥ Ben

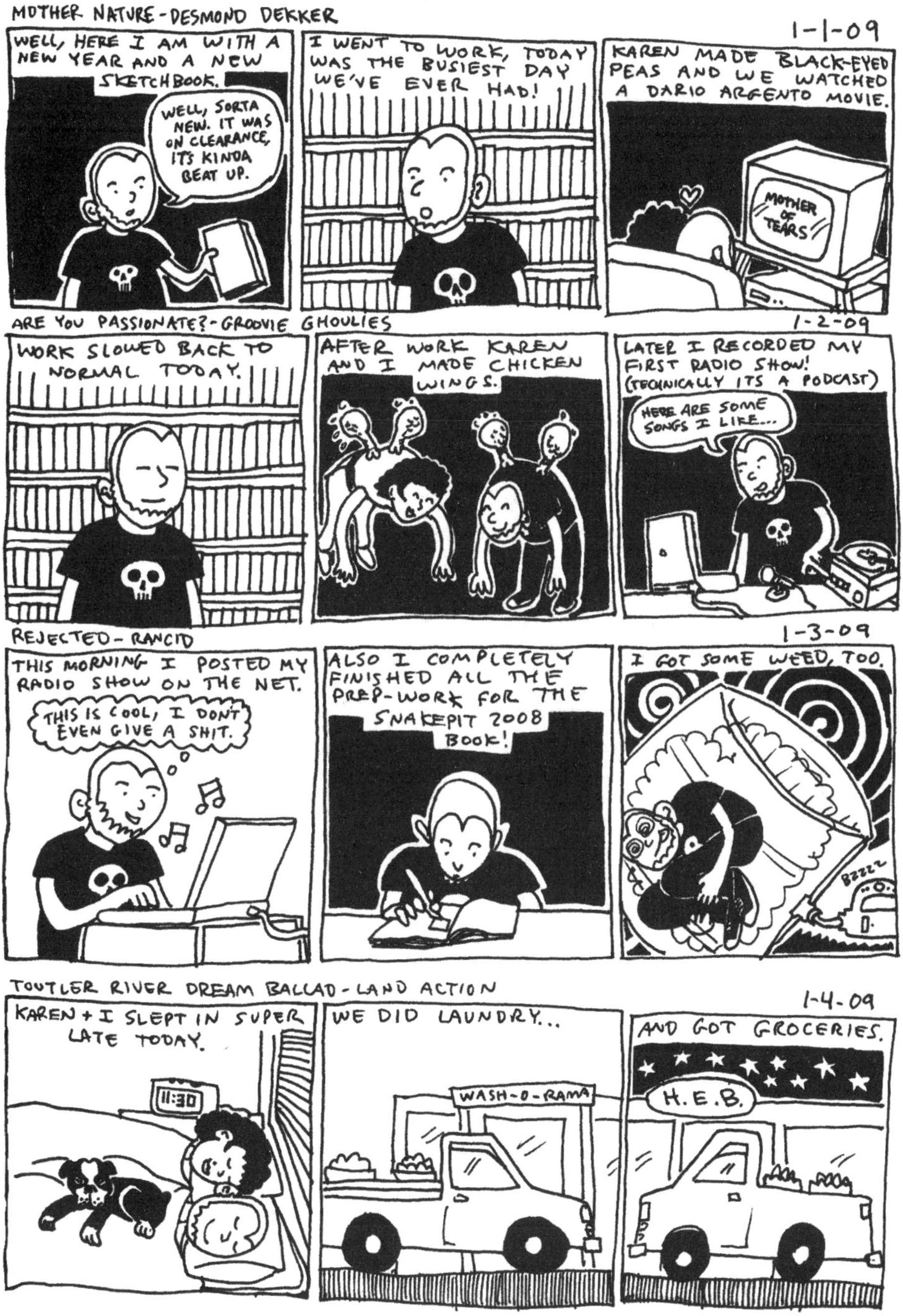
MOTHER NATURE - DESMOND DEKKER
1-1-09
WELL, HERE I AM WITH A NEW YEAR AND A NEW SKETCHBOOK.
WELL, SORTA NEW. IT WAS ON CLEARANCE, IT'S KINDA BEAT UP.
I WENT TO WORK, TODAY WAS THE BUSIEST DAY WE'VE EVER HAD!
KAREN MADE BLACK-EYED PEAS AND WE WATCHED A DARIO ARGENTO MOVIE.
MOTHER OF TEARS
ARE YOU PASSIONATE? - GROOVIE GHOULIES
1-2-09
WORK SLOWED BACK TO NORMAL TODAY.
AFTER WORK KAREN AND I MADE CHICKEN WINGS.
LATER I RECORDED MY FIRST RADIO SHOW! (TECHNICALLY ITS A PODCAST)
HERE ARE SOME SONGS I LIKE....
REJECTED - RANCID
1-3-09
THIS MORNING I POSTED MY RADIO SHOW ON THE NET.
THIS IS COOL, I DON'T EVEN GIVE A SHIT.
ALSO I COMPLETELY FINISHED ALL THE PREP-WORK FOR THE SNAKEPIT 2008 BOOK!
I GOT SOME WEED, TOO.
BZZZZ
TOUTLER RIVER DREAM BALLAD - LAND ACTION
1-4-09
KAREN + I SLEPT IN SUPER LATE TODAY.
11:30
WE DID LAUNDRY...
WASH-O-RAMA
AND GOT GROCERIES.
H.E.B.

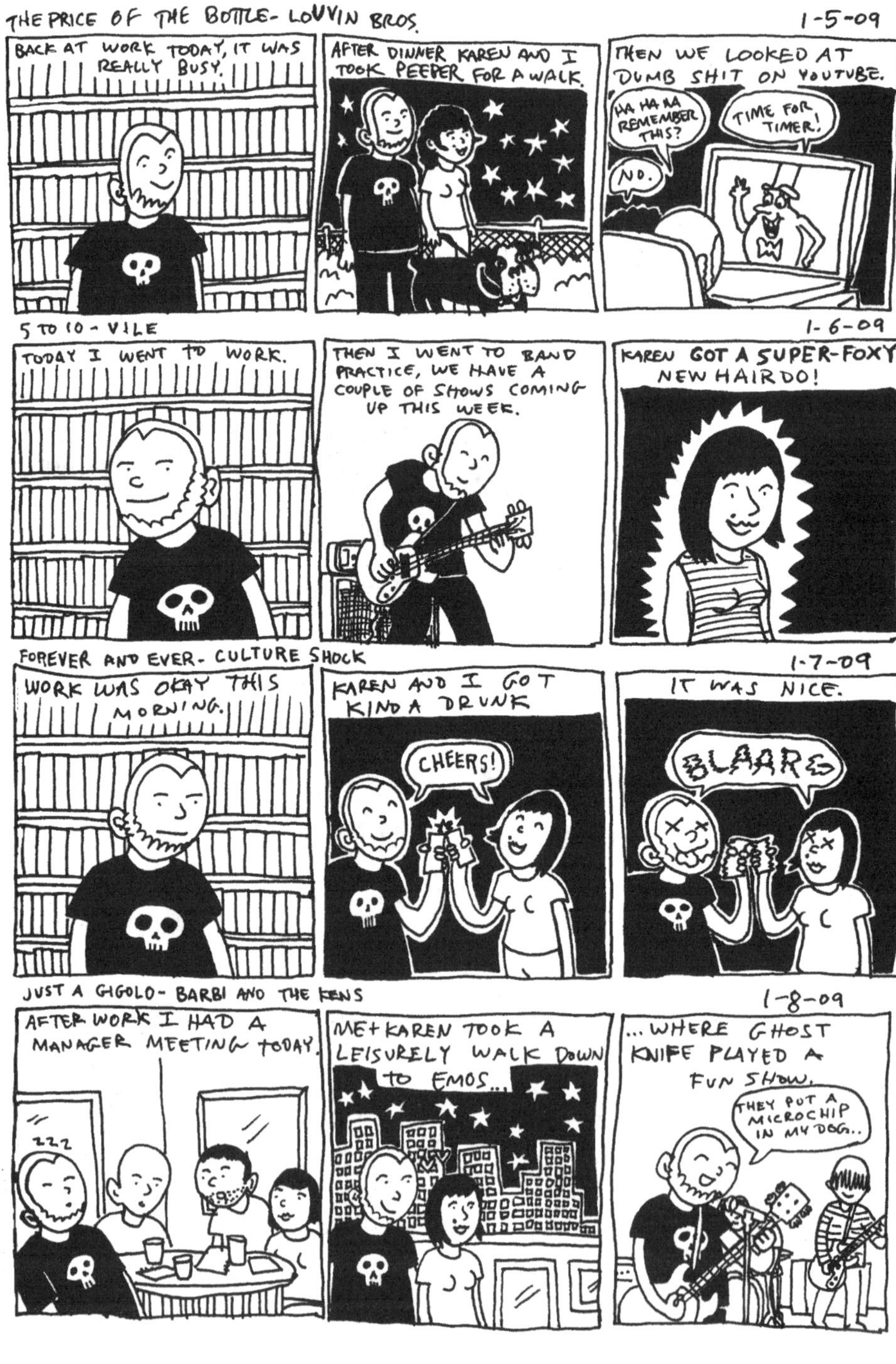
THE PRICE OF THE BOTTLE - LOUVIN BROS.
1-5-09
BACK AT WORK TODAY, IT WAS REALLY BUSY.
AFTER DINNER KAREN AND I TOOK PEEPER FOR A WALK.
THEN WE LOOKED AT DUMB SHIT ON YOUTUBE.
HA HA HA REMEMBER THIS?
NO.
TIME FOR TIMER!
5 TO 10 - VILE
1-6-09
TODAY I WENT TO WORK.
THEN I WENT TO BAND PRACTICE, WE HAVE A COUPLE OF SHOWS COMING UP THIS WEEK.
KAREN GOT A SUPER-FOXY NEW HAIRDO!
FOREVER AND EVER - CULTURE SHOCK
1-7-09
WORK WAS OKAY THIS MORNING.
KAREN AND I GOT KINDA DRUNK
CHEERS!
IT WAS NICE.
BLAARG
JUST A GIGOLO - BARBI AND THE KENS
1-8-09
AFTER WORK I HAD A MANAGER MEETING TODAY.
ZZZ
ME + KAREN TOOK A LEISURELY WALK DOWN TO EMOS...
...WHERE GHOST KNIFE PLAYED A FUN SHOW.
THEY PUT A MICROCHIP IN MY DOG...

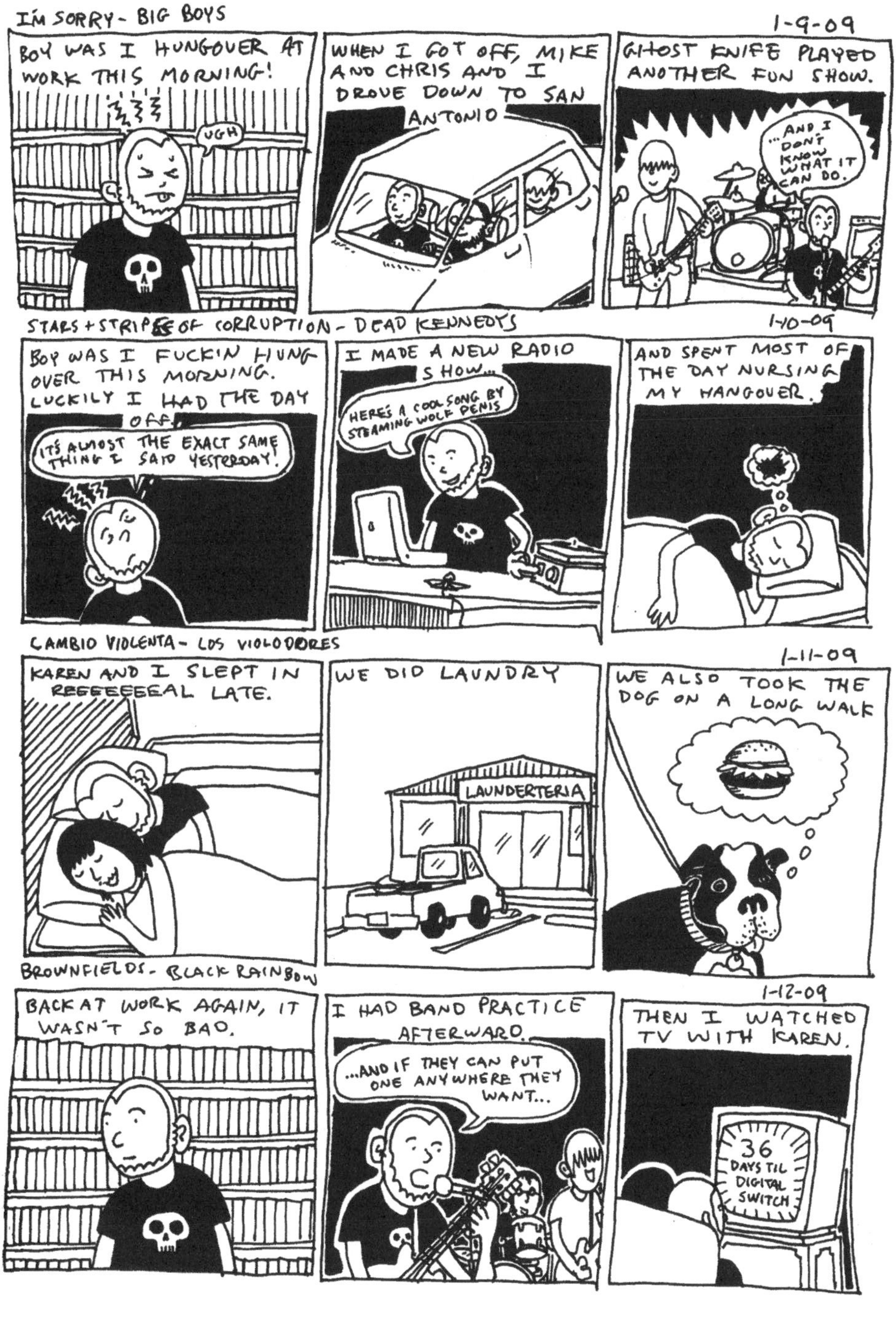
I'M SORRY - BIG BOYS
1-9-09
BOY WAS I HUNGOVER AT WORK THIS MORNING!
UGH
WHEN I GOT OFF, MIKE AND CHRIS AND I DROVE DOWN TO SAN ANTONIO
GHOST KNIFE PLAYED ANOTHER FUN SHOW.
...AND I DON'T KNOW WHAT IT CAN DO.
STARS + STRIPES OF CORRUPTION - DEAD KENNEDYS
1-10-09
BOY WAS I FUCKIN HUNG OVER THIS MORNING. LUCKILY I HAD THE DAY OFF.
IT'S ALMOST THE EXACT SAME THING I SAID YESTERDAY!
I MADE A NEW RADIO SHOW...
HERE'S A COOL SONG BY STEAMING WOLF PENIS
AND SPENT MOST OF THE DAY NURSING MY HANGOVER.
CAMBIO VIOLENTA - LOS VIOLODORES
1-11-09
KAREN AND I SLEPT IN REEEEEEEAL LATE.
WE DID LAUNDRY
LAUNDERTERIA
WE ALSO TOOK THE DOG ON A LONG WALK
BROWNFIELDS - BLACK RAINBOW
1-12-09
BACK AT WORK AGAIN, IT WASN'T SO BAD.
I HAD BAND PRACTICE AFTERWARD.
...AND IF THEY CAN PUT ONE ANYWHERE THEY WANT...
THEN I WATCHED TV WITH KAREN.
36 DAYS TIL DIGITAL SWITCH

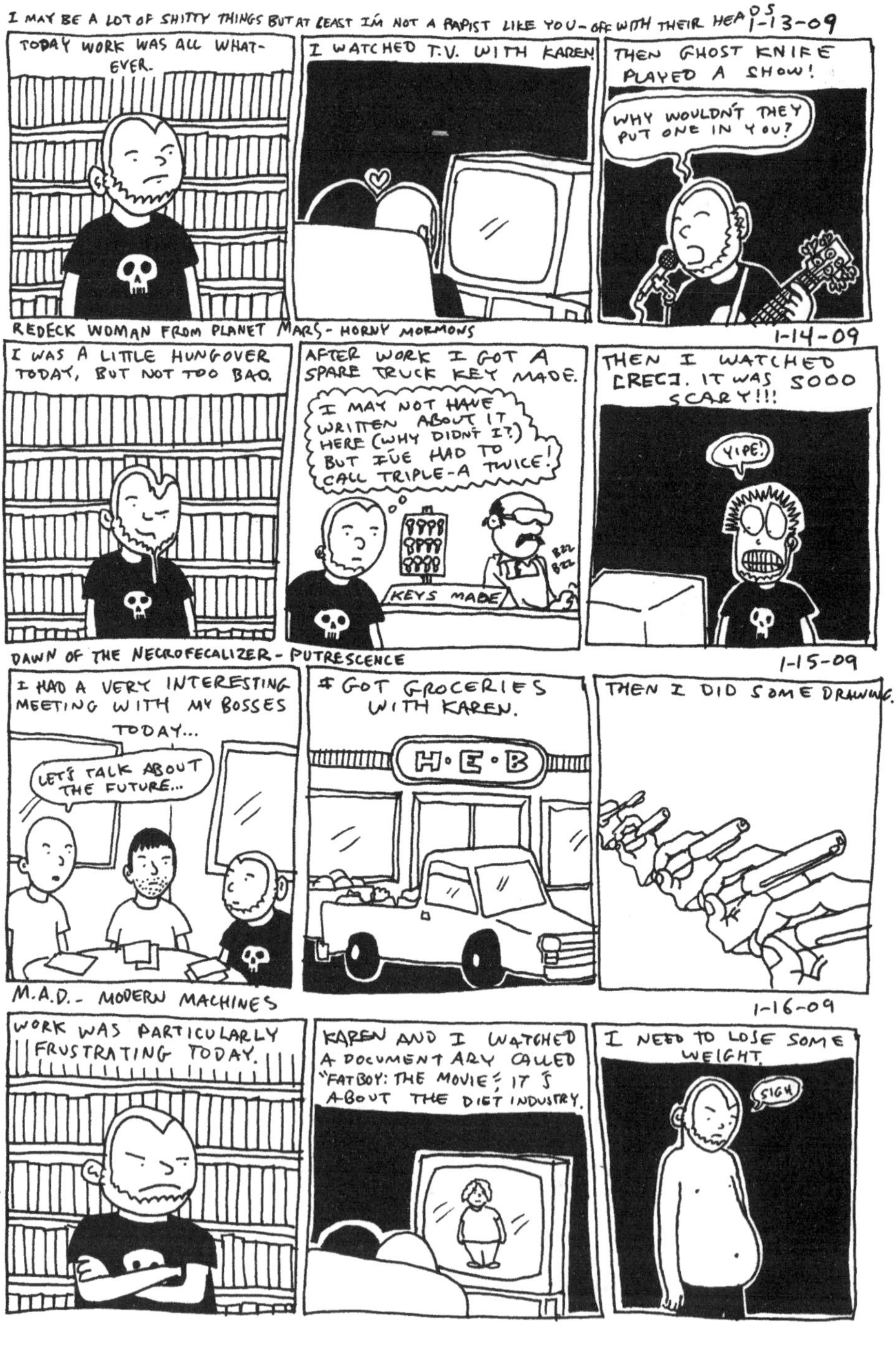
I MAY BE A LOT OF SHITTY THINGS BUT AT LEAST I'M NOT A RAPIST LIKE YOU - OFF WITH THEIR HEADS
1-13-09
TODAY WORK WAS ALL WHATEVER.
I WATCHED T.V. WITH KAREN!
THEN GHOST KNIFE PLAYED A SHOW!
WHY WOULDN'T THEY PUT ONE IN YOU?
REDECK WOMAN FROM PLANET MARS - HORNY MORMONS
1-14-09
I WAS A LITTLE HUNGOVER TODAY, BUT NOT TOO BAD.
AFTER WORK I GOT A SPARE TRUCK KEY MADE.
I MAY NOT HAVE WRITTEN ABOUT IT HERE (WHY DIDN'T I?) BUT I'VE HAD TO CALL TRIPLE-A TWICE!
KEYS MADE
BZZ BZZ
THEN I WATCHED [REC]. IT WAS SOOO SCARY!!!
YIPE!
DAWN OF THE NECROFECALIZER - PUTRESCENCE
1-15-09
I HAD A VERY INTERESTING MEETING WITH MY BOSSES TODAY...
LET'S TALK ABOUT THE FUTURE...
I GOT GROCERIES WITH KAREN.
H·E·B
THEN I DID SOME DRAWING.
M.A.D. - MODERN MACHINES
1-16-09
WORK WAS PARTICULARLY FRUSTRATING TODAY.
KAREN AND I WATCHED A DOCUMENTARY CALLED "FATBOY: THE MOVIE", IT'S ABOUT THE DIET INDUSTRY.
I NEED TO LOSE SOME WEIGHT.
SIGH

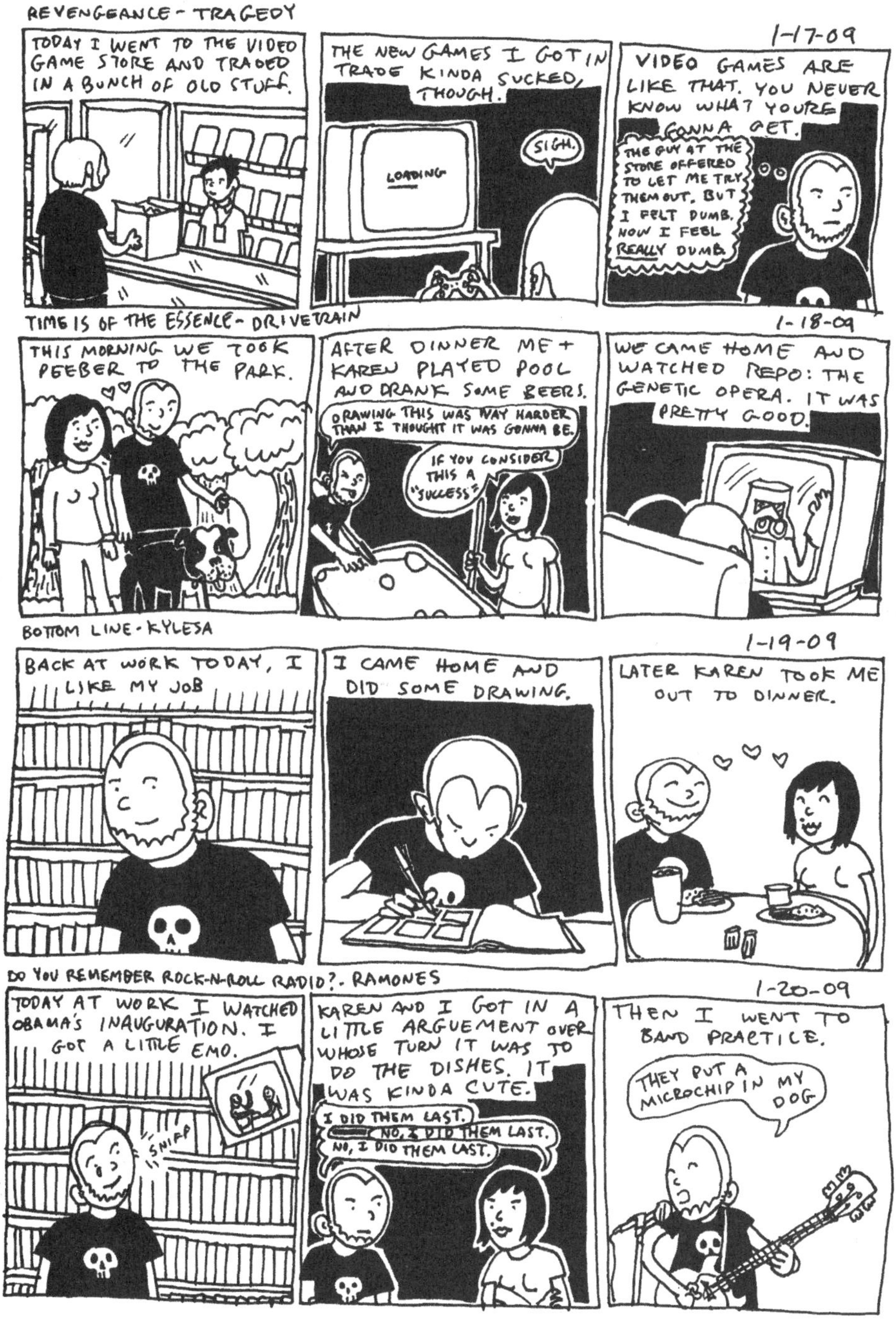
REVENGEANCE - TRAGEDY
1-17-09
TODAY I WENT TO THE VIDEO GAME STORE AND TRADED IN A BUNCH OF OLD STUFF.
THE NEW GAMES I GOT IN TRADE KINDA SUCKED, THOUGH.
LOADING
SIGH.
VIDEO GAMES ARE LIKE THAT. YOU NEVER KNOW WHAT YOU'RE GONNA GET.
THE GUY AT THE STORE OFFERED TO LET ME TRY THEM OUT, BUT I FELT DUMB. NOW I FEEL REALLY DUMB.
TIME IS OF THE ESSENCE - DRIVETRAIN
1-18-09
THIS MORNING WE TOOK PEEBER TO THE PARK.
AFTER DINNER ME + KAREN PLAYED POOL AND DRANK SOME BEERS.
DRAWING THIS WAS WAY HARDER THAN I THOUGHT IT WAS GONNA BE.
IF YOU CONSIDER THIS A "SUCCESS"
WE CAME HOME AND WATCHED REPO: THE GENETIC OPERA. IT WAS PRETTY GOOD.
BOTTOM LINE - KYLESA
1-19-09
BACK AT WORK TODAY, I LIKE MY JOB
I CAME HOME AND DID SOME DRAWING.
LATER KAREN TOOK ME OUT TO DINNER.
DO YOU REMEMBER ROCK-N-ROLL RADIO? - RAMONES
1-20-09
TODAY AT WORK I WATCHED OBAMA'S INAUGURATION. I GOT A LITTLE EMO.
SNIFF
KAREN AND I GOT IN A LITTLE ARGUEMENT OVER WHOSE TURN IT WAS TO DO THE DISHES. IT WAS KINDA CUTE.
I DID THEM LAST.
NO, I DID THEM LAST.
NO, I DID THEM LAST.
THEN I WENT TO BAND PRACTICE.
THEY PUT A MICROCHIP IN MY DOG

SCUM- NAPALM DEATH

| WORK WAS OKAY TODAY. | AFTERWARDS I TOOK PEEBER FOR A LONG WALK. | THEN I HUNG OUT WITH MIKE + CLARKE FOR A LITTLE WHILE. |

PAY NO MIND- BECK

| WORK WAS PAINLESS TODAY. | I'D TOLD MY SELF LAST WEEK THAT I WASN'T GONNA BUY ANY MORE WEED TIL AFTER VALENTINES DAY. | BUT I CAVED TODAY. |

WORLD O' FILTH- GWAR

| TODAY AT WORK I PROMOTED MIKE TO ASSISTANT MANAGER. | LATER I WENT AND SAW RANDA DO STAND-UP COMEDY! IT WAS REALLY FUNNY! | AFTERWARDS WE PARTIED AT HER HOUSE. |

RED EYE - DEVO

| THIS MORNING I RECORDED A NEW PODCAST BUT THE DUMB WEBSITE WOULDN'T LET ME UP LOAD IT. | KAREN AND I WENT AND SAW SEVERED HEAD OF STATE! THEY RULED!! | WE STAYED UP REAL LATE PARTYIN. |

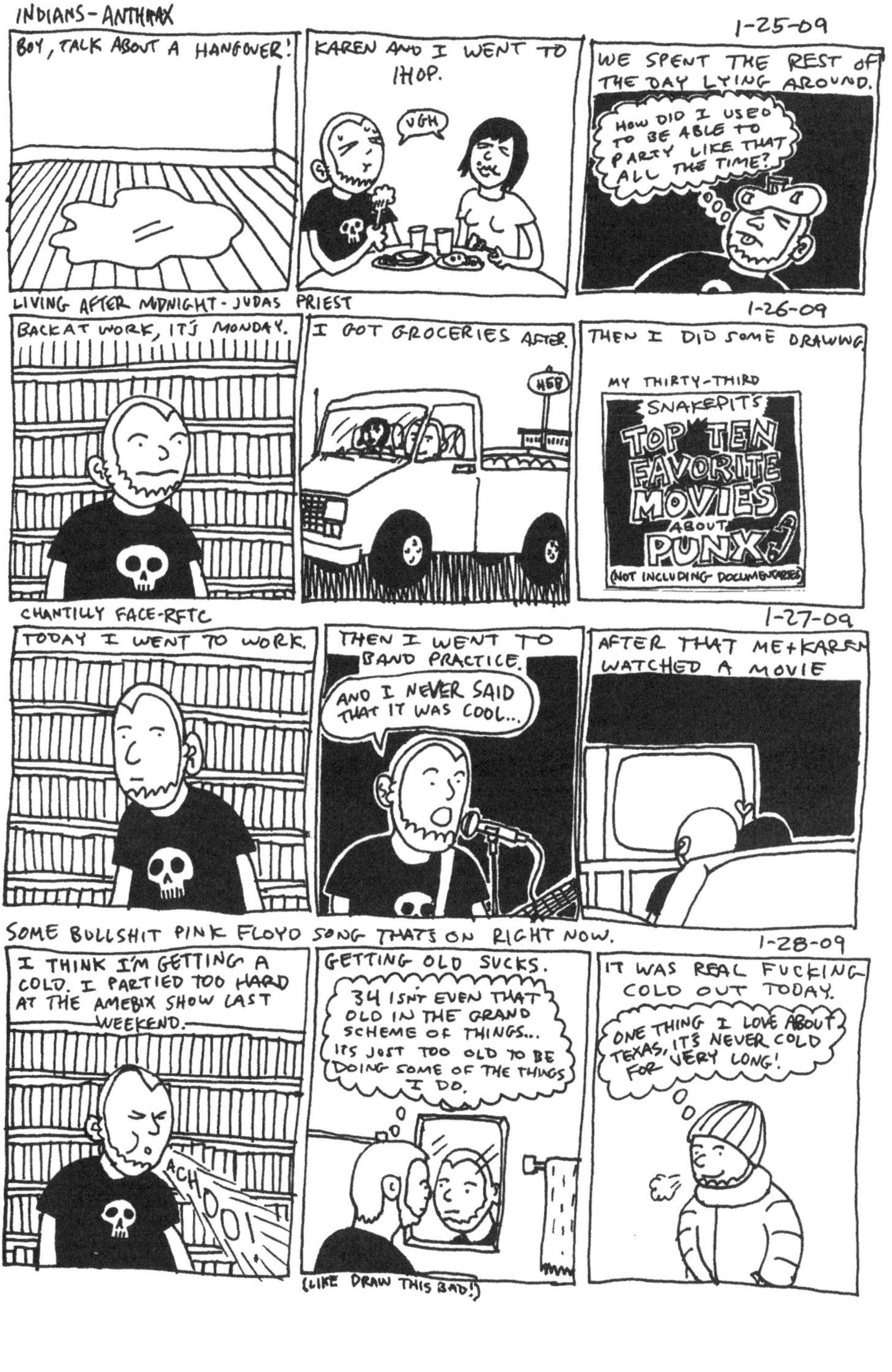
INDIANS - ANTHRAX
1-25-09
BOY, TALK ABOUT A HANGOVER!
KAREN AND I WENT TO IHOP.
UGH
WE SPENT THE REST OF THE DAY LYING AROUND.
HOW DID I USED TO BE ABLE TO PARTY LIKE THAT ALL THE TIME?
LIVING AFTER MIDNIGHT - JUDAS PRIEST
1-26-09
BACK AT WORK, IT'S MONDAY.
I GOT GROCERIES AFTER.
HEB
THEN I DID SOME DRAWING
MY THIRTY-THIRD
SNAKEPIT'S
TOP TEN FAVORITE MOVIES ABOUT PUNX
(NOT INCLUDING DOCUMENTARIES)
CHANTILLY FACE - RFTC
1-27-09
TODAY I WENT TO WORK.
THEN I WENT TO BAND PRACTICE.
AND I NEVER SAID THAT IT WAS COOL...
AFTER THAT ME+KAREN WATCHED A MOVIE
SOME BULLSHIT PINK FLOYD SONG THAT'S ON RIGHT NOW.
1-28-09
I THINK I'M GETTING A COLD. I PARTIED TOO HARD AT THE AMEBIX SHOW LAST WEEKEND.
ACHOO!
GETTING OLD SUCKS.
34 ISN'T EVEN THAT OLD IN THE GRAND SCHEME OF THINGS... ITS JUST TOO OLD TO BE DOING SOME OF THE THINGS I DO.
(LIKE DRAW THIS BAD!)
IT WAS REAL FUCKING COLD OUT TODAY.
ONE THING I LOVE ABOUT TEXAS, IT'S NEVER COLD FOR VERY LONG!

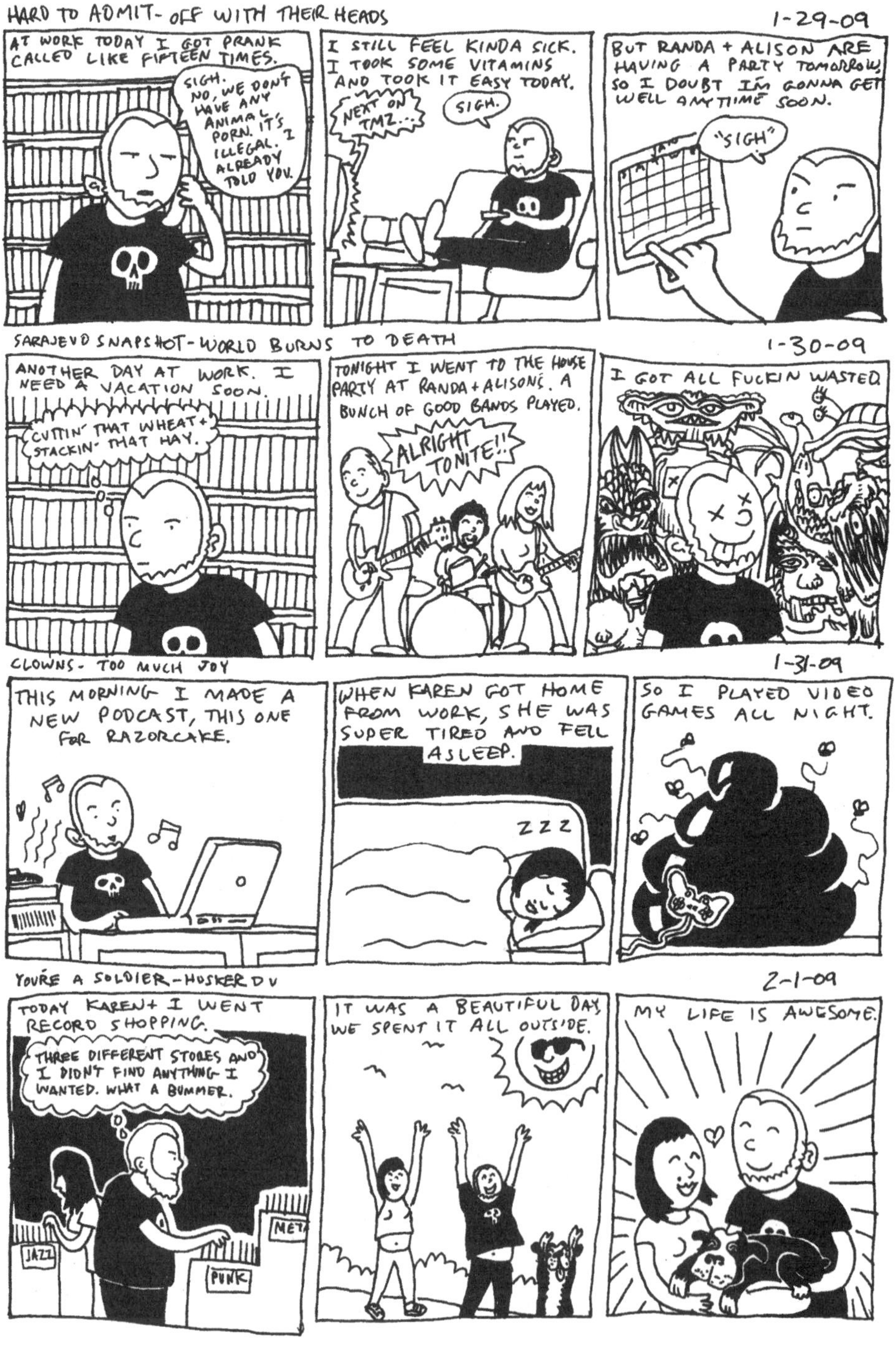
HARD TO ADMIT- OFF WITH THEIR HEADS
1-29-09
AT WORK TODAY I GOT PRANK CALLED LIKE FIFTEEN TIMES.
SIGH. NO, WE DON'T HAVE ANY ANIMAL PORN. IT'S ILLEGAL. I ALREADY TOLD YOU.
I STILL FEEL KINDA SICK. I TOOK SOME VITAMINS AND TOOK IT EASY TODAY.
NEXT ON TMZ...
SIGH.
BUT RANDA + ALISON ARE HAVING A PARTY TOMORROW, SO I DOUBT I'M GONNA GET WELL ANYTIME SOON.
"SIGH"
SARAJEVO SNAPSHOT- WORLD BURNS TO DEATH
1-30-09
ANOTHER DAY AT WORK. I NEED A VACATION SOON.
CUTTIN' THAT WHEAT + STACKIN' THAT HAY.
TONIGHT I WENT TO THE HOUSE PARTY AT RANDA + ALISON'S. A BUNCH OF GOOD BANDS PLAYED.
ALRIGHT TONITE!!
I GOT ALL FUCKIN WASTED.
CLOWNS- TOO MUCH JOY
1-31-09
THIS MORNING I MADE A NEW PODCAST, THIS ONE FOR RAZORCAKE.
WHEN KAREN GOT HOME FROM WORK, SHE WAS SUPER TIRED AND FELL ASLEEP.
ZZZ
SO I PLAYED VIDEO GAMES ALL NIGHT.
YOU'RE A SOLDIER- HUSKER DU
2-1-09
TODAY KAREN + I WENT RECORD SHOPPING.
THREE DIFFERENT STORES AND I DIDN'T FIND ANYTHING I WANTED. WHAT A BUMMER.
JAZZ
PUNK
META
IT WAS A BEAUTIFUL DAY, WE SPENT IT ALL OUTSIDE.
MY LIFE IS AWESOME.

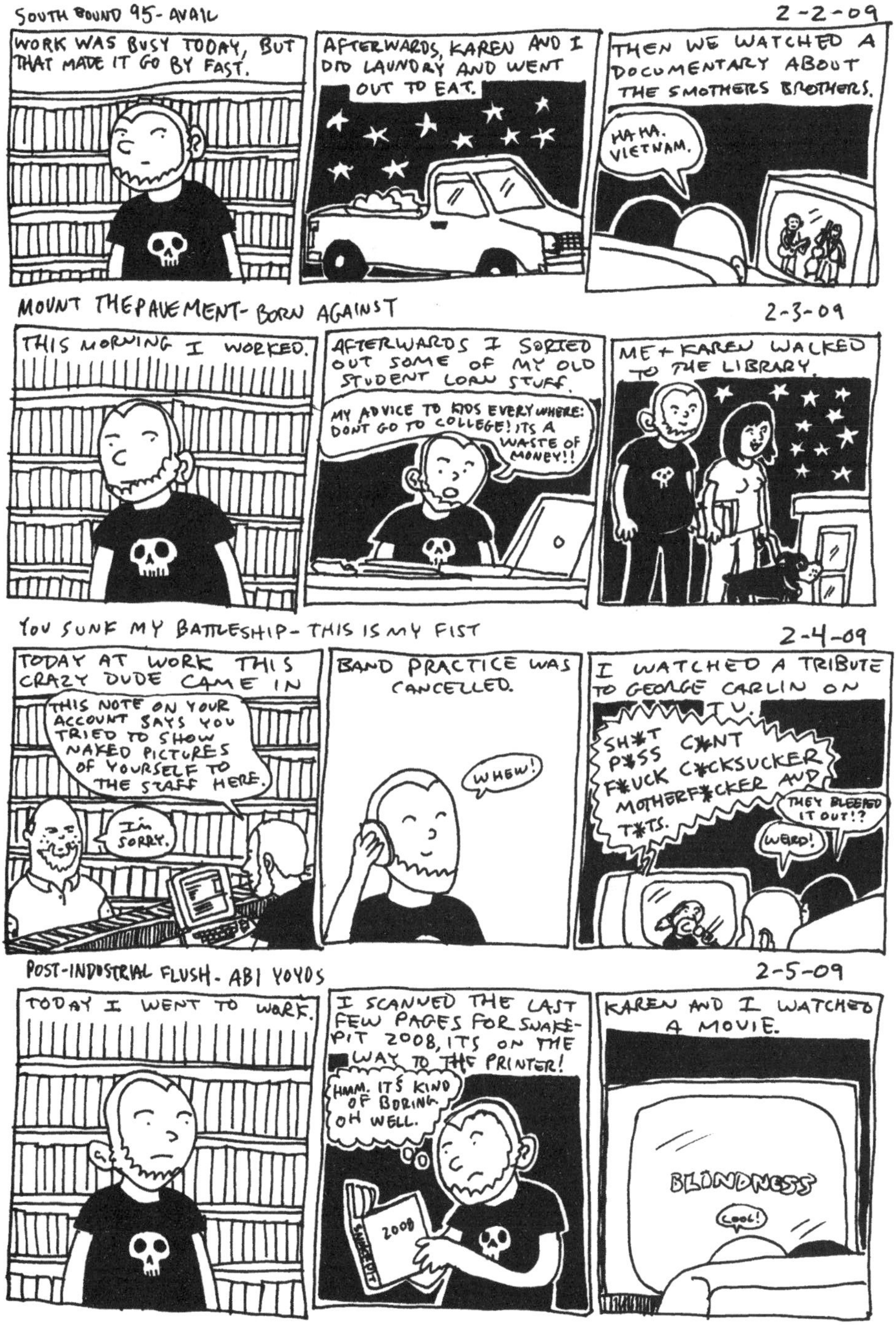
SOUTH BOUND 95- AVAIL
2-2-09
WORK WAS BUSY TODAY, BUT THAT MADE IT GO BY FAST.
AFTERWARDS, KAREN AND I DID LAUNDRY AND WENT OUT TO EAT.
THEN WE WATCHED A DOCUMENTARY ABOUT THE SMOTHERS BROTHERS.
HA HA. VIETNAM.
MOUNT THEPAVEMENT- BORN AGAINST
2-3-09
THIS MORNING I WORKED.
AFTERWARDS I SORTED OUT SOME OF MY OLD STUDENT LOAN STUFF.
MY ADVICE TO KIDS EVERYWHERE: DONT GO TO COLLEGE! ITS A WASTE OF MONEY!!
ME + KAREN WALKED TO THE LIBRARY.
YOU SUNK MY BATTLESHIP- THIS IS MY FIST
2-4-09
TODAY AT WORK THIS CRAZY DUDE CAME IN
THIS NOTE ON YOUR ACCOUNT SAYS YOU TRIED TO SHOW NAKED PICTURES OF YOURSELF TO THE STAFF HERE.
I'M SORRY.
BAND PRACTICE WAS CANCELLED.
WHEW!
I WATCHED A TRIBUTE TO GEORGE CARLIN ON T.V.
SH*T C*NT P*SS F*UCK C*CKSUCKER MOTHERF*CKER AND T*TS.
THEY BLEEPED IT OUT!?
WEIRD!
POST-INDUSTRIAL FLUSH- ABI YOYOS
2-5-09
TODAY I WENT TO WORK.
I SCANNED THE LAST FEW PAGES FOR SNAKE-PIT 2008, ITS ON THE WAY TO THE PRINTER!
HMM. ITS KIND OF BORING. OH WELL.
2008
SNAKEPIT
KAREN AND I WATCHED A MOVIE.
BLINDNESS
COOL!

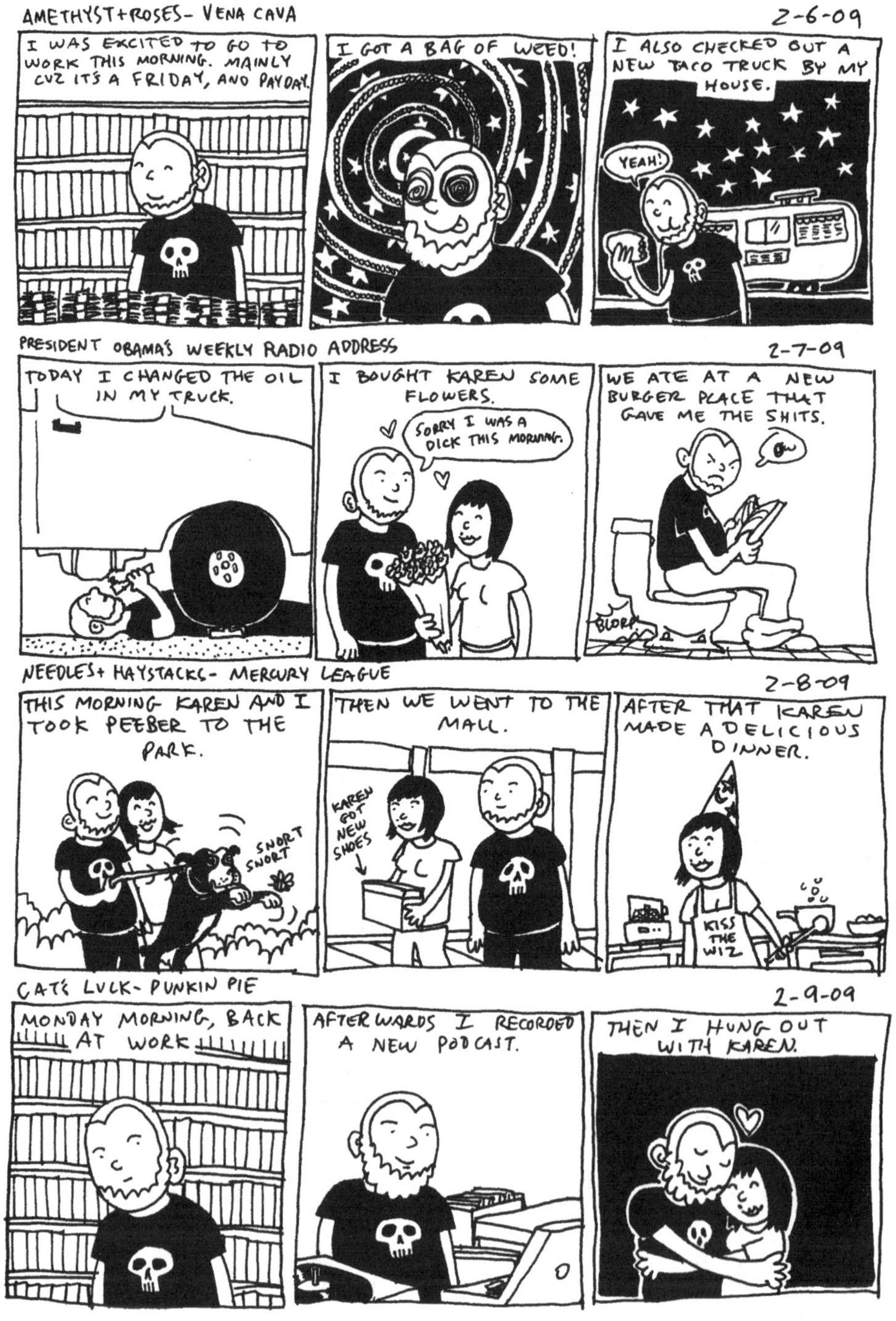
AMETHYST+ROSES- VENA CAVA
2-6-09
I WAS EXCITED TO GO TO WORK THIS MORNING. MAINLY CUZ IT'S A FRIDAY, AND PAYDAY.
I GOT A BAG OF WEED!
I ALSO CHECKED OUT A NEW TACO TRUCK BY MY HOUSE.
YEAH!
PRESIDENT OBAMA'S WEEKLY RADIO ADDRESS
2-7-09
TODAY I CHANGED THE OIL IN MY TRUCK.
I BOUGHT KAREN SOME FLOWERS.
SORRY I WAS A DICK THIS MORNING.
WE ATE AT A NEW BURGER PLACE THAT GAVE ME THE SHITS.
OW
BLORP
NEEDLES+ HAYSTACKS- MERCURY LEAGUE
2-8-09
THIS MORNING KAREN AND I TOOK PEEBER TO THE PARK.
SNORT SNORT
THEN WE WENT TO THE MALL.
KAREN GOT NEW SHOES
AFTER THAT KAREN MADE A DELICIOUS DINNER.
KISS THE WIZ
CAT'S LUCK- PUNKIN PIE
2-9-09
MONDAY MORNING, BACK AT WORK
AFTERWARDS I RECORDED A NEW PODCAST.
THEN I HUNG OUT WITH KAREN.

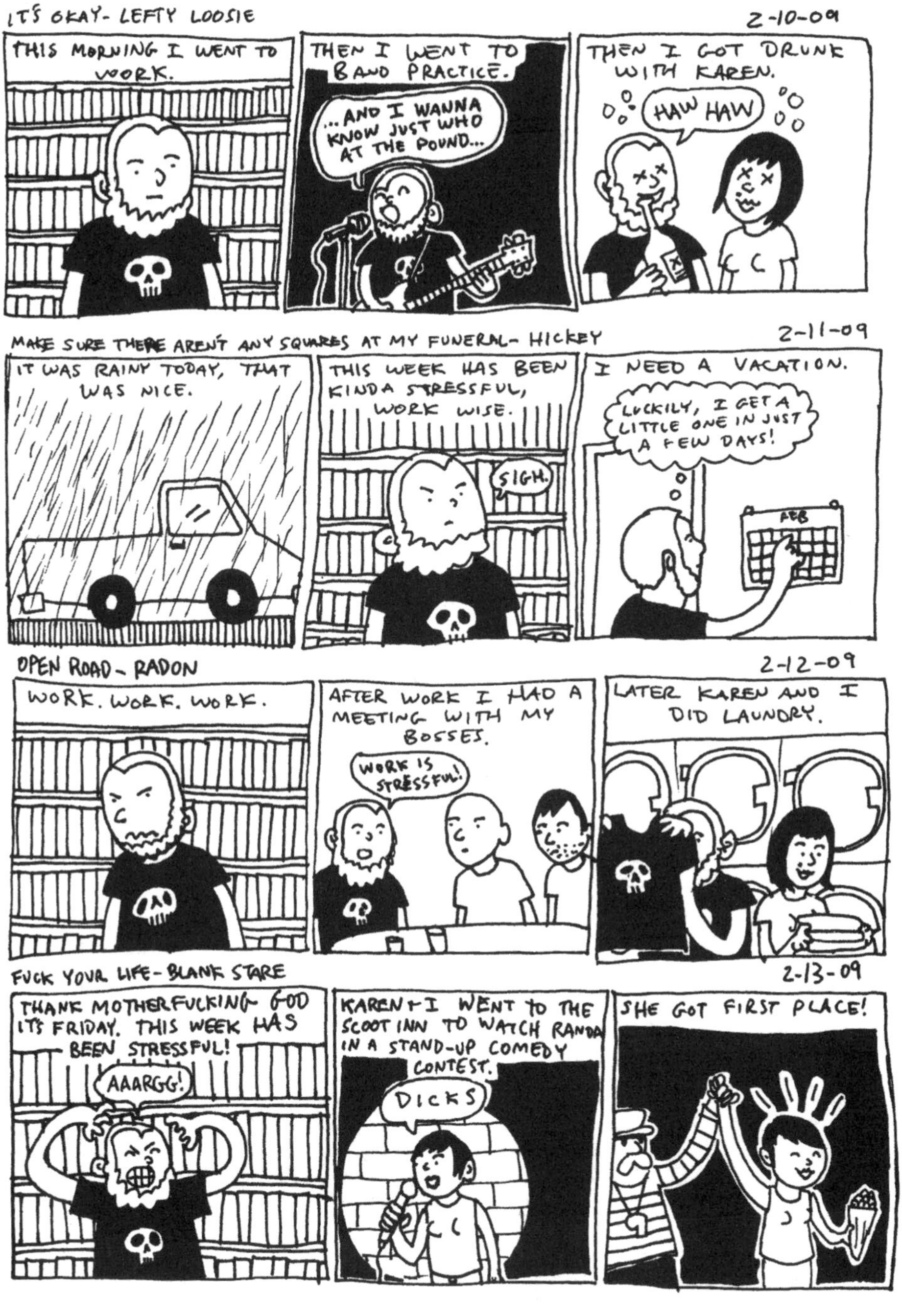
IT'S OKAY- LEFTY LOOSIE
2-10-09
THIS MORNING I WENT TO WORK.
THEN I WENT TO BAND PRACTICE.
...AND I WANNA KNOW JUST WHO AT THE POUND...
THEN I GOT DRUNK WITH KAREN.
HAW HAW
MAKE SURE THERE AREN'T ANY SQUARES AT MY FUNERAL- HICKEY
2-11-09
IT WAS RAINY TODAY, THAT WAS NICE.
THIS WEEK HAS BEEN KINDA STRESSFUL, WORK WISE.
SIGH.
I NEED A VACATION.
LUCKILY, I GET A LITTLE ONE IN JUST A FEW DAYS!
FEB
OPEN ROAD- RADON
2-12-09
WORK. WORK. WORK.
AFTER WORK I HAD A MEETING WITH MY BOSSES.
WORK IS STRESSFUL!
LATER KAREN AND I DID LAUNDRY.
FUCK YOUR LIFE- BLANK STARE
2-13-09
THANK MOTHERFUCKING GOD IT'S FRIDAY. THIS WEEK HAS BEEN STRESSFUL!
AAARGG!
KAREN+I WENT TO THE SCOOT INN TO WATCH RANDA IN A STAND-UP COMEDY CONTEST.
DICKS
SHE GOT FIRST PLACE!

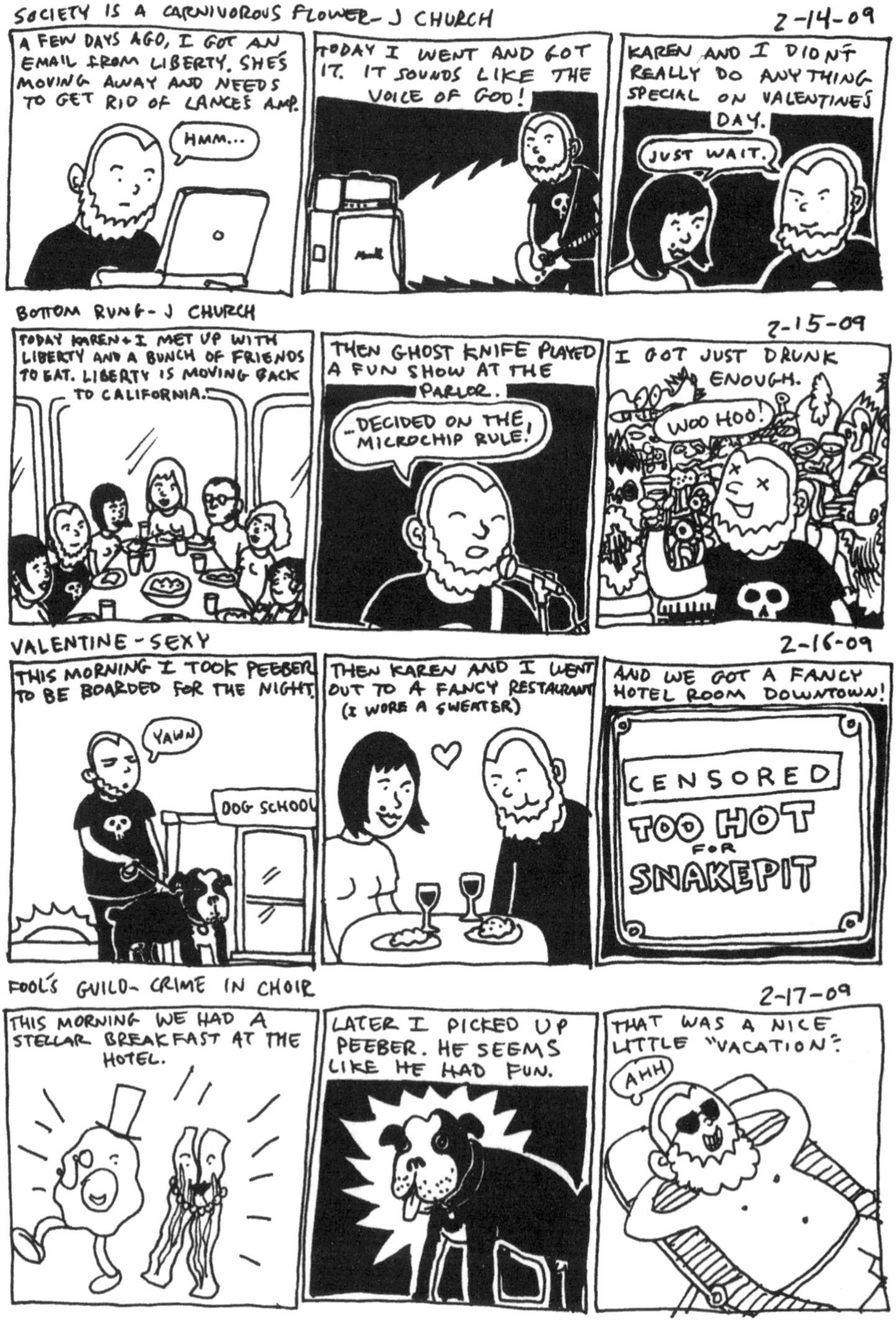
SOCIETY IS A CARNIVOROUS FLOWER- J CHURCH
2-14-09
A FEW DAYS AGO, I GOT AN EMAIL FROM LIBERTY. SHE'S MOVING AWAY AND NEEDS TO GET RID OF LANCE'S AMP.
HMM...
TODAY I WENT AND GOT IT. IT SOUNDS LIKE THE VOICE OF GOD!
KAREN AND I DIDN'T REALLY DO ANYTHING SPECIAL ON VALENTINE'S DAY.
JUST WAIT.
BOTTOM RUNG- J CHURCH
2-15-09
TODAY KAREN + I MET UP WITH LIBERTY AND A BUNCH OF FRIENDS TO EAT. LIBERTY IS MOVING BACK TO CALIFORNIA.
THEN GHOST KNIFE PLAYED A FUN SHOW AT THE PARLOR.
...DECIDED ON THE MICROCHIP RULE!
I GOT JUST DRUNK ENOUGH.
WOO HOO!
VALENTINE - SEXY
2-16-09
THIS MORNING I TOOK PEEBER TO BE BOARDED FOR THE NIGHT.
YAWN
DOG SCHOOL
THEN KAREN AND I WENT OUT TO A FANCY RESTAURANT (I WORE A SWEATER)
AND WE GOT A FANCY HOTEL ROOM DOWNTOWN!
CENSORED
TOO HOT FOR SNAKEPIT
FOOL'S GUILD- CRIME IN CHOIR
2-17-09
THIS MORNING WE HAD A STELLAR BREAKFAST AT THE HOTEL.
LATER I PICKED UP PEEBER. HE SEEMS LIKE HE HAD FUN.
THAT WAS A NICE LITTLE "VACATION".
AHH

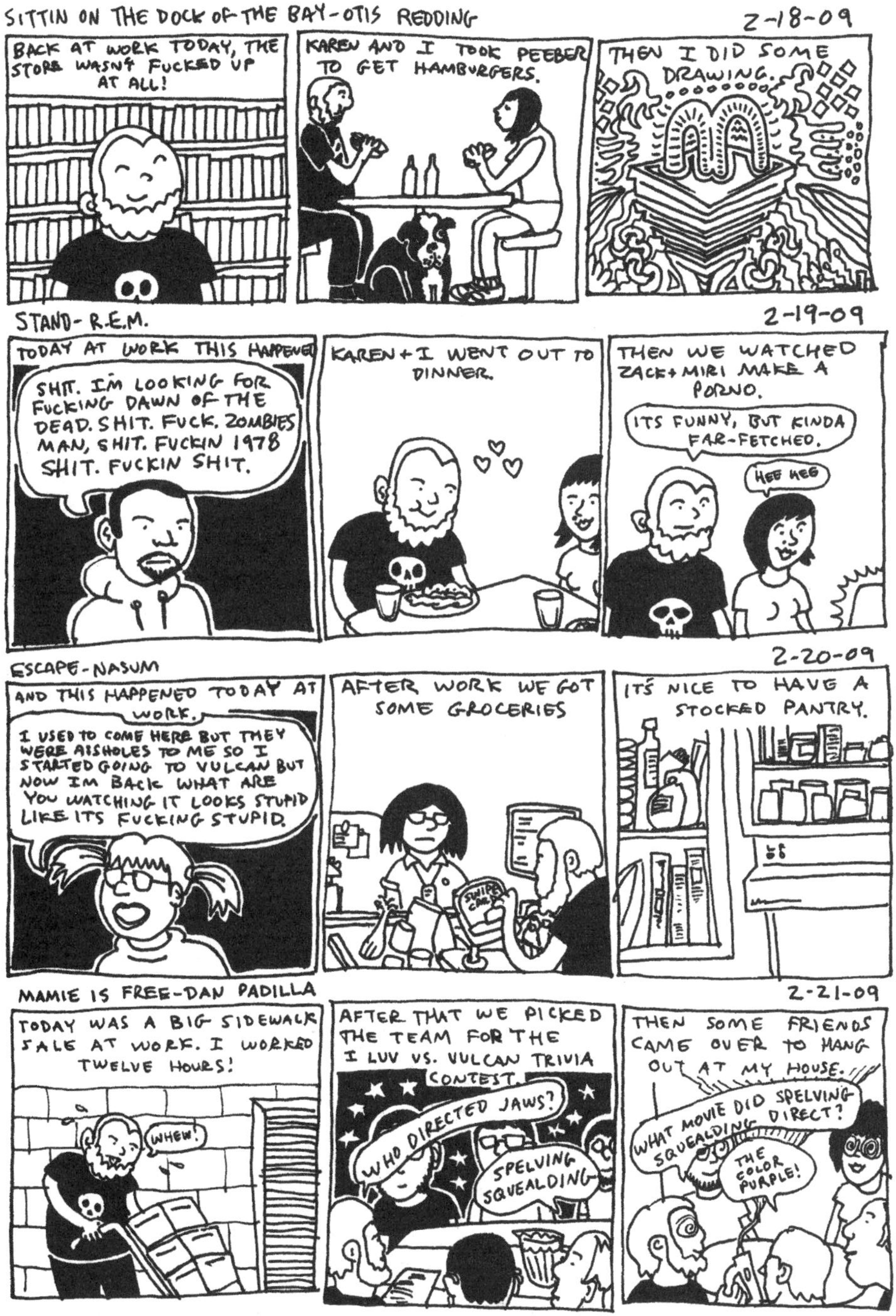
SITTIN ON THE DOCK OF THE BAY - OTIS REDDING
2-18-09
BACK AT WORK TODAY, THE STORE WASN'T FUCKED UP AT ALL!
KAREN AND I TOOK PEEBER TO GET HAMBURGERS.
THEN I DID SOME DRAWING.
STAND - R.E.M.
2-19-09
TODAY AT WORK THIS HAPPENED
SHIT. I'M LOOKING FOR FUCKING DAWN OF THE DEAD. SHIT. FUCK. ZOMBIES MAN, SHIT. FUCKIN 1978 SHIT. FUCKIN SHIT.
KAREN + I WENT OUT TO DINNER.
THEN WE WATCHED ZACK + MIRI MAKE A PORNO.
ITS FUNNY, BUT KINDA FAR-FETCHED.
HEE HEE
ESCAPE - NASUM
2-20-09
AND THIS HAPPENED TODAY AT WORK.
I USED TO COME HERE BUT THEY WERE ASSHOLES TO ME SO I STARTED GOING TO VULCAN BUT NOW IM BACK WHAT ARE YOU WATCHING IT LOOKS STUPID LIKE ITS FUCKING STUPID.
AFTER WORK WE GOT SOME GROCERIES
SWIPE CARD
IT'S NICE TO HAVE A STOCKED PANTRY.
MAMIE IS FREE - DAN PADILLA
2-21-09
TODAY WAS A BIG SIDEWALK SALE AT WORK. I WORKED TWELVE HOURS!
WHEW!
AFTER THAT WE PICKED THE TEAM FOR THE I LUV VS. VULCAN TRIVIA CONTEST.
WHO DIRECTED JAWS?
SPELVING SQUEALDING
THEN SOME FRIENDS CAME OVER TO HANG OUT AT MY HOUSE.
WHAT MOVIE DID SPELVING SQUEALDING DIRECT?
THE COLOR PURPLE!

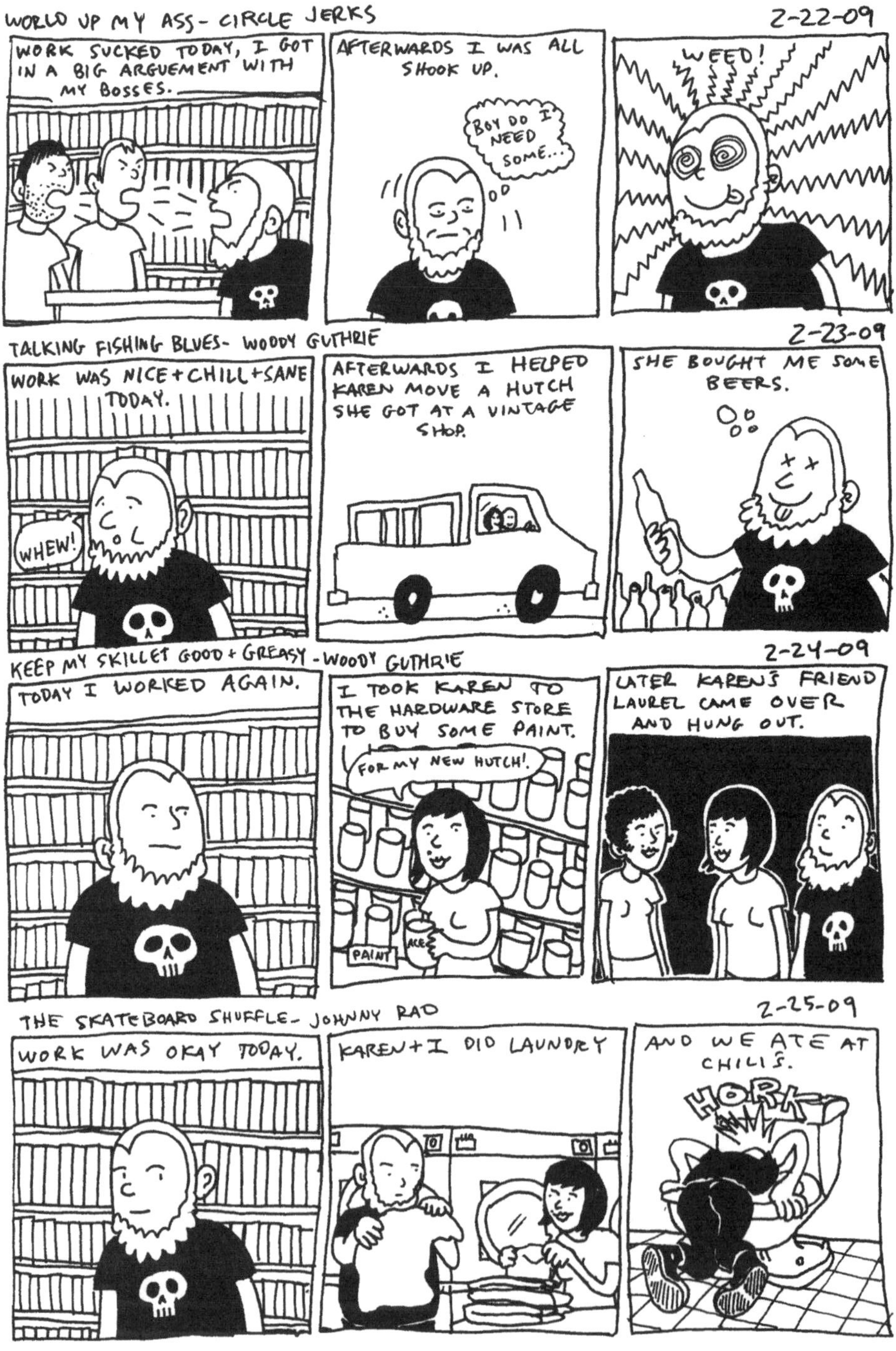
WORLD UP MY ASS - CIRCLE JERKS
2-22-09
WORK SUCKED TODAY, I GOT IN A BIG ARGUEMENT WITH MY BOSSES.
AFTERWARDS I WAS ALL SHOOK UP.
BOY DO I NEED SOME...
WEED!
TALKING FISHING BLUES - WOODY GUTHRIE
2-23-09
WORK WAS NICE + CHILL + SANE TODAY.
WHEW!
AFTERWARDS I HELPED KAREN MOVE A HUTCH SHE GOT AT A VINTAGE SHOP.
SHE BOUGHT ME SOME BEERS.
KEEP MY SKILLET GOOD + GREASY - WOODY GUTHRIE
2-24-09
TODAY I WORKED AGAIN.
I TOOK KAREN TO THE HARDWARE STORE TO BUY SOME PAINT.
FOR MY NEW HUTCH!
PAINT
ACE
LATER KAREN'S FRIEND LAUREL CAME OVER AND HUNG OUT.
THE SKATEBOARD SHUFFLE - JOHNNY RAD
2-25-09
WORK WAS OKAY TODAY.
KAREN + I DID LAUNDRY
AND WE ATE AT CHILI'S.
HORK

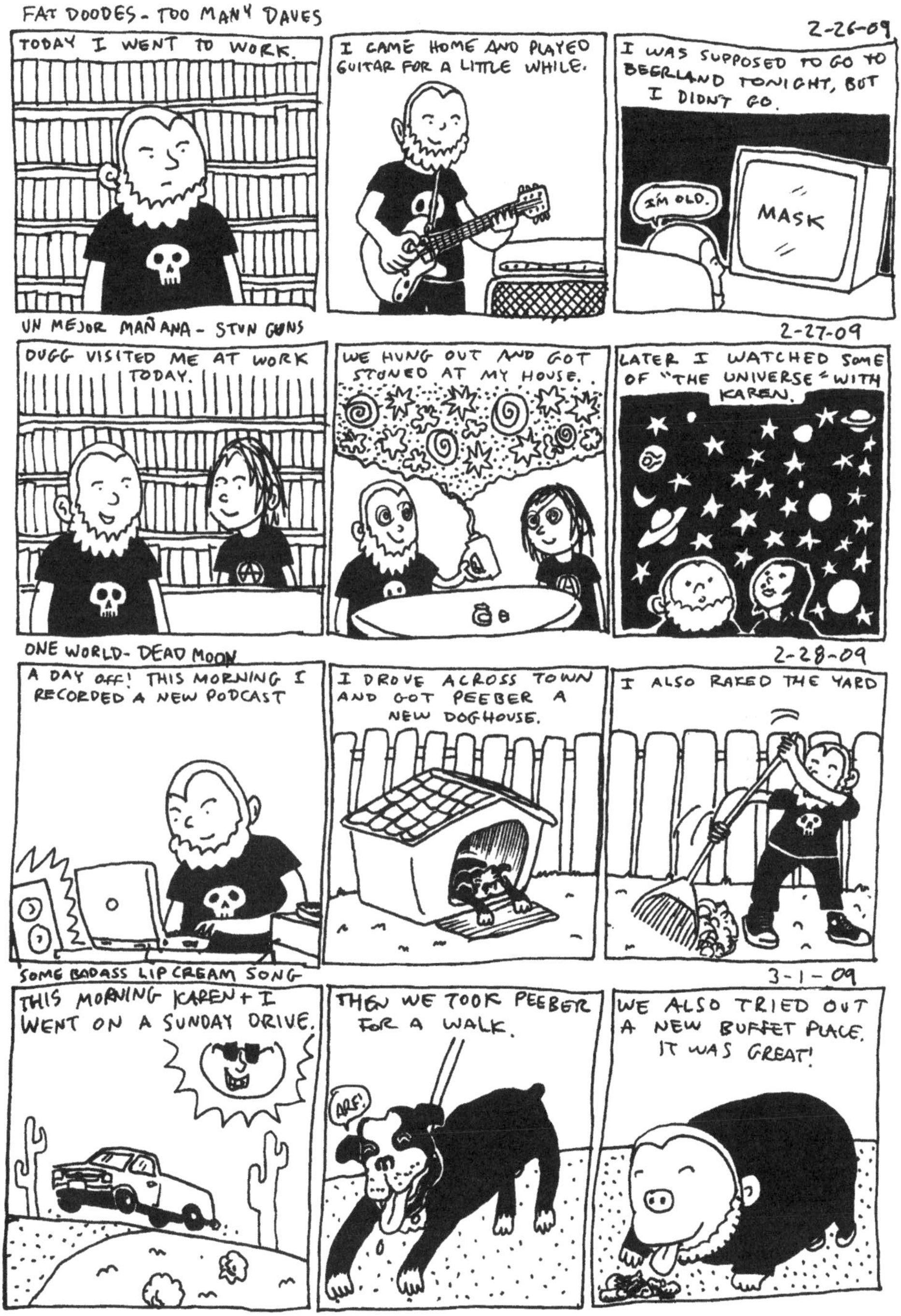
FAT DOODES - TOO MANY DAVES
2-26-09
TODAY I WENT TO WORK.
I CAME HOME AND PLAYED GUITAR FOR A LITTLE WHILE.
I WAS SUPPOSED TO GO TO BEERLAND TONIGHT, BUT I DIDN'T GO.
I'M OLD.
MASK
UN MEJOR MAÑANA - STUN GUNS
2-27-09
DUGG VISITED ME AT WORK TODAY.
WE HUNG OUT AND GOT STONED AT MY HOUSE.
LATER I WATCHED SOME OF "THE UNIVERSE" WITH KAREN.
ONE WORLD - DEAD MOON
2-28-09
A DAY OFF! THIS MORNING I RECORDED A NEW PODCAST
I DROVE ACROSS TOWN AND GOT PEEBER A NEW DOGHOUSE.
I ALSO RAKED THE YARD
SOME BADASS LIP CREAM SONG
3-1-09
THIS MORNING KAREN + I WENT ON A SUNDAY DRIVE.
THEN WE TOOK PEEBER FOR A WALK.
ARF!
WE ALSO TRIED OUT A NEW BUFFET PLACE. IT WAS GREAT!

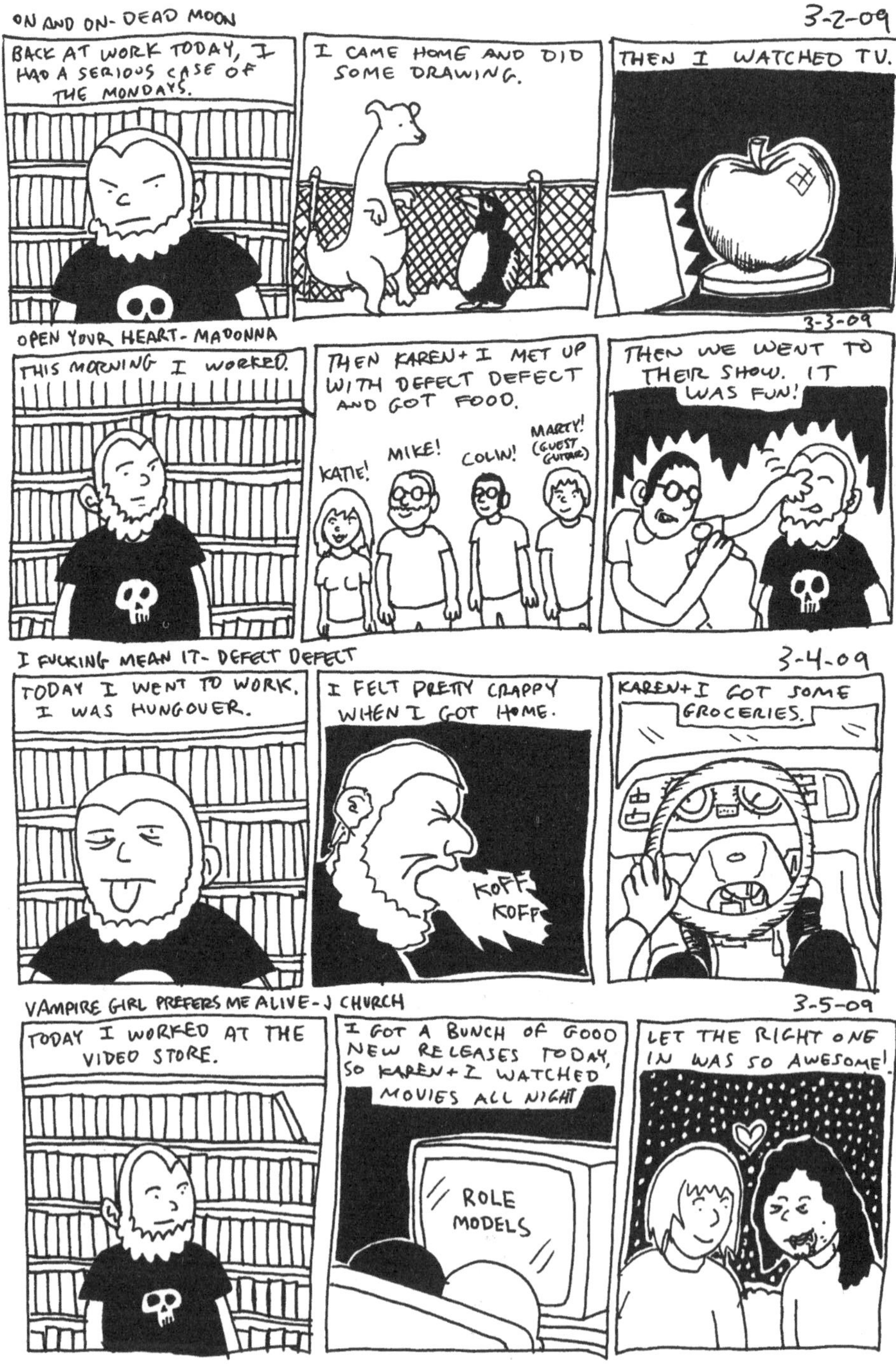
ON AND ON- DEAD MOON
3-2-09
BACK AT WORK TODAY, I HAD A SERIOUS CASE OF THE MONDAYS.
I CAME HOME AND DID SOME DRAWING.
THEN I WATCHED T.V.
OPEN YOUR HEART- MADONNA
3-3-09
THIS MORNING I WORKED.
THEN KAREN+I MET UP WITH DEFECT DEFECT AND GOT FOOD.
KATIE!
MIKE!
COLIN!
MARTY! (GUEST GUITAR)
THEN WE WENT TO THEIR SHOW. IT WAS FUN!
I FUCKING MEAN IT- DEFECT DEFECT
3-4-09
TODAY I WENT TO WORK. I WAS HUNGOVER.
I FELT PRETTY CRAPPY WHEN I GOT HOME.
KOFF KOFF
KAREN+I GOT SOME GROCERIES.
VAMPIRE GIRL PREFERS ME ALIVE- J CHURCH
3-5-09
TODAY I WORKED AT THE VIDEO STORE.
I GOT A BUNCH OF GOOD NEW RELEASES TODAY, SO KAREN+I WATCHED MOVIES ALL NIGHT
ROLE MODELS
LET THE RIGHT ONE IN WAS SO AWESOME!

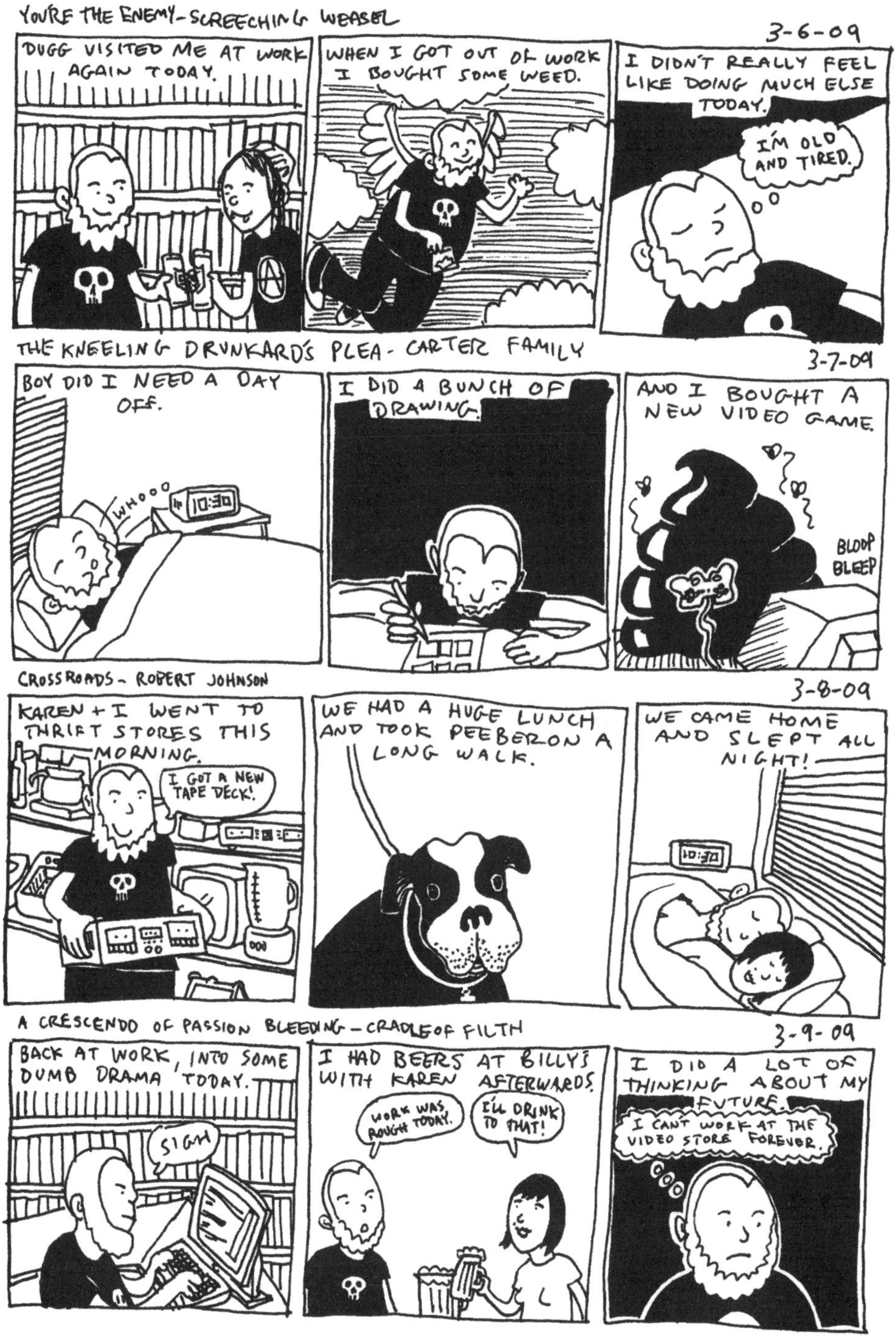
YOU'RE THE ENEMY - SCREECHING WEASEL
3-6-09
DUGG VISITED ME AT WORK AGAIN TODAY.
WHEN I GOT OUT OF WORK I BOUGHT SOME WEED.
I DIDN'T REALLY FEEL LIKE DOING MUCH ELSE TODAY.
I'M OLD AND TIRED.
THE KNEELING DRUNKARD'S PLEA - CARTER FAMILY
3-7-09
BOY DID I NEED A DAY OFF.
WHOOO
10:30
I DID A BUNCH OF DRAWING.
AND I BOUGHT A NEW VIDEO GAME.
BLOOP
BLEEP
CROSSROADS - ROBERT JOHNSON
3-8-09
KAREN + I WENT TO THRIFT STORES THIS MORNING.
I GOT A NEW TAPE DECK!
WE HAD A HUGE LUNCH AND TOOK PEEBERON A LONG WALK.
WE CAME HOME AND SLEPT ALL NIGHT!
A CRESCENDO OF PASSION BLEEDING - CRADLE OF FILTH
3-9-09
BACK AT WORK, INTO SOME DUMB DRAMA TODAY.
SIGH
I HAD BEERS AT BILLY'S WITH KAREN AFTERWARDS.
WORK WAS ROUGH TODAY.
I'LL DRINK TO THAT!
I DID A LOT OF THINKING ABOUT MY FUTURE.
I CAN'T WORK AT THE VIDEO STORE FOREVER.

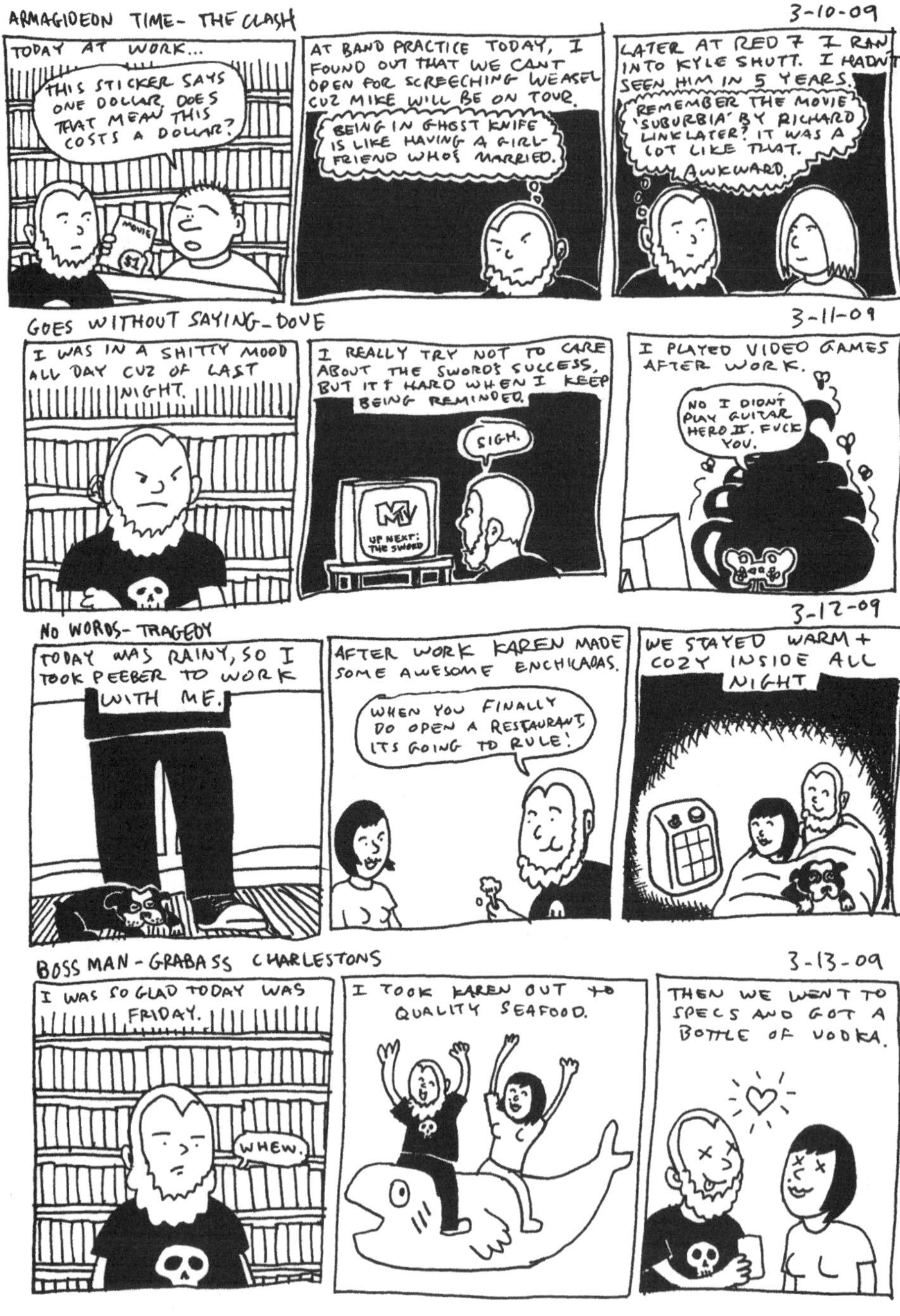
ARMAGIDEON TIME - THE CLASH
3-10-09
TODAY AT WORK...
THIS STICKER SAYS ONE DOLLAR. DOES THAT MEAN THIS COSTS A DOLLAR?
MOVIE
$1
AT BAND PRACTICE TODAY, I FOUND OUT THAT WE CANT OPEN FOR SCREECHING WEASEL CUZ MIKE WILL BE ON TOUR.
BEING IN GHOST KNIFE IS LIKE HAVING A GIRLFRIEND WHOS MARRIED.
LATER AT RED 7 I RAN INTO KYLE SHUTT. I HADN'T SEEN HIM IN 5 YEARS.
REMEMBER THE MOVIE 'SUBURBIA' BY RICHARD LINKLATER? IT WAS A LOT LIKE THAT.
AWKWARD.
GOES WITHOUT SAYING - DOVE
3-11-09
I WAS IN A SHITTY MOOD ALL DAY CUZ OF LAST NIGHT.
I REALLY TRY NOT TO CARE ABOUT THE SWORD'S SUCCESS, BUT IT'S HARD WHEN I KEEP BEING REMINDED.
SIGH.
MTV
UP NEXT: THE SWORD
I PLAYED VIDEO GAMES AFTER WORK.
NO I DIDN'T PLAY GUITAR HERO II. FUCK YOU.
NO WORDS - TRAGEDY
3-12-09
TODAY WAS RAINY, SO I TOOK PEEBER TO WORK WITH ME.
AFTER WORK KAREN MADE SOME AWESOME ENCHILADAS.
WHEN YOU FINALLY DO OPEN A RESTAURANT, ITS GOING TO RULE!
WE STAYED WARM + COZY INSIDE ALL NIGHT
BOSS MAN - GRABASS CHARLESTONS
3-13-09
I WAS SO GLAD TODAY WAS FRIDAY.
WHEW.
I TOOK KAREN OUT TO QUALITY SEAFOOD.
THEN WE WENT TO SPECS AND GOT A BOTTLE OF VODKA.

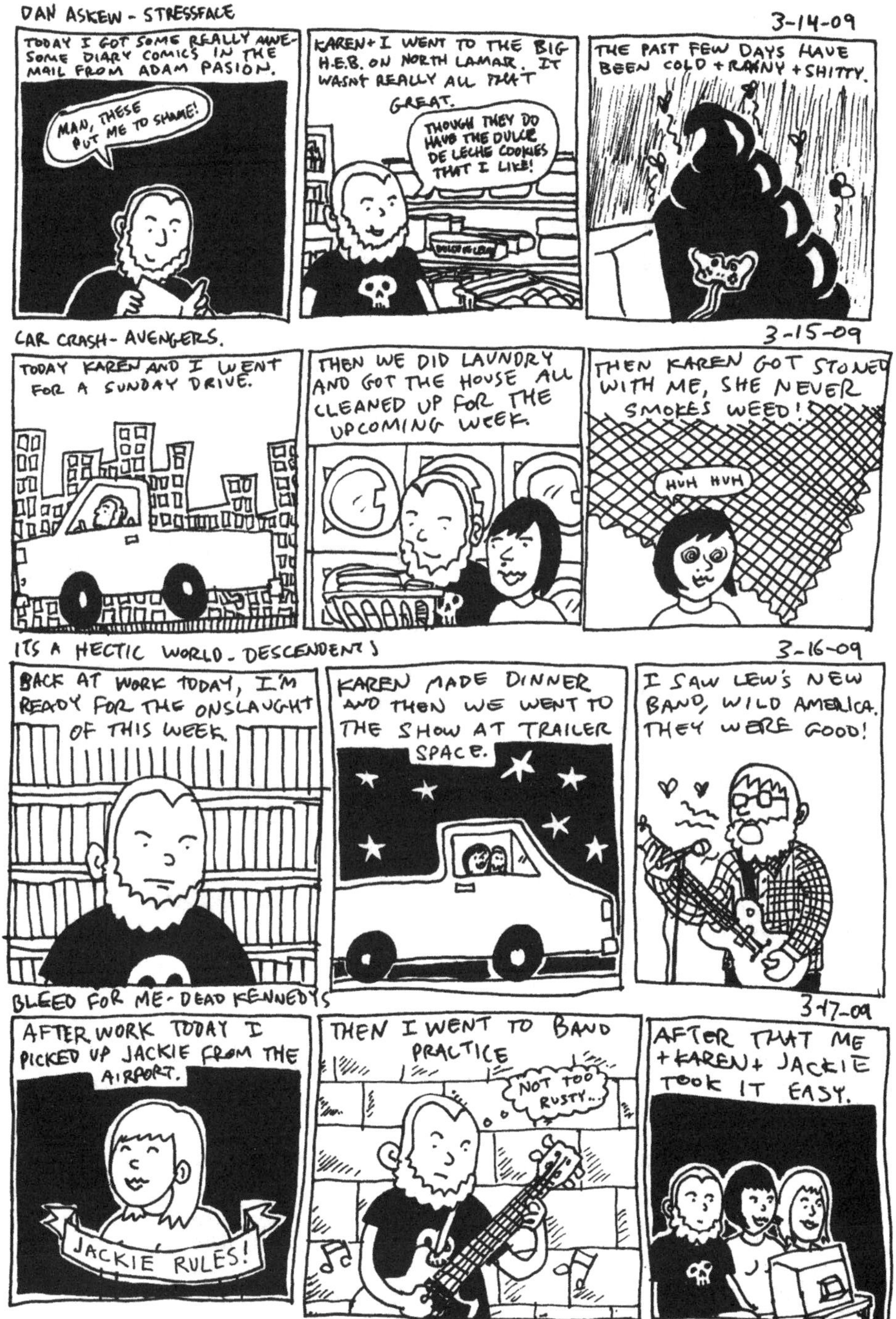
DAN ASKEW - STRESSFACE
3-14-09
TODAY I GOT SOME REALLY AWESOME DIARY COMICS IN THE MAIL FROM ADAM PASION.
MAN, THESE PUT ME TO SHAME!
KAREN+I WENT TO THE BIG H.E.B. ON NORTH LAMAR. IT WASN'T REALLY ALL THAT GREAT.
THOUGH THEY DO HAVE THE DULCE DE LECHE COOKIES THAT I LIKE!
THE PAST FEW DAYS HAVE BEEN COLD + RAINY + SHITTY.
CAR CRASH - AVENGERS.
3-15-09
TODAY KAREN AND I WENT FOR A SUNDAY DRIVE.
THEN WE DID LAUNDRY AND GOT THE HOUSE ALL CLEANED UP FOR THE UPCOMING WEEK.
THEN KAREN GOT STONED WITH ME, SHE NEVER SMOKES WEED!
HUH HUH
ITS A HECTIC WORLD - DESCENDENTS
3-16-09
BACK AT WORK TODAY, I'M READY FOR THE ONSLAUGHT OF THIS WEEK.
KAREN MADE DINNER AND THEN WE WENT TO THE SHOW AT TRAILER SPACE.
I SAW LEW'S NEW BAND, WILD AMERICA. THEY WERE GOOD!
BLEED FOR ME - DEAD KENNEDYS
3-17-09
AFTER WORK TODAY I PICKED UP JACKIE FROM THE AIRPORT.
JACKIE RULES!
THEN I WENT TO BAND PRACTICE
NOT TOO RUSTY...
AFTER THAT ME + KAREN + JACKIE TOOK IT EASY.

REFUSE/RESIST- SEPULTURA 3-18-09

WORK WAS SUPER SLOW TODAY.

GHOST KNIFE PLAYED A REALLY SHITTY SXSW SHOW.

"THEY PUT A MICROCHIP IN MY DOG..."

THEN I SAW SHELL SHAG! THEY WERE SO GOOD!

HAPPINESS

BAD MOUTH- FUGAZI 3-19-09

BACK AT WORK THIS MORNING, MY HANGOVER WAS TOLERABLE.

ER..

I WENT TO THE STAR- CLEANER PARTY ALL DAY.

WOW, THE VIVIAN GIRLS AREN'T JUST A BUNCH OF OVERRATED HYPE, THEY'RE ACTUALLY REALLY GOOD!

IT WAS FUN + LONG!

FISH TACOS 98- SCARED OF CHAKA 3-20-09

I HAD THE MORNING OFF WORK, I WENT TO THE SHOW AT RANDA + ALISON'S HOUSE.

SERIOUS, TRACERS.

THEN I SAW SHELL SHAG + THIS BIKE IS A PIPE BOMB PLAY A RAD HOUSE SHOW!

THIS IS WHAT I WANT

THEN I WORKED TIL 3 AM.

YAWN.

SOFTCORE- JAWBREAKER 3-21-09

I WAS BACK AT WORK THIS MORNING, SIX HOURS AFTER I CLOCKED OUT LAST NIGHT.

OH GOD I FUCKING HATE SXSW.

I FELT SO TIRED AND SHITTY WHEN I GOT HOME, I DIDN'T DO ANYTHING.

DILLINGER 4 PLAYED TONIGHT, I DIDN'T EVEN GO TO THAT!

PADDY'S BEEN IN TOWN FOR DAYS AND I HAVEN'T EVEN SEEN HIM.

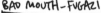

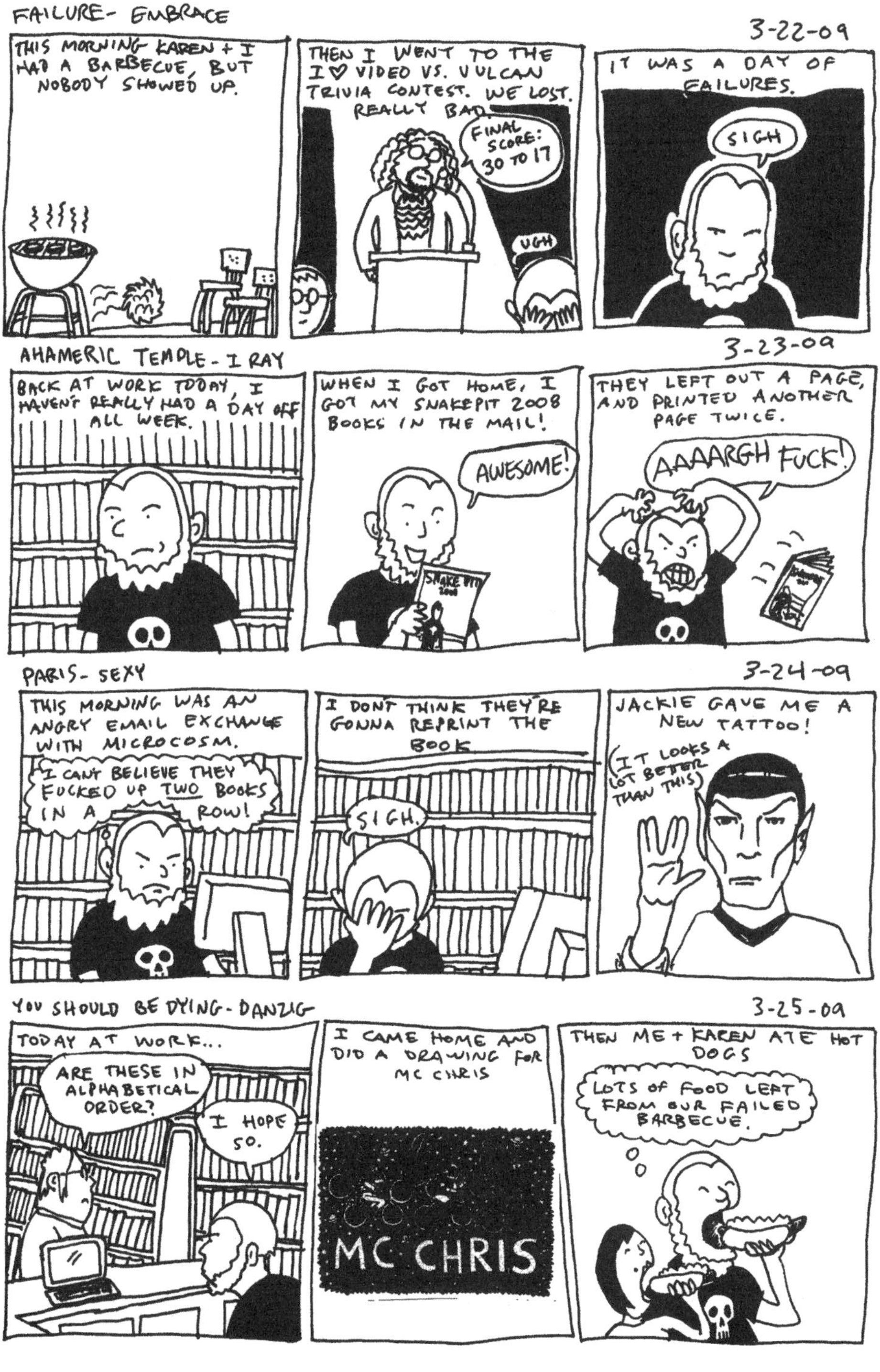
FAILURE - EMBRACE
3-22-09
THIS MORNING KAREN + I HAD A BARBECUE, BUT NOBODY SHOWED UP.
THEN I WENT TO THE I ♡ VIDEO VS. VULCAN TRIVIA CONTEST. WE LOST. REALLY BAD.
FINAL SCORE: 30 TO 17
UGH
IT WAS A DAY OF FAILURES.
SIGH
AHAMERIC TEMPLE - I RAY
3-23-09
BACK AT WORK TODAY, I HAVEN'T REALLY HAD A DAY OFF ALL WEEK.
WHEN I GOT HOME, I GOT MY SNAKEPIT 2008 BOOKS IN THE MAIL!
AWESOME!
SNAKE PIT 2008
THEY LEFT OUT A PAGE, AND PRINTED ANOTHER PAGE TWICE.
AAAARGH FUCK!
PARIS - SEXY
3-24-09
THIS MORNING WAS AN ANGRY EMAIL EXCHANGE WITH MICROCOSM.
I CANT BELIEVE THEY FUCKED UP TWO BOOKS IN A ROW!
I DONT THINK THEY'RE GONNA REPRINT THE BOOK
SIGH.
JACKIE GAVE ME A NEW TATTOO!
(IT LOOKS A LOT BETTER THAN THIS)
YOU SHOULD BE DYING - DANZIG
3-25-09
TODAY AT WORK...
ARE THESE IN ALPHABETICAL ORDER?
I HOPE SO.
I CAME HOME AND DID A DRAWING FOR MC CHRIS
MC CHRIS
THEN ME + KAREN ATE HOT DOGS
LOTS OF FOOD LEFT FROM OUR FAILED BARBECUE.

DREAM WARRIORS- DOKKEN   3-26-09

WORK WENT BY PRETTY FAST TODAY.

BAND PRACTICE WAS CANCELLED, TOO.

AWESOME!!

I WONDER WHY I'M ALWAYS STOKED WHEN THERE'S NO BAND PRACTICE?

THAT'S GOTTA MEAN SOMETHING.

HEATER MOVES + EYES - MELVINS   3-27-09

MY LAST OF A 14-DAY WORK WEEK. UGH!

TO MAKE IT WORSE, I HAD A MEETING AFTERWARD.

SIGH.

I SPENT MY EVENING IN A DRUG-INDUCED HAZE

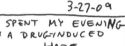

JOHNNY- THIS BIKE IS A PIPE BOMB   3-28-09

TODAY I CLEANED THE HOUSE AND DID SOME DRAWING.

KAREN + I WENT OVER TO MIKE ROD'S FOR HIS BIRTHDAY.

HAPPY BIRTHDAY

I ♥ MIKE ROD

WE GOT DRUNK!

LIAR'S HOOK - TOYS THAT KILL   3-29-09

TODAY KAREN + I DROVE DOWN TO SAN ANTONIO.

WE DID THE TOURISTY STUFF, SAW THE ALAMO AND THE RIVER WALK AND STUFF.

WE WENT HOME AND I HAD BAND PRACTICE.

...AND THEY SAY THAT ITS TOO SMALL TO SEE...

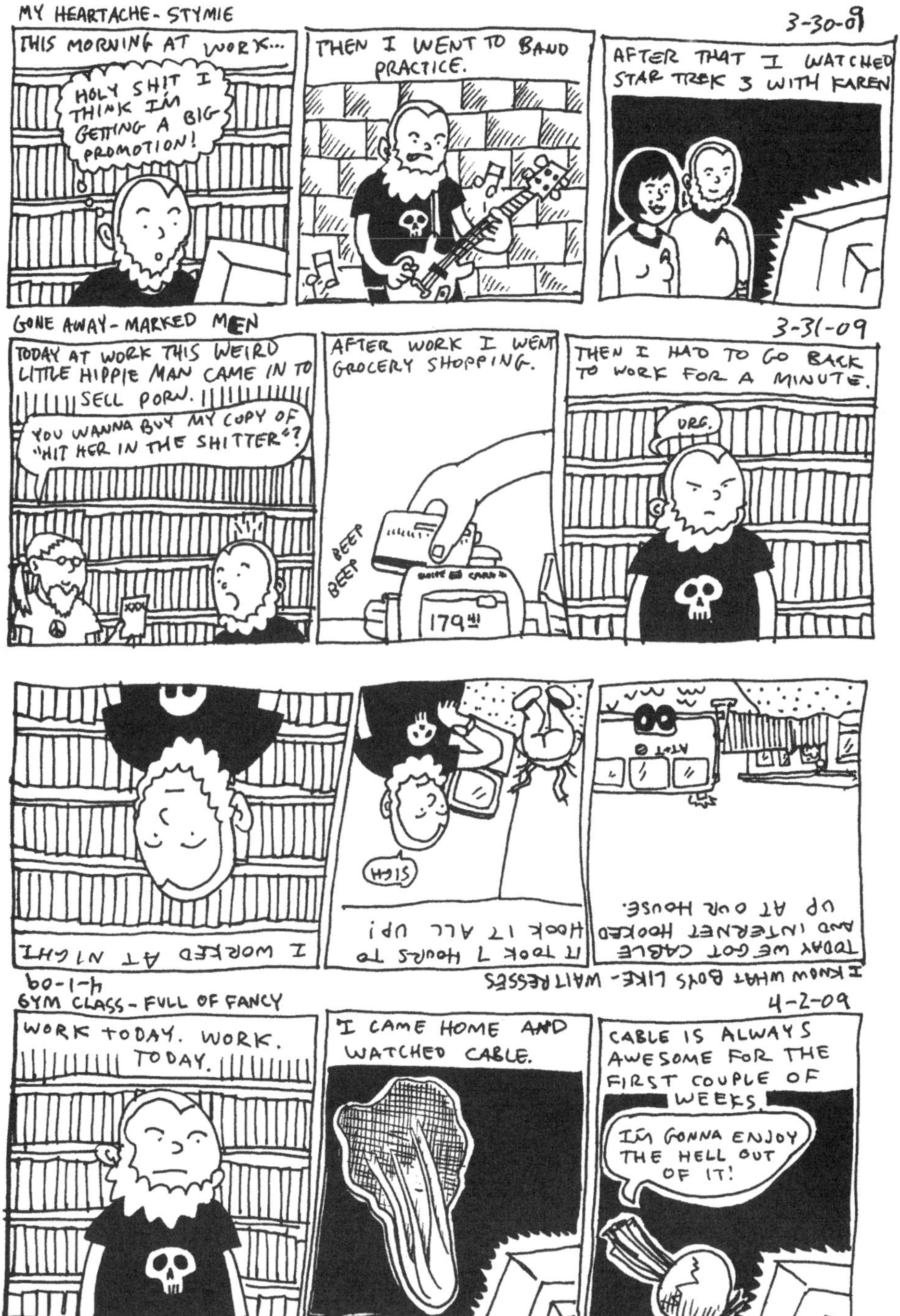
MY HEARTACHE - STYMIE
3-30-09
THIS MORNING AT WORK...
HOLY SHIT I THINK I'M GETTING A BIG PROMOTION!
THEN I WENT TO BAND PRACTICE.
AFTER THAT I WATCHED STAR TREK 3 WITH KAREN
GONE AWAY - MARKED MEN
3-31-09
TODAY AT WORK THIS WEIRD LITTLE HIPPIE MAN CAME IN TO SELL PORN.
YOU WANNA BUY MY COPY OF "HIT HER IN THE SHITTER"?
XXX
AFTER WORK I WENT GROCERY SHOPPING.
BEEP BEEP
179.45
THEN I HAD TO GO BACK TO WORK FOR A MINUTE.
URG.
I KNOW WHAT BOYS LIKE - WAITRESSES
4-1-09
TODAY WE GOT CABLE AND INTERNET HOOKED UP AT OUR HOUSE.
AT&T
IT TOOK 7 HOURS TO HOOK IT ALL UP!
SIGH
I WORKED AT NIGHT
GYM CLASS - FULL OF FANCY
4-2-09
WORK TODAY. WORK. TODAY.
I CAME HOME AND WATCHED CABLE.
CABLE IS ALWAYS AWESOME FOR THE FIRST COUPLE OF WEEKS.
I'M GONNA ENJOY THE HELL OUT OF IT!

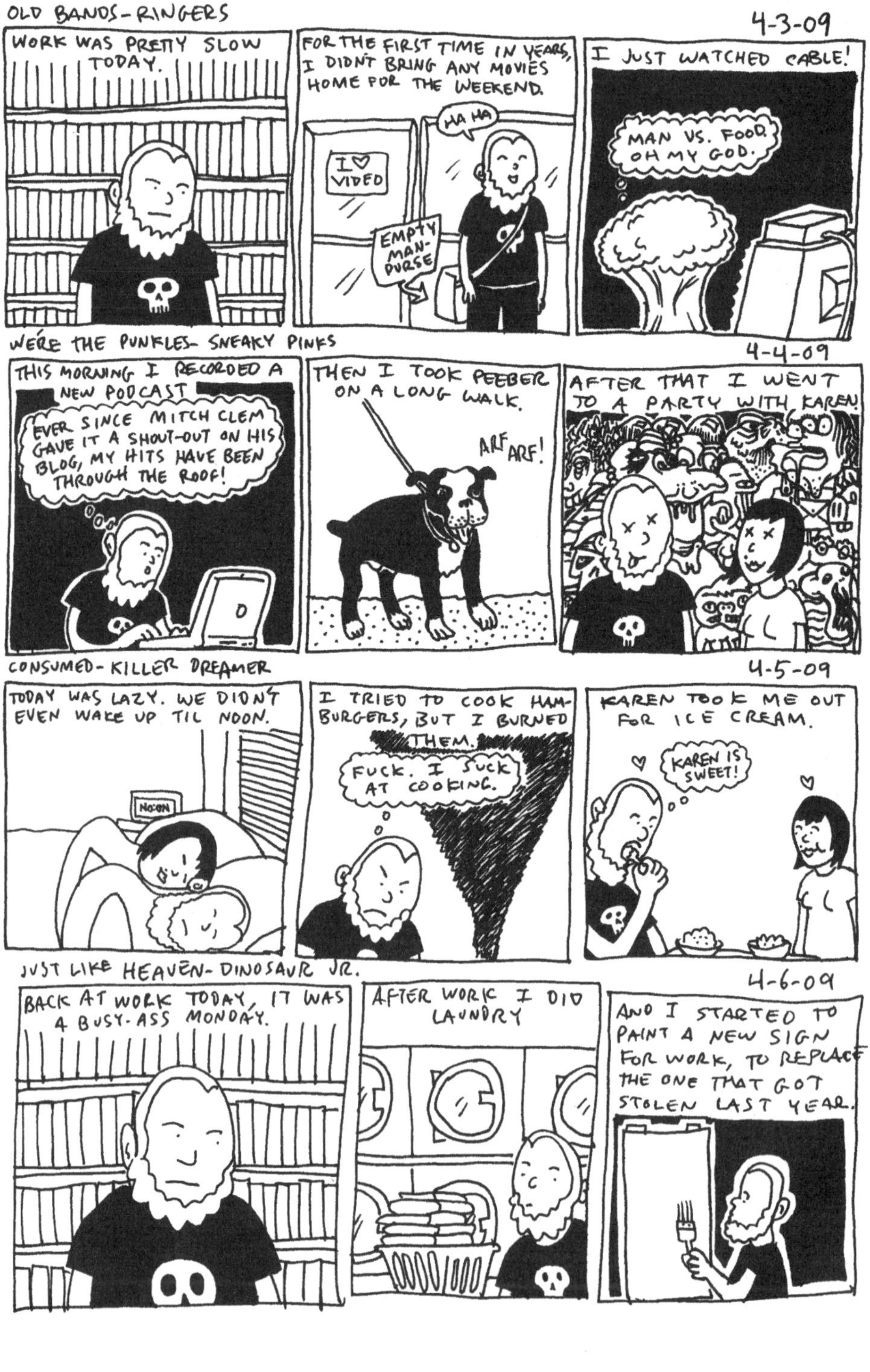

OLD BANDS-RINGERS
4-3-09
WORK WAS PRETTY SLOW TODAY.
FOR THE FIRST TIME IN YEARS, I DIDN'T BRING ANY MOVIES HOME FOR THE WEEKEND.
I ♡ VIDEO
HA HA
EMPTY MAN-PURSE
I JUST WATCHED CABLE!
MAN VS. FOOD. OH MY GOD.
WE'RE THE PUNKLES- SNEAKY PINKS
4-4-09
THIS MORNING I RECORDED A NEW PODCAST
EVER SINCE MITCH CLEM GAVE IT A SHOUT-OUT ON HIS BLOG, MY HITS HAVE BEEN THROUGH THE ROOF!
THEN I TOOK PEEBER ON A LONG WALK.
ARF ARF!
AFTER THAT I WENT TO A PARTY WITH KAREN!
CONSUMED- KILLER DREAMER
4-5-09
TODAY WAS LAZY. WE DIDN'T EVEN WAKE UP TIL NOON.
NOON
I TRIED TO COOK HAMBURGERS, BUT I BURNED THEM.
FUCK. I SUCK AT COOKING.
KAREN TOOK ME OUT FOR ICE CREAM.
KAREN IS SWEET!
JUST LIKE HEAVEN- DINOSAUR JR.
4-6-09
BACK AT WORK TODAY, IT WAS A BUSY-ASS MONDAY.
AFTER WORK I DID LAUNDRY
AND I STARTED TO PAINT A NEW SIGN FOR WORK, TO REPLACE THE ONE THAT GOT STOLEN LAST YEAR.

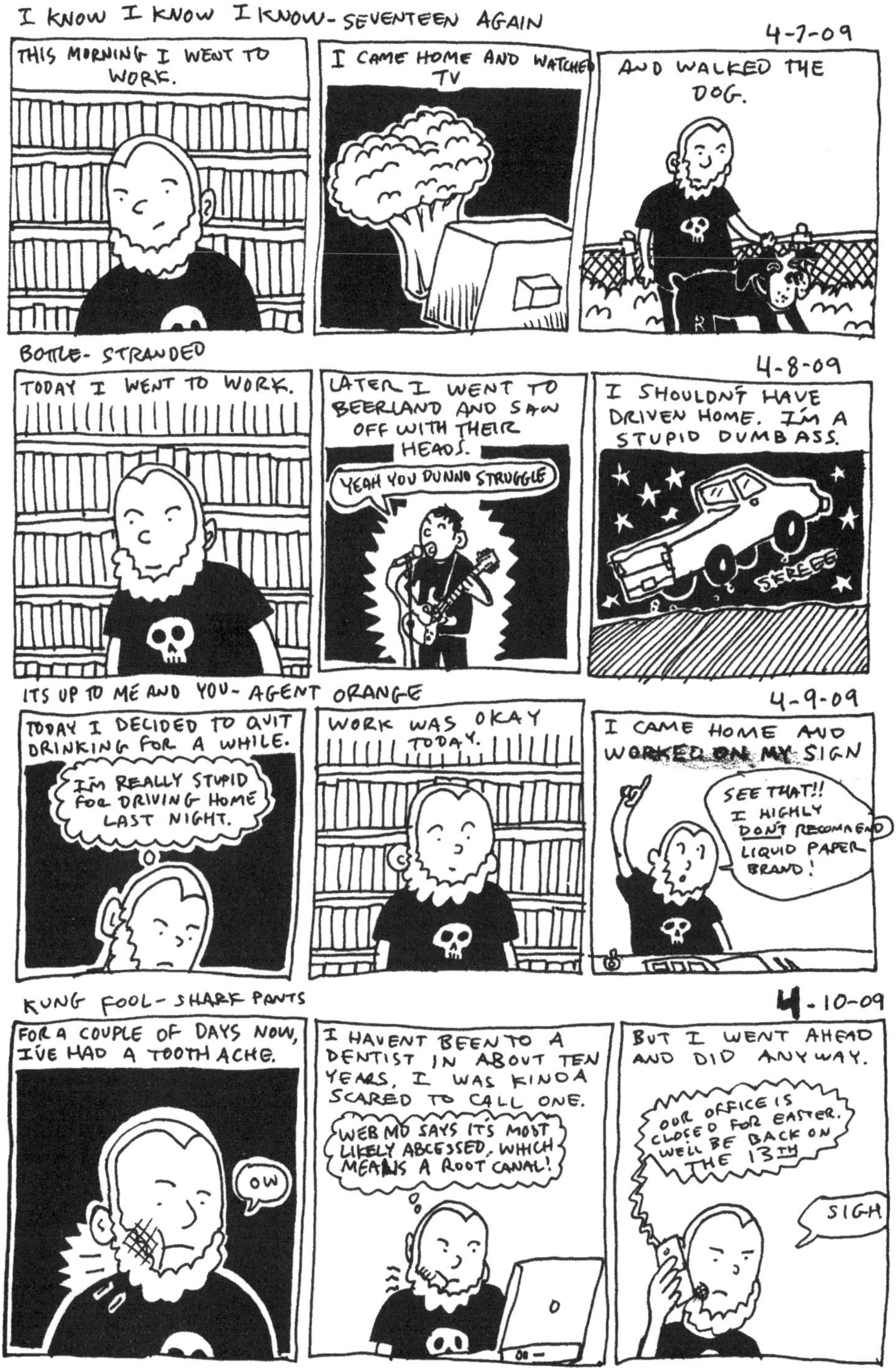
I KNOW I KNOW I KNOW - SEVENTEEN AGAIN
4-7-09
THIS MORNING I WENT TO WORK.
I CAME HOME AND WATCHED TV
AND WALKED THE DOG.
BOTTLE - STRANDED
4-8-09
TODAY I WENT TO WORK.
LATER I WENT TO BEERLAND AND SAW OFF WITH THEIR HEADS.
YEAH YOU DUNNO STRUGGLE
I SHOULDN'T HAVE DRIVEN HOME. I'M A STUPID DUMBASS.
SCREEE
ITS UP TO ME AND YOU - AGENT ORANGE
4-9-09
TODAY I DECIDED TO QUIT DRINKING FOR A WHILE.
I'M REALLY STUPID FOR DRIVING HOME LAST NIGHT.
WORK WAS OKAY TODAY.
I CAME HOME AND WORKED ON MY SIGN
SEE THAT!! I HIGHLY DON'T RECOMMEND LIQUID PAPER BRAND!
KUNG FOOL - SHARK PANTS
4-10-09
FOR A COUPLE OF DAYS NOW, I'VE HAD A TOOTH ACHE.
OW
I HAVENT BEEN TO A DENTIST IN ABOUT TEN YEARS. I WAS KINDA SCARED TO CALL ONE.
WEB MD SAYS ITS MOST LIKELY ABCESSED, WHICH MEANS A ROOT CANAL!
BUT I WENT AHEAD AND DID ANYWAY.
OUR OFFICE IS CLOSED FOR EASTER. WE'LL BE BACK ON THE 13TH
SIGH

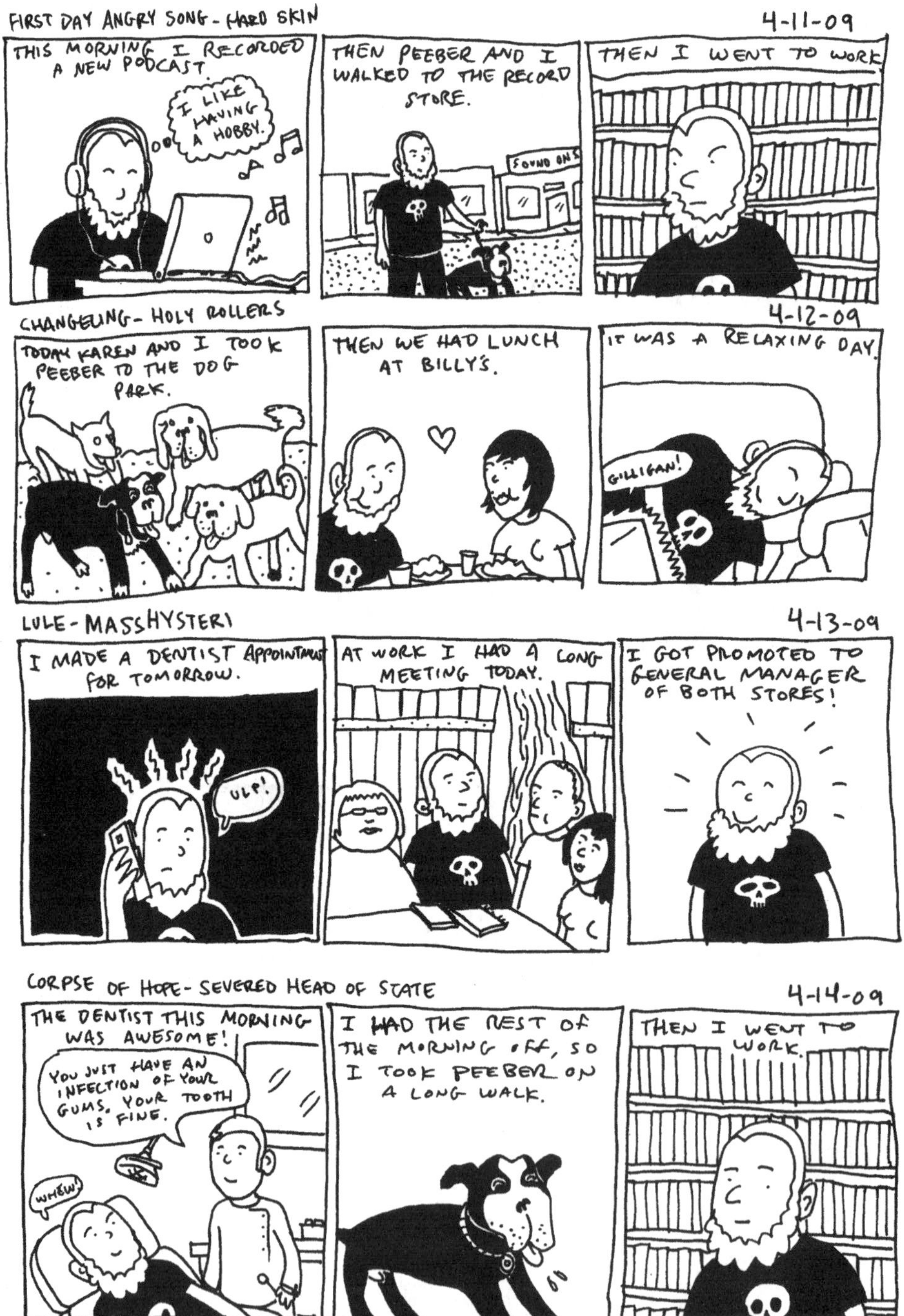

FIRST DAY ANGRY SONG - HARD SKIN
4-11-09
THIS MORNING I RECORDED A NEW PODCAST.
I LIKE HAVING A HOBBY.
THEN PEEBER AND I WALKED TO THE RECORD STORE.
SOUND ON S
THEN I WENT TO WORK.
CHANGELING - HOLY ROLLERS
4-12-09
TODAY KAREN AND I TOOK PEEBER TO THE DOG PARK.
THEN WE HAD LUNCH AT BILLY'S.
IT WAS A RELAXING DAY.
GILLIGAN!
LULE - MASSHYSTERI
4-13-09
I MADE A DENTIST APPOINTMENT FOR TOMORROW.
ULP!
AT WORK I HAD A LONG MEETING TODAY.
I GOT PROMOTED TO GENERAL MANAGER OF BOTH STORES!
CORPSE OF HOPE - SEVERED HEAD OF STATE
4-14-09
THE DENTIST THIS MORNING WAS AWESOME!
YOU JUST HAVE AN INFECTION OF YOUR GUMS. YOUR TOOTH IS FINE.
WHEW!
I HAD THE REST OF THE MORNING OFF, SO I TOOK PEEBER ON A LONG WALK.
THEN I WENT TO WORK.

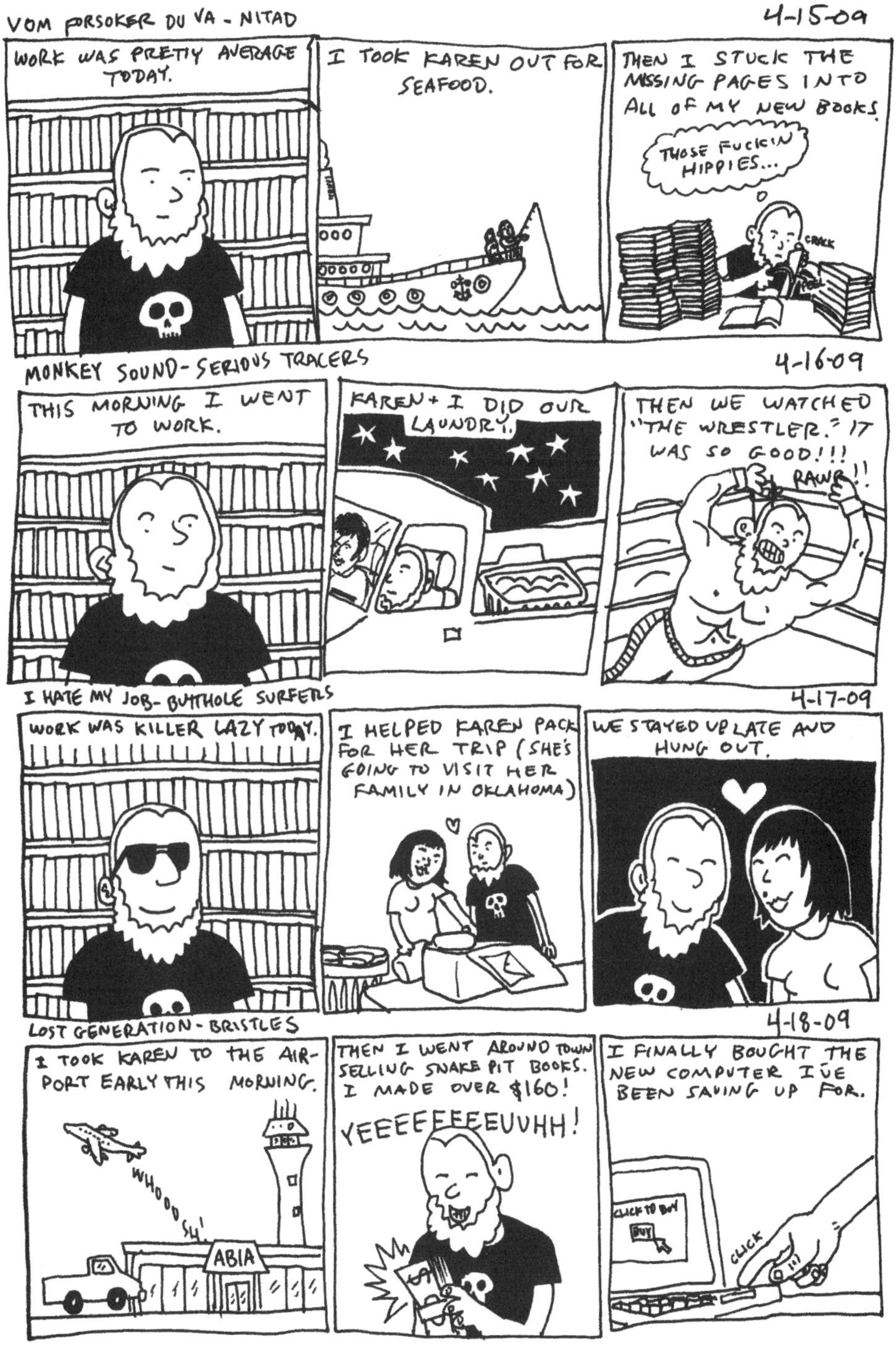
VOM FORSOKER DU VA - NITAD
4-15-09
WORK WAS PRETTY AVERAGE TODAY.
I TOOK KAREN OUT FOR SEAFOOD.
THEN I STUCK THE MISSING PAGES INTO ALL OF MY NEW BOOKS.
THOSE FUCKIN HIPPIES...
CRACK
PEEL
MONKEY SOUND - SERIOUS TRACERS
4-16-09
THIS MORNING I WENT TO WORK.
KAREN + I DID OUR LAUNDRY.
THEN WE WATCHED "THE WRESTLER." IT WAS SO GOOD!!!
RAWR!!
I HATE MY JOB - BUTTHOLE SURFERS
4-17-09
WORK WAS KILLER LAZY TODAY.
I HELPED KAREN PACK FOR HER TRIP (SHE'S GOING TO VISIT HER FAMILY IN OKLAHOMA)
WE STAYED UP LATE AND HUNG OUT.
LOST GENERATION - BRISTLES
4-18-09
I TOOK KAREN TO THE AIRPORT EARLY THIS MORNING.
WHOOOSH!
ABIA
THEN I WENT AROUND TOWN SELLING SNAKE PIT BOOKS. I MADE OVER $160!
YEEEEEEEEEUVHH!
I FINALLY BOUGHT THE NEW COMPUTER I'VE BEEN SAVING UP FOR.
CLICK TO BUY
BUY
CLICK

GUESS WHO'S RUNNING THE SHOW - THATCHER ON ACID

4-19-09

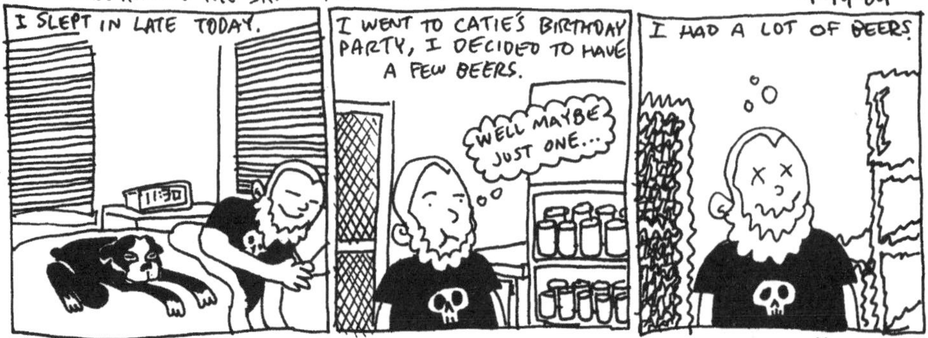
I SLEPT IN LATE TODAY.
11:30
I WENT TO CATIE'S BIRTHDAY PARTY, I DECIDED TO HAVE A FEW BEERS.
WELL MAYBE JUST ONE...
I HAD A LOT OF BEERS.

4-20-09

ATTITUDE - THE BRAT

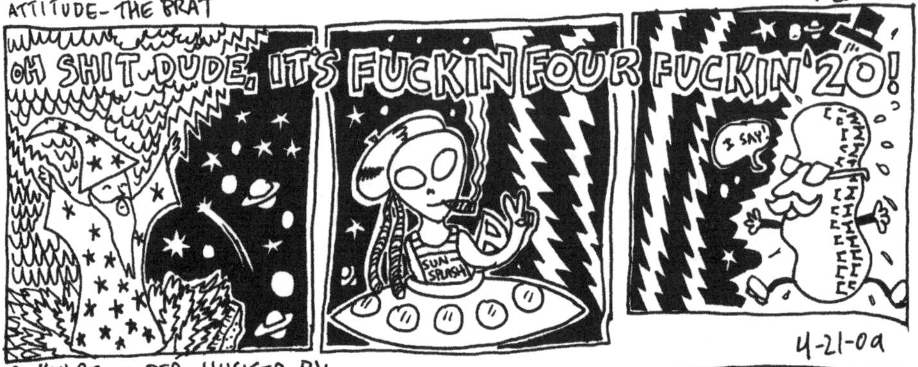
OH SHIT DUDE, IT'S FUCKIN FOUR FUCKIN '20!
SUN SPLASH
I SAY!

4-21-09

DO YOU REMEMBER - HUSKER DU

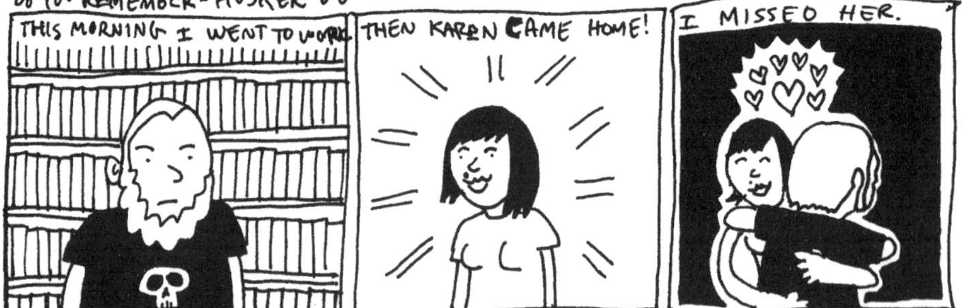
THIS MORNING I WENT TO WORK
THEN KAREN CAME HOME!
I MISSED HER.

TAMP IT IN - ADDSC

4-22-09

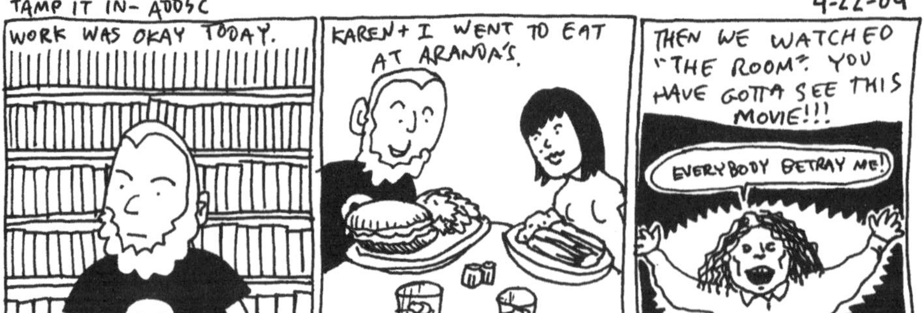
WORK WAS OKAY TODAY.
KAREN + I WENT TO EAT AT ARANDA'S.
THEN WE WATCHED "THE ROOM". YOU HAVE GOTTA SEE THIS MOVIE!!!
EVERYBODY BETRAY ME!

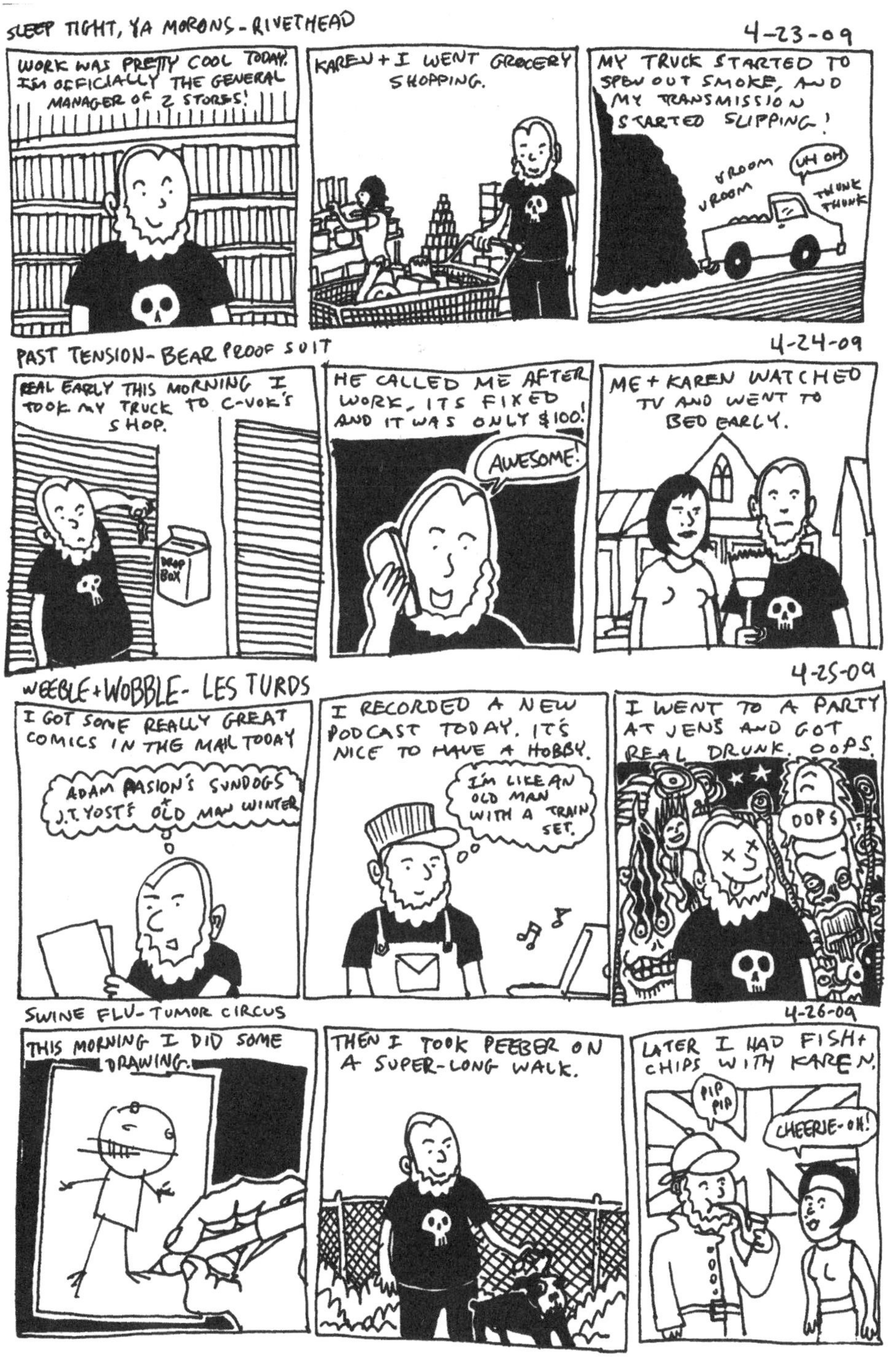
SLEEP TIGHT, YA MORONS - RIVETHEAD
4-23-09
WORK WAS PRETTY COOL TODAY. I'M OFFICIALLY THE GENERAL MANAGER OF 2 STORES!
KAREN + I WENT GROCERY SHOPPING.
MY TRUCK STARTED TO SPEW OUT SMOKE, AND MY TRANSMISSION STARTED SLIPPING!
VROOM VROOM
UH OH
THUNK THUNK
PAST TENSION - BEAR PROOF SUIT
4-24-09
REAL EARLY THIS MORNING I TOOK MY TRUCK TO C-VOK'S SHOP.
DROP BOX
HE CALLED ME AFTER WORK, ITS FIXED AND IT WAS ONLY $100!
AWESOME!
ME + KAREN WATCHED TV AND WENT TO BED EARLY.
WEEBLE + WOBBLE - LES TURDS
4-25-09
I GOT SOME REALLY GREAT COMICS IN THE MAIL TODAY
ADAM PASION'S SUNDOGS + J.T. YOST'S OLD MAN WINTER
I RECORDED A NEW PODCAST TODAY. IT'S NICE TO HAVE A HOBBY.
I'M LIKE AN OLD MAN WITH A TRAIN SET.
I WENT TO A PARTY AT JEN'S AND GOT REAL DRUNK. OOPS.
OOPS
SWINE FLU - TUMOR CIRCUS
4-26-09
THIS MORNING I DID SOME DRAWING.
THEN I TOOK PEEBER ON A SUPER-LONG WALK.
LATER I HAD FISH + CHIPS WITH KAREN.
PIP PIP
CHEERIE-OH!

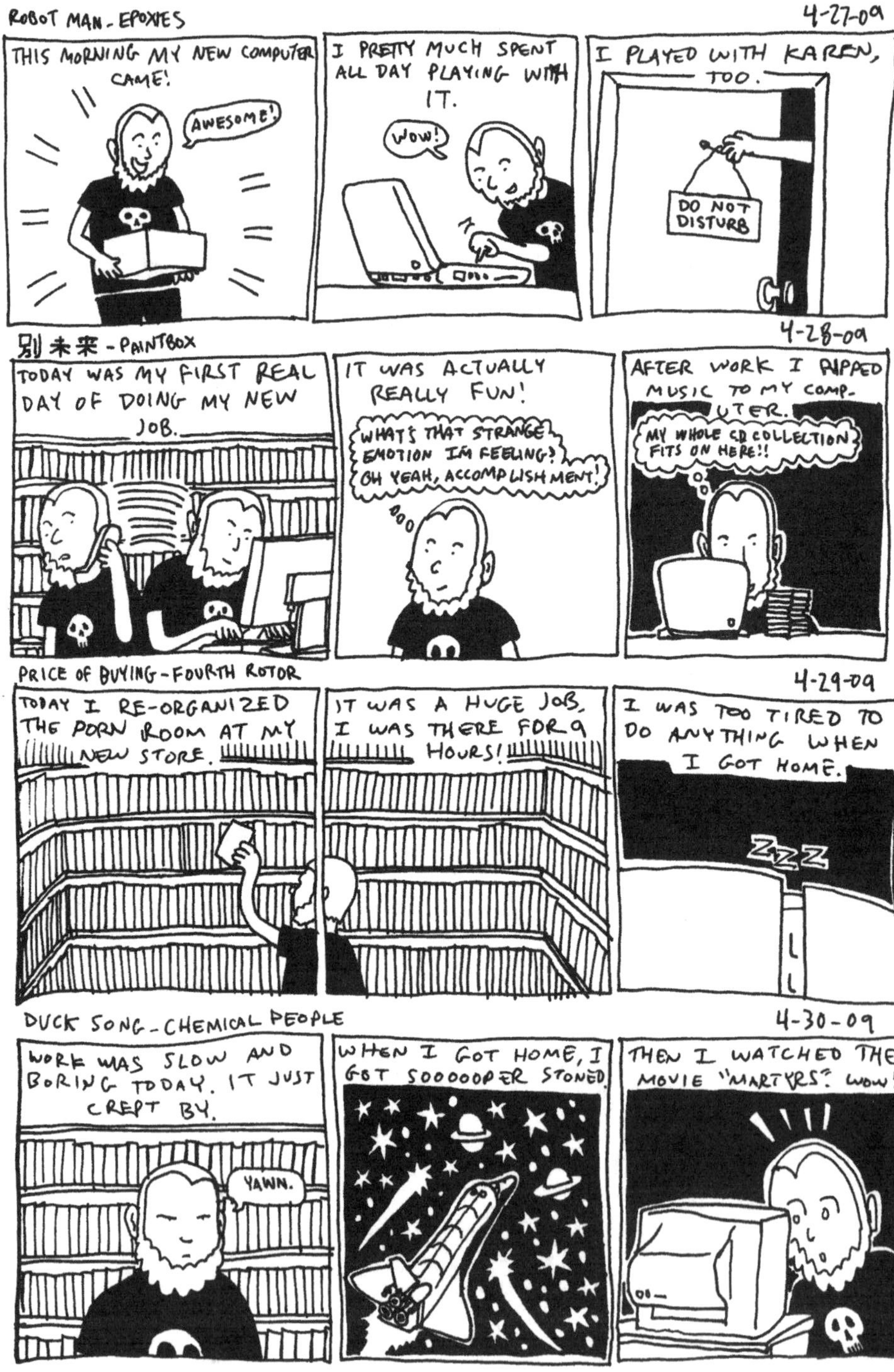
ROBOT MAN - EPOXIES
4-27-09
THIS MORNING MY NEW COMPUTER CAME!
AWESOME!
I PRETTY MUCH SPENT ALL DAY PLAYING WITH IT.
WOW!
I PLAYED WITH KAREN, TOO.
DO NOT DISTURB
别未来 - PAINTBOX
4-28-09
TODAY WAS MY FIRST REAL DAY OF DOING MY NEW JOB.
IT WAS ACTUALLY REALLY FUN!
WHAT'S THAT STRANGE EMOTION I'M FEELING? OH YEAH, ACCOMPLISHMENT!
AFTER WORK I RIPPED MUSIC TO MY COMPUTER.
MY WHOLE CD COLLECTION FITS ON HERE!!
PRICE OF BUYING - FOURTH ROTOR
4-29-09
TODAY I RE-ORGANIZED THE PORN ROOM AT MY NEW STORE.
IT WAS A HUGE JOB. I WAS THERE FOR 9 HOURS!
I WAS TOO TIRED TO DO ANYTHING WHEN I GOT HOME.
ZZZ
DUCK SONG - CHEMICAL PEOPLE
4-30-09
WORK WAS SLOW AND BORING TODAY. IT JUST CREPT BY.
YAWN.
WHEN I GOT HOME, I GOT SOOOOOPER STONED.
THEN I WATCHED THE MOVIE "MARTYRS." WOW!

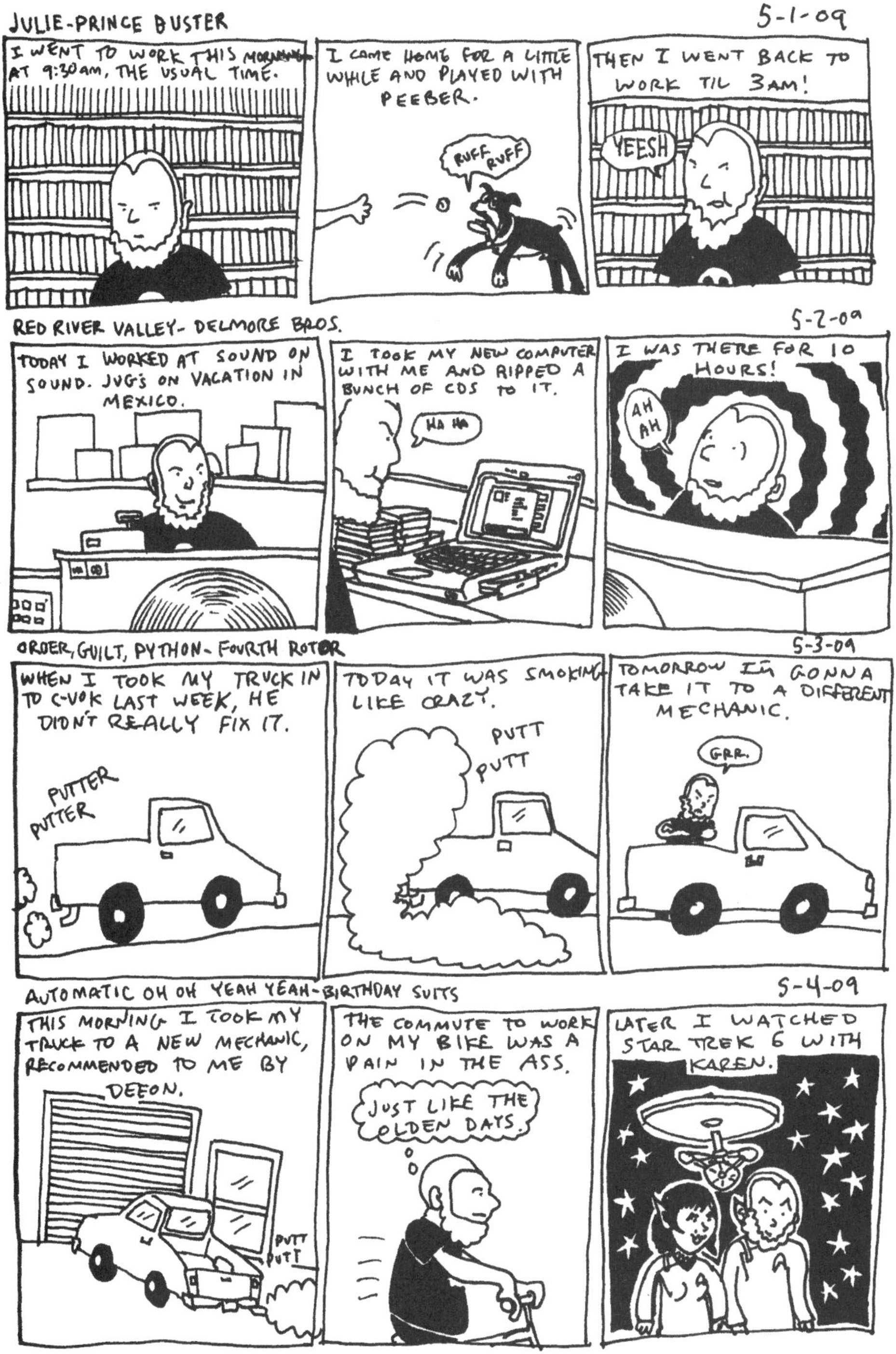
JULIE-PRINCE BUSTER
5-1-09
I WENT TO WORK THIS MORNING AT 9:30am, THE USUAL TIME.
I CAME HOME FOR A LITTLE WHILE AND PLAYED WITH PEEBER.
RUFF RUFF
THEN I WENT BACK TO WORK TIL 3AM!
YEESH
RED RIVER VALLEY- DELMORE BROS.
5-2-09
TODAY I WORKED AT SOUND ON SOUND. JUG'S ON VACATION IN MEXICO.
I TOOK MY NEW COMPUTER WITH ME AND RIPPED A BUNCH OF CDS TO IT.
HA HA
I WAS THERE FOR 10 HOURS!
AH AH
ORDER, GUILT, PYTHON- FOURTH ROTOR
5-3-09
WHEN I TOOK MY TRUCK IN TO C-VOK LAST WEEK, HE DIDN'T REALLY FIX IT.
PUTTER PUTTER
TODAY IT WAS SMOKING LIKE CRAZY.
PUTT PUTT
TOMORROW I'M GONNA TAKE IT TO A DIFFERENT MECHANIC.
GRR.
AUTOMATIC OH OH YEAH YEAH- BIRTHDAY SUITS
5-4-09
THIS MORNING I TOOK MY TRUCK TO A NEW MECHANIC, RECOMMENDED TO ME BY DEEON.
PUTT PUTT
THE COMMUTE TO WORK ON MY BIKE WAS A PAIN IN THE ASS.
JUST LIKE THE OLDEN DAYS.
LATER I WATCHED STAR TREK 6 WITH KAREN.

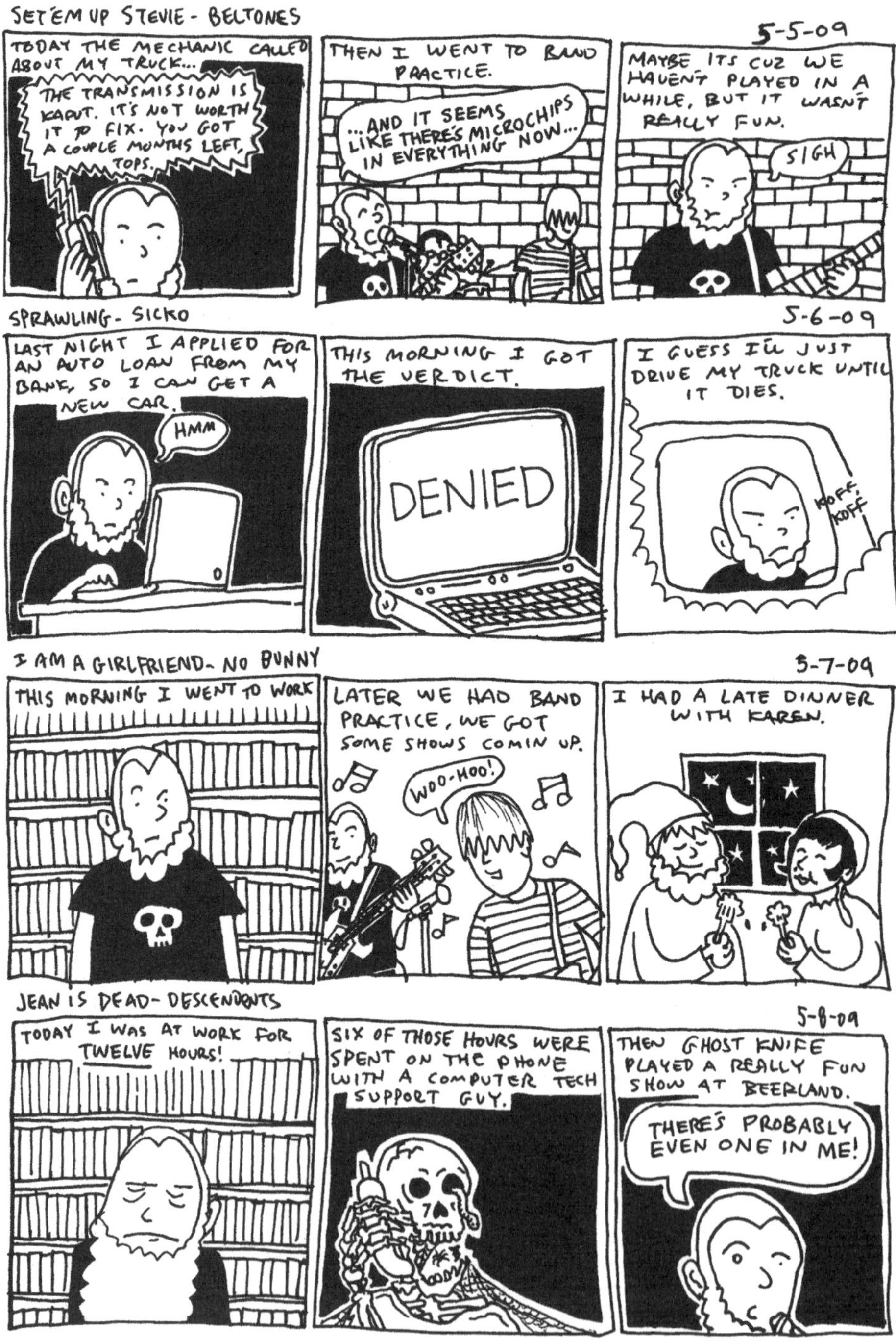
SET'EM UP STEVIE - BELTONES
5-5-09
TODAY THE MECHANIC CALLED ABOUT MY TRUCK...
THE TRANSMISSION IS KAPUT. IT'S NOT WORTH IT TO FIX. YOU GOT A COUPLE MONTHS LEFT, TOPS.
THEN I WENT TO BAND PRACTICE.
...AND IT SEEMS LIKE THERE'S MICROCHIPS IN EVERYTHING NOW...
MAYBE ITS CUZ WE HAVEN'T PLAYED IN A WHILE, BUT IT WASN'T REALLY FUN.
SIGH
SPRAWLING - SICKO
5-6-09
LAST NIGHT I APPLIED FOR AN AUTO LOAN FROM MY BANK, SO I CAN GET A NEW CAR.
HMM
THIS MORNING I GOT THE VERDICT.
DENIED
I GUESS I'LL JUST DRIVE MY TRUCK UNTIL IT DIES.
KOFF, KOFF
I AM A GIRLFRIEND - NO BUNNY
5-7-09
THIS MORNING I WENT TO WORK
LATER WE HAD BAND PRACTICE, WE GOT SOME SHOWS COMIN UP.
WOO-HOO!
I HAD A LATE DINNER WITH KAREN.
JEAN IS DEAD - DESCENDENTS
5-8-09
TODAY I WAS AT WORK FOR TWELVE HOURS!
SIX OF THOSE HOURS WERE SPENT ON THE PHONE WITH A COMPUTER TECH SUPPORT GUY.
THEN GHOST KNIFE PLAYED A REALLY FUN SHOW AT BEERLAND.
THERE'S PROBABLY EVEN ONE IN ME!

WE RUN - DAN PADILLA

THIS MORNING I TOOK PEEBER FOR A WALK.	THEN MIKE + CHRIS PICKED ME UP + WE WENT TO DENTON.	THE SHOW WAS FUN!

TO DENTON

WONDERFUL RAINBOW - LIGHTNING BOLT

I WOKE UP ALL SHITTY + HUNG-OVER THIS MORNING.	THE DRIVE BACK TO AUSTIN SEEMED TO TAKE FOREVER.	TONIGHT KAREN + I SAW STAR TREK AT THE IMAX!

HOW DID I USED TO DO THIS ALL THE TIME?

(WE DID STAY AT THIS COOL HOUSE WITH A GIANT TV)

MAD MEN

IS IT REALLY 7:30?

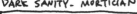

DARK SANITY - MORTICIAN

WORK WAS SO LONG TODAY. IT DIDN'T HELP THAT I GOT 4 HOURS OF SLEEP. AFTER STAR TREK WAS OVER LAST NIGHT, I HAD TO GO IN TO WORK AT 3:AM.	AFTER WORK I WENT SHOE SHOPPING WITH KAREN.	THEN GHOST KNIFE PLAYED A SHOW AT 1808

THESE LOOK KINDA DUMB. I DUNNO IF I LIKE THEM

1808 SUCKS

ST. PANCRAS - QUINTESSENCE

WORK TODAY WAS MUCH BETTER. I LIKE WORKING AT THE AIRPORT STORE.	I CAME HOME AND DID NOTHING. IT WAS RAD.	THEN KAREN + I DID LAUNDRY.

IT'S DIFFERENT!

PUTTER PUTTER

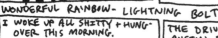

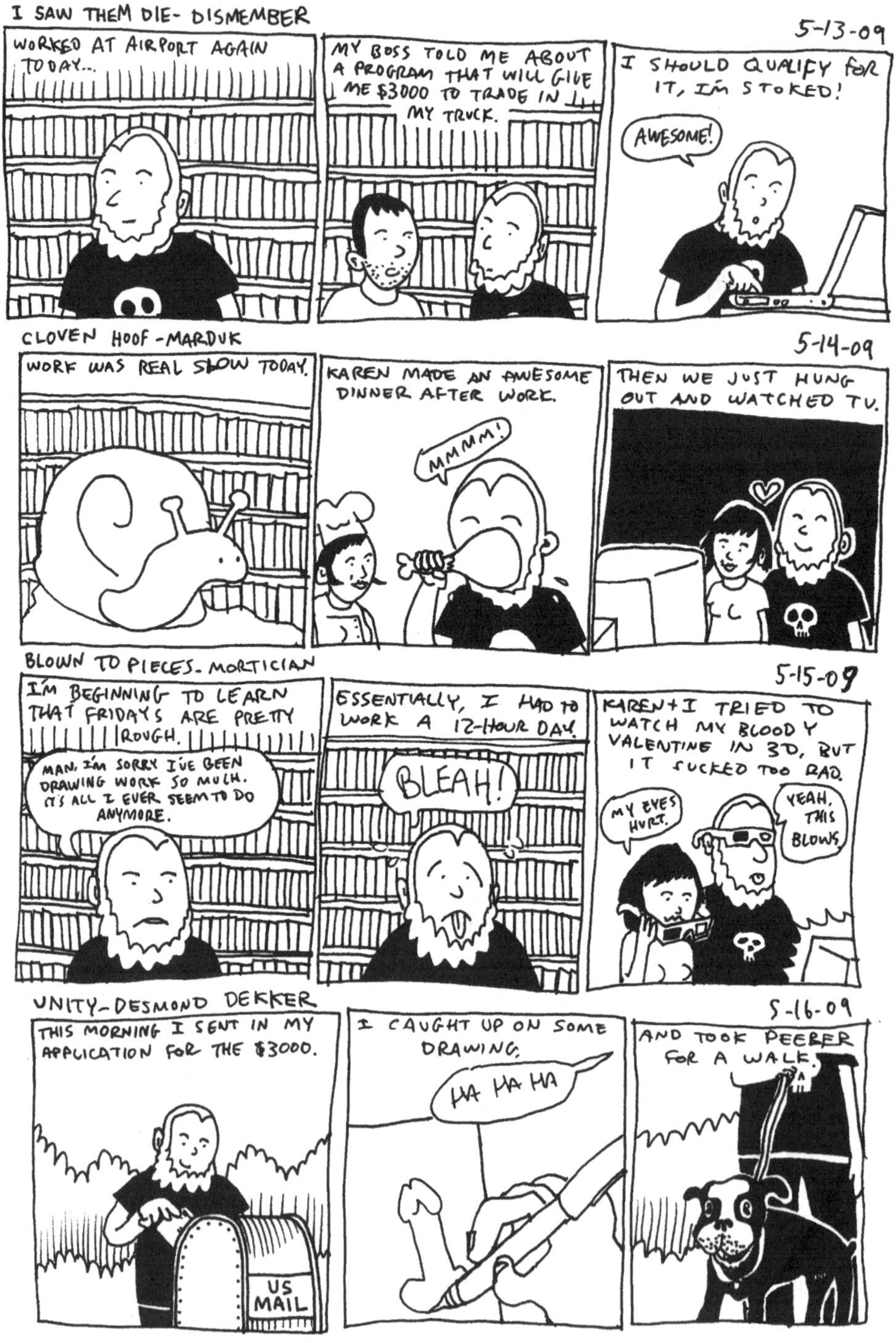
I SAW THEM DIE- DISMEMBER
5-13-09
WORKED AT AIRPORT AGAIN TODAY...
MY BOSS TOLD ME ABOUT A PROGRAM THAT WILL GIVE ME $3000 TO TRADE IN MY TRUCK.
I SHOULD QUALIFY FOR IT, I'M STOKED!
AWESOME!
CLOVEN HOOF - MARDUK
5-14-09
WORK WAS REAL SLOW TODAY.
KAREN MADE AN AWESOME DINNER AFTER WORK.
MMMM!
THEN WE JUST HUNG OUT AND WATCHED TV.
BLOWN TO PIECES - MORTICIAN
5-15-09
I'M BEGINNING TO LEARN THAT FRIDAYS ARE PRETTY ROUGH.
MAN, I'M SORRY I'VE BEEN DRAWING WORK SO MUCH. IT'S ALL I EVER SEEM TO DO ANYMORE.
ESSENTIALLY, I HAD TO WORK A 12-HOUR DAY.
BLEAH!
KAREN + I TRIED TO WATCH MY BLOODY VALENTINE IN 3D, BUT IT SUCKED TOO BAD.
MY EYES HURT.
YEAH. THIS BLOWS.
UNITY - DESMOND DEKKER
5-16-09
THIS MORNING I SENT IN MY APPLICATION FOR THE $3000.
US MAIL
I CAUGHT UP ON SOME DRAWING.
HA HA HA
AND TOOK PEEBER FOR A WALK.

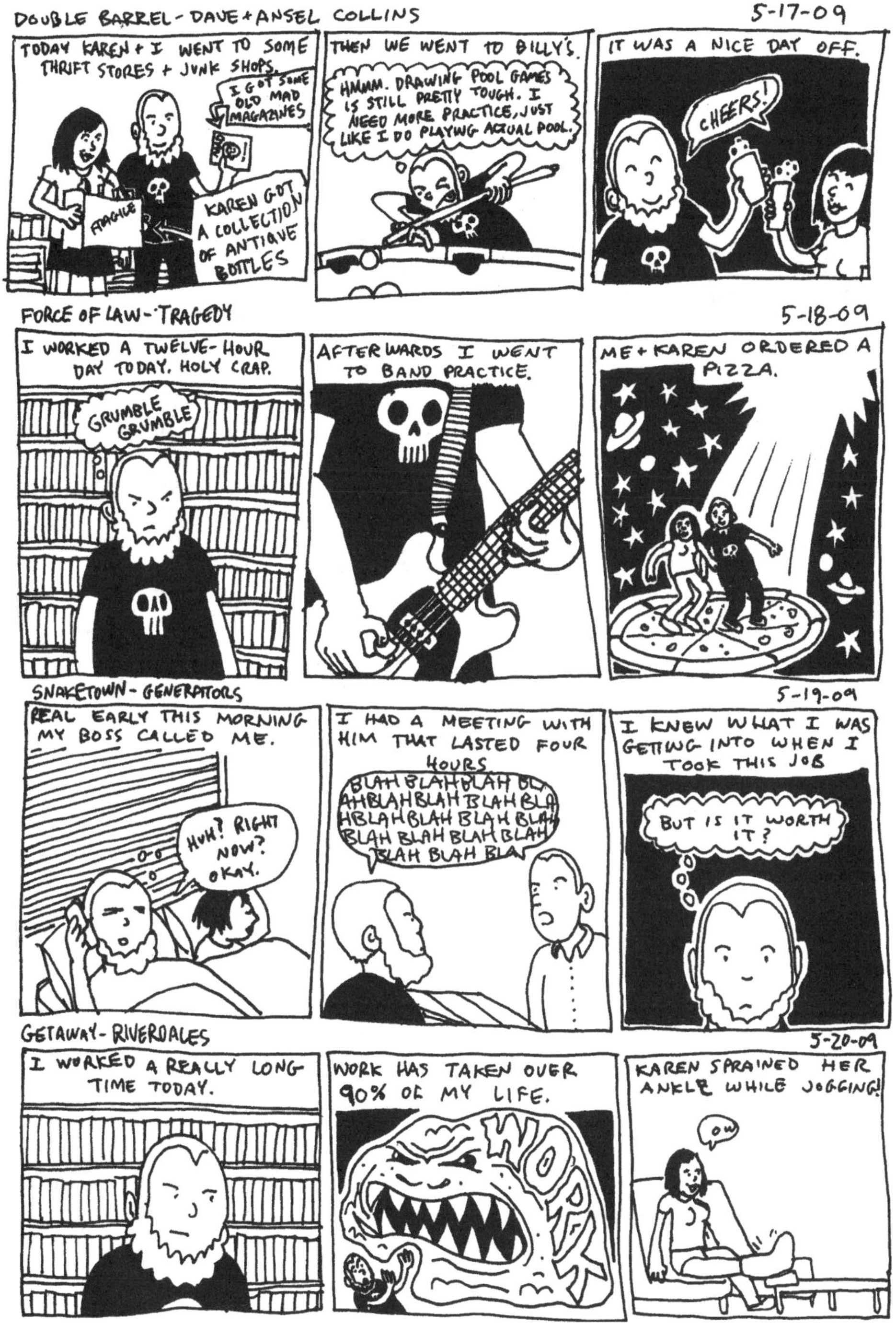
DOUBLE BARREL - DAVE + ANSEL COLLINS
5-17-09
TODAY KAREN + I WENT TO SOME THRIFT STORES + JUNK SHOPS.
I GOT SOME OLD MAD MAGAZINES
FRAGILE
KAREN GOT A COLLECTION OF ANTIQUE BOTTLES
THEN WE WENT TO BILLY'S.
HMMM. DRAWING POOL GAMES IS STILL PRETTY TOUGH. I NEED MORE PRACTICE, JUST LIKE I DO PLAYING ACTUAL POOL.
IT WAS A NICE DAY OFF.
CHEERS!
FORCE OF LAW - TRAGEDY
5-18-09
I WORKED A TWELVE-HOUR DAY TODAY. HOLY CRAP.
GRUMBLE GRUMBLE
AFTERWARDS I WENT TO BAND PRACTICE.
ME + KAREN ORDERED A PIZZA.
SNAKETOWN - GENERATORS
5-19-09
REAL EARLY THIS MORNING MY BOSS CALLED ME.
HUH? RIGHT NOW? OKAY.
I HAD A MEETING WITH HIM THAT LASTED FOUR HOURS.
BLAH BLAH BLAH BLAH BLAH BLAH BLAH BLAH BLAH BLAH BLAH BLAH BLAH BLAH BLAH BLAH BLAH BLAH BLAH BLAH BLAH
I KNEW WHAT I WAS GETTING INTO WHEN I TOOK THIS JOB
BUT IS IT WORTH IT?
GETAWAY - RIVERDALES
5-20-09
I WORKED A REALLY LONG TIME TODAY.
WORK HAS TAKEN OVER 90% OF MY LIFE.
WORK
KAREN SPRAINED HER ANKLE WHILE JOGGING!
OW

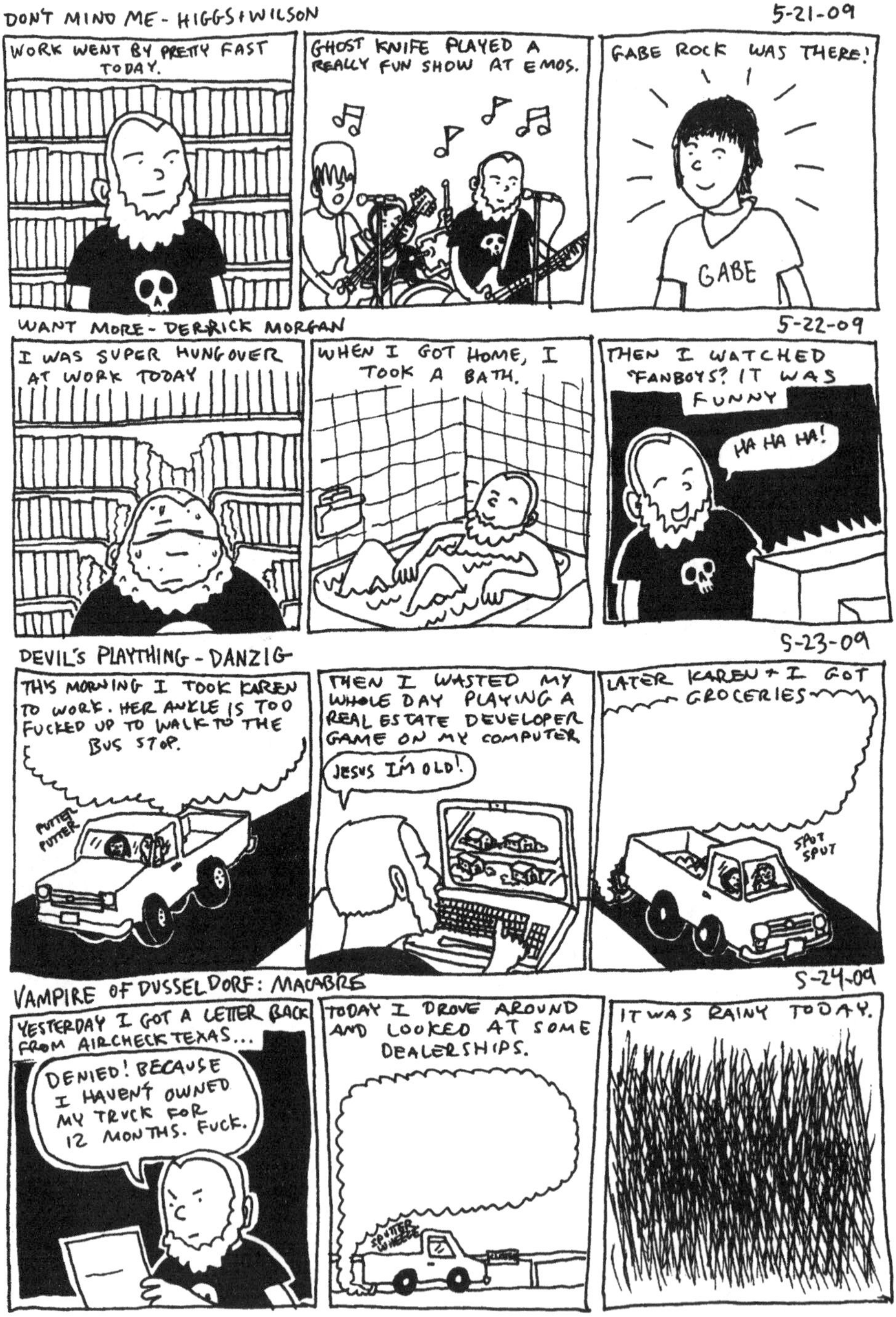
DON'T MIND ME - HIGGS + WILSON
5-21-09
WORK WENT BY PRETTY FAST TODAY.
GHOST KNIFE PLAYED A REALLY FUN SHOW AT EMOS.
GABE ROCK WAS THERE!
GABE
WANT MORE - DERRICK MORGAN
5-22-09
I WAS SUPER HUNGOVER AT WORK TODAY
WHEN I GOT HOME, I TOOK A BATH.
THEN I WATCHED "FANBOYS." IT WAS FUNNY
HA HA HA!
DEVIL'S PLAYTHING - DANZIG
5-23-09
THIS MORNING I TOOK KAREN TO WORK. HER ANKLE IS TOO FUCKED UP TO WALK TO THE BUS STOP.
PUTTER PUTTER
THEN I WASTED MY WHOLE DAY PLAYING A REAL ESTATE DEVELOPER GAME ON MY COMPUTER
JESUS I'M OLD!
LATER KAREN + I GOT GROCERIES
SPUT SPUT
VAMPIRE OF DUSSELDORF: MACABRE
5-24-09
YESTERDAY I GOT A LETTER BACK FROM AIRCHECK TEXAS...
DENIED! BECAUSE I HAVEN'T OWNED MY TRUCK FOR 12 MONTHS. FUCK.
TODAY I DROVE AROUND AND LOOKED AT SOME DEALERSHIPS.
SPUTTER WHEEZE
IT WAS RAINY TODAY.

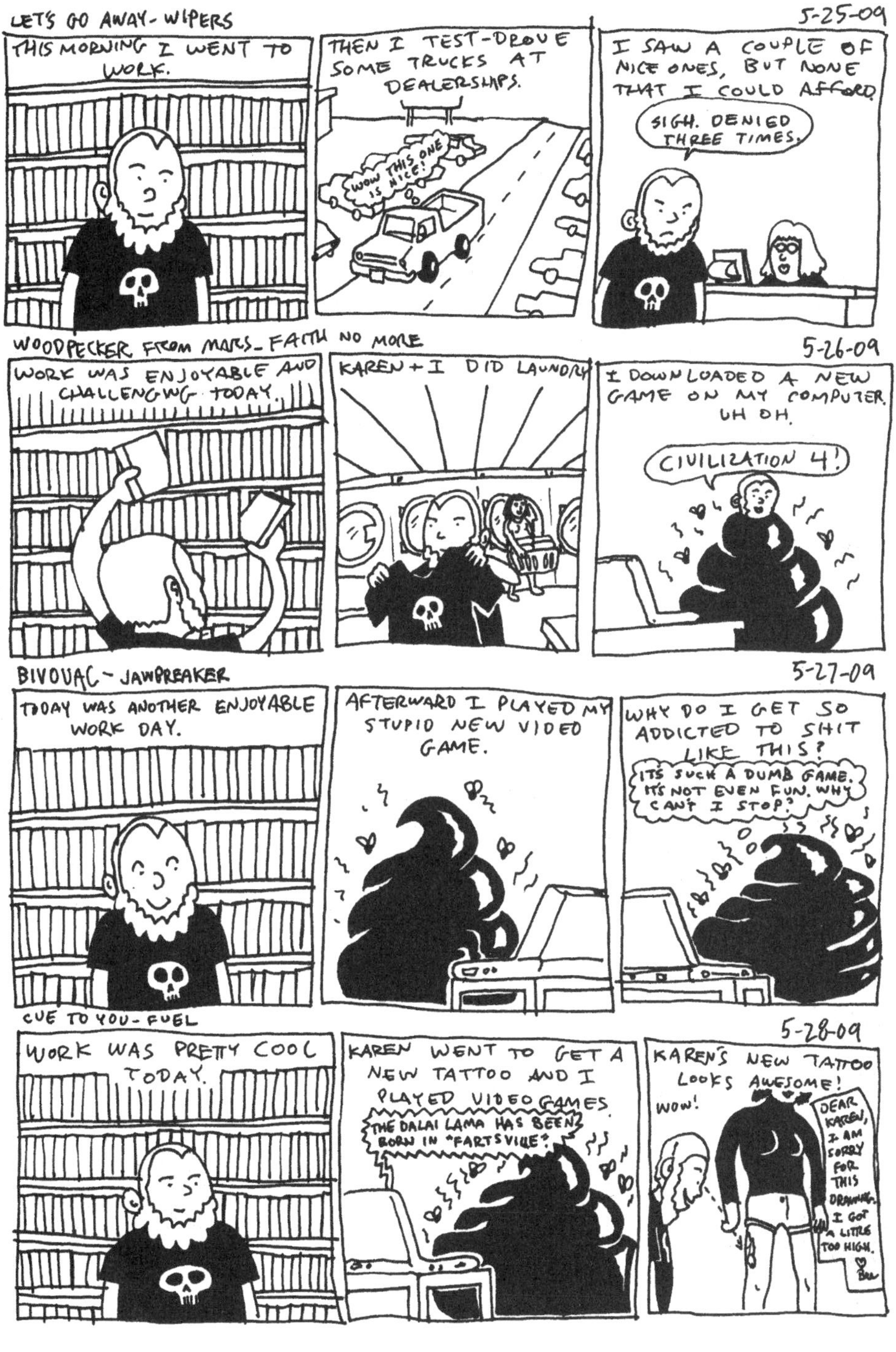
LET'S GO AWAY - WIPERS
5-25-09
THIS MORNING I WENT TO WORK.
THEN I TEST-DROVE SOME TRUCKS AT DEALERSHIPS.
WOW THIS ONE IS NICE!
I SAW A COUPLE OF NICE ONES, BUT NONE THAT I COULD AFFORD.
SIGH. DENIED THREE TIMES.
WOODPECKER FROM MARS - FAITH NO MORE
5-26-09
WORK WAS ENJOYABLE AND CHALLENGING TODAY.
KAREN + I DID LAUNDRY
I DOWNLOADED A NEW GAME ON MY COMPUTER. UH OH.
CIVILIZATION 4!
BIVOUAC - JAWBREAKER
5-27-09
TODAY WAS ANOTHER ENJOYABLE WORK DAY.
AFTERWARD I PLAYED MY STUPID NEW VIDEO GAME.
WHY DO I GET SO ADDICTED TO SHIT LIKE THIS?
IT'S SUCH A DUMB GAME. IT'S NOT EVEN FUN. WHY CAN'T I STOP?
CUE TO YOU - FUEL
5-28-09
WORK WAS PRETTY COOL TODAY.
KAREN WENT TO GET A NEW TATTOO AND I PLAYED VIDEO GAMES.
THE DALAI LAMA HAS BEEN BORN IN "FARTSVILLE"
KAREN'S NEW TATTOO LOOKS AWESOME!
WOW!
DEAR KAREN, I AM SORRY FOR THIS DRAWING. I GOT A LITTLE TOO HIGH.

LIV OCH DÖD - MASSHYSTERI

5-29-09

AT WORK TODAY THEY FUCKED UP MY PAYCHECK FOR THE FIFTH WEEK IN A ROW!!!
GOD DAMMIT!

MY FORM OF "SILENT PROTEST" WAS TO GO HOME EARLY
THIS'LL SHOW 'EM!

BUT I STILL HAD TO GO IN LATER AT NIGHT AND WORK.
SIGH.

LOCOFOCO MOTHER-FUCKER - FLESHIES

5-30-09

A DAY OFF! I CAUGHT UP ON SOME DRAWING...

CLEANED THE KITCHEN...

AND PLAYED VIDEO GAMES.
I DON'T GIVE A FUCK WHAT YOU THINK!

DAY OF DARKNESS - DEICIDE

5-31-09

THE ONLY THING BETTER THAN A DAY OFF IS A DAY OFF WITH KAREN!

WE WENT TO SOME THRIFT STORES.
GOODWILL

AND WENT OUT FOR DINNER.
I LOVE MY GIRLFRIEND.

FREAK MACHINE - MAN IS THE BASTARD

6-1-09

BACK AT WORK TODAY, I WAS BUSY AS HELL!

KAREN + I MADE BURGERS ON THE GRILL FOR DINNER.
HEY!

SHE READ A BOOK WHILE I PLAYED VIDEO GAMES.

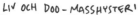

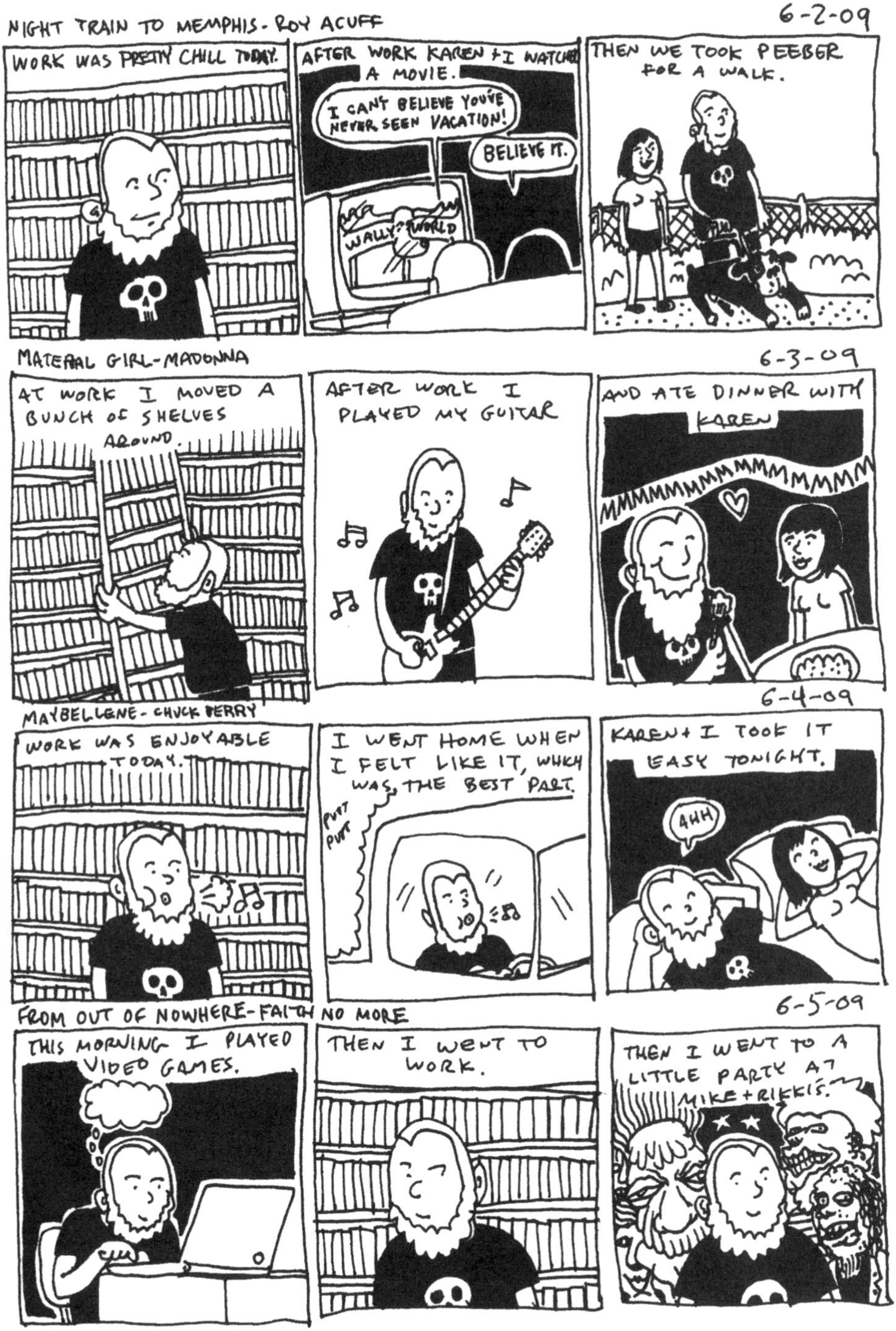
NIGHT TRAIN TO MEMPHIS - ROY ACUFF
6-2-09
WORK WAS PRETTY CHILL TODAY.
AFTER WORK KAREN + I WATCHED A MOVIE.
I CAN'T BELIEVE YOU'VE NEVER SEEN VACATION!
BELIEVE IT.
WALLY WORLD
THEN WE TOOK PEEBER FOR A WALK.
MATERIAL GIRL - MADONNA
6-3-09
AT WORK I MOVED A BUNCH OF SHELVES AROUND.
AFTER WORK I PLAYED MY GUITAR
AND ATE DINNER WITH KAREN
MMMMMMMMMMMMMMMMMMM
MAYBELLENE - CHUCK BERRY
6-4-09
WORK WAS ENJOYABLE TODAY.
I WENT HOME WHEN I FELT LIKE IT, WHICH WAS THE BEST PART.
PUTT PUTT
KAREN + I TOOK IT EASY TONIGHT.
AHH
FROM OUT OF NOWHERE - FAITH NO MORE
6-5-09
THIS MORNING I PLAYED VIDEO GAMES.
THEN I WENT TO WORK.
THEN I WENT TO A LITTLE PARTY AT MIKE + RIKKI'S.

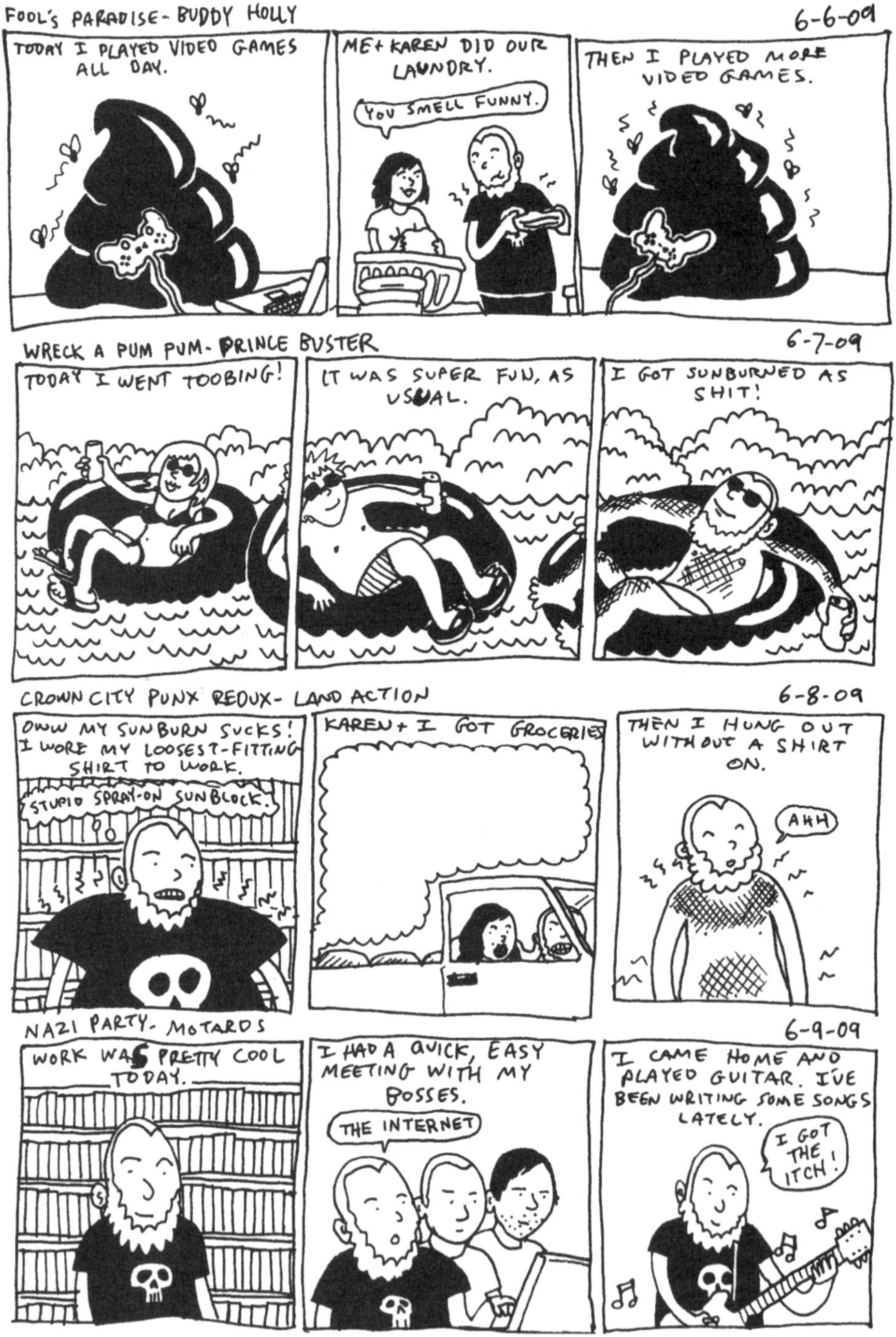
FOOL'S PARADISE- BUDDY HOLLY
6-6-09
TODAY I PLAYED VIDEO GAMES ALL DAY.
ME+ KAREN DID OUR LAUNDRY.
YOU SMELL FUNNY.
THEN I PLAYED MORE VIDEO GAMES.
WRECK A PUM PUM- PRINCE BUSTER
6-7-09
TODAY I WENT TOOBING!
IT WAS SUPER FUN, AS USUAL.
I GOT SUNBURNED AS SHIT!
CROWN CITY PUNX REDUX- LAND ACTION
6-8-09
OWW MY SUNBURN SUCKS! I WORE MY LOOSEST-FITTING SHIRT TO WORK.
STUPID SPRAY-ON SUNBLOCK.
KAREN+ I GOT GROCERIES
THEN I HUNG OUT WITHOUT A SHIRT ON.
AHH
NAZI PARTY- MOTARDS
6-9-09
WORK WAS PRETTY COOL TODAY.
I HAD A QUICK, EASY MEETING WITH MY BOSSES.
THE INTERNET
I CAME HOME AND PLAYED GUITAR. I'VE BEEN WRITING SOME SONGS LATELY.
I GOT THE ITCH!

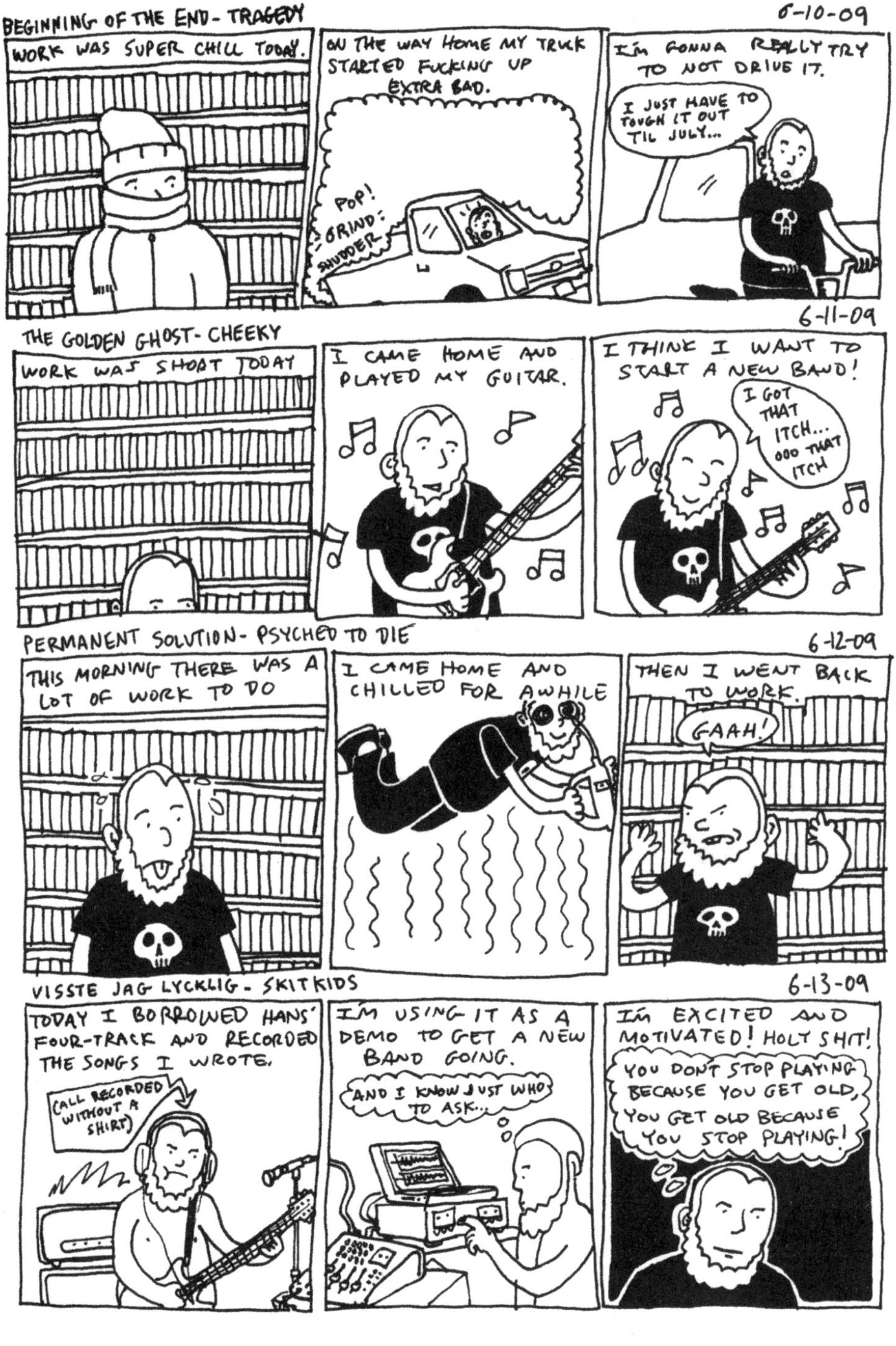
BEGINNING OF THE END - TRAGEDY
6-10-09
WORK WAS SUPER CHILL TODAY.
ON THE WAY HOME MY TRUCK STARTED FUCKING UP EXTRA BAD.
POP! GRIND: SHUDDER
I'M GONNA REALLY TRY TO NOT DRIVE IT.
I JUST HAVE TO TOUGH IT OUT TIL JULY...
THE GOLDEN GHOST - CHEEKY
6-11-09
WORK WAS SHORT TODAY
I CAME HOME AND PLAYED MY GUITAR.
I THINK I WANT TO START A NEW BAND!
I GOT THAT ITCH... OOO THAT ITCH
PERMANENT SOLUTION - PSYCHED TO DIE
6-12-09
THIS MORNING THERE WAS A LOT OF WORK TO DO
I CAME HOME AND CHILLED FOR AWHILE
THEN I WENT BACK TO WORK.
GAAH!
VISSTE JAG LYCKLIG - SKITKIDS
6-13-09
TODAY I BORROWED HANS' FOUR-TRACK AND RECORDED THE SONGS I WROTE.
(ALL RECORDED WITHOUT A SHIRT)
I'M USING IT AS A DEMO TO GET A NEW BAND GOING.
AND I KNOW JUST WHO TO ASK...
I'M EXCITED AND MOTIVATED! HOLY SHIT!
YOU DON'T STOP PLAYING BECAUSE YOU GET OLD, YOU GET OLD BECAUSE YOU STOP PLAYING!

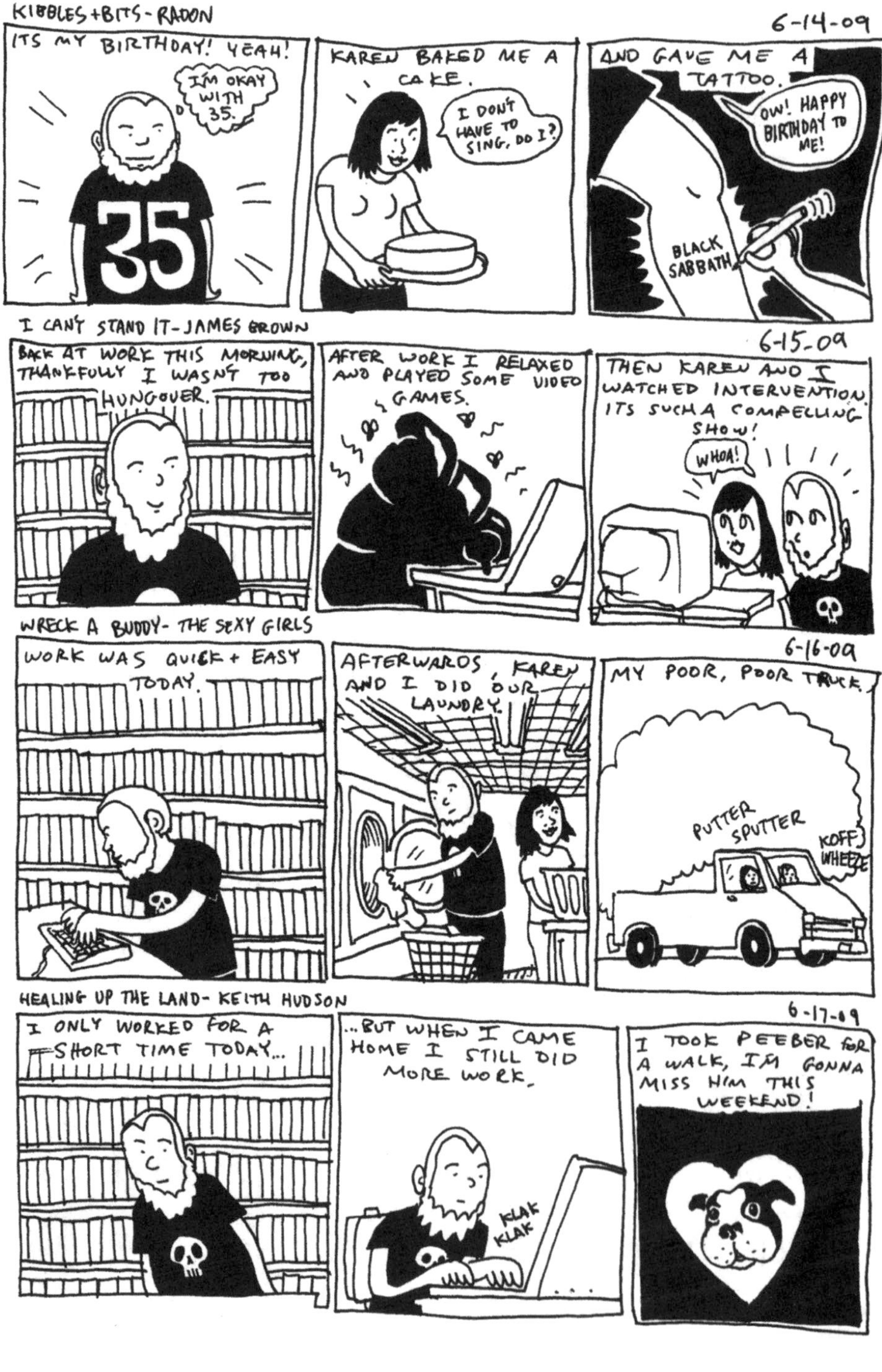
KIBBLES + BITS - RADON
6-14-09
ITS MY BIRTHDAY! YEAH!
I'M OKAY WITH 35.
35
KAREN BAKED ME A CAKE.
I DON'T HAVE TO SING, DO I?
AND GAVE ME A TATTOO.
OW! HAPPY BIRTHDAY TO ME!
BLACK SABBATH
I CAN'T STAND IT - JAMES BROWN
6-15-09
BACK AT WORK THIS MORNING, THANKFULLY I WASN'T TOO HUNGOVER.
AFTER WORK I RELAXED AND PLAYED SOME VIDEO GAMES.
THEN KAREN AND I WATCHED INTERVENTION. ITS SUCH A COMPELLING SHOW!
WHOA!
WRECK A BUDDY - THE SEXY GIRLS
6-16-09
WORK WAS QUICK + EASY TODAY.
AFTERWARDS, KAREN AND I DID OUR LAUNDRY.
MY POOR, POOR TRUCK.
PUTTER SPUTTER
KOFF WHEEZE
HEALING UP THE LAND - KEITH HUDSON
6-17-09
I ONLY WORKED FOR A SHORT TIME TODAY...
...BUT WHEN I CAME HOME I STILL DID MORE WORK.
KLAK KLAK
I TOOK PEEBER FOR A WALK, I'M GONNA MISS HIM THIS WEEKEND!

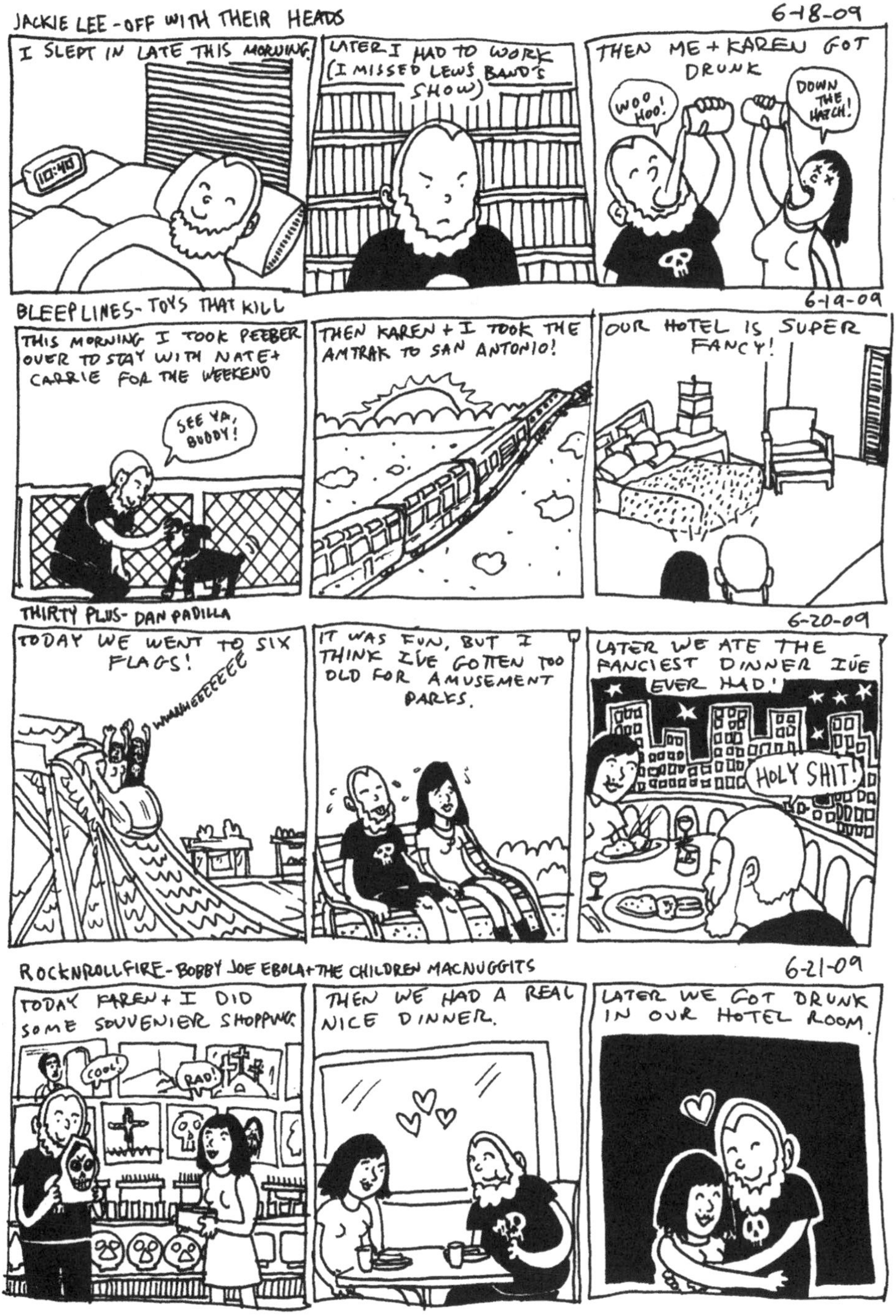

JACKIE LEE - OFF WITH THEIR HEADS
6-18-09
I SLEPT IN LATE THIS MORNING.
10:40
LATER I HAD TO WORK (I MISSED LEW'S BAND'S SHOW)
THEN ME + KAREN GOT DRUNK
WOO HOO!
DOWN THE HATCH!
BLEEPLINES - TOYS THAT KILL
6-19-09
THIS MORNING I TOOK PEEBER OVER TO STAY WITH NATE + CARRIE FOR THE WEEKEND
SEE YA, BUDDY!
THEN KAREN + I TOOK THE AMTRAK TO SAN ANTONIO!
OUR HOTEL IS SUPER FANCY!
THIRTY PLUS - DAN PADILLA
6-20-09
TODAY WE WENT TO SIX FLAGS!
IT WAS FUN, BUT I THINK I'VE GOTTEN TOO OLD FOR AMUSEMENT PARKS.
LATER WE ATE THE FANCIEST DINNER I'VE EVER HAD!
HOLY SHIT!
ROCKNROLLFIRE - BOBBY JOE EBOLA + THE CHILDREN MACNUGGITS
6-21-09
TODAY KAREN + I DID SOME SOUVENIER SHOPPING.
COOL!
RAD!
THEN WE HAD A REAL NICE DINNER.
LATER WE GOT DRUNK IN OUR HOTEL ROOM.

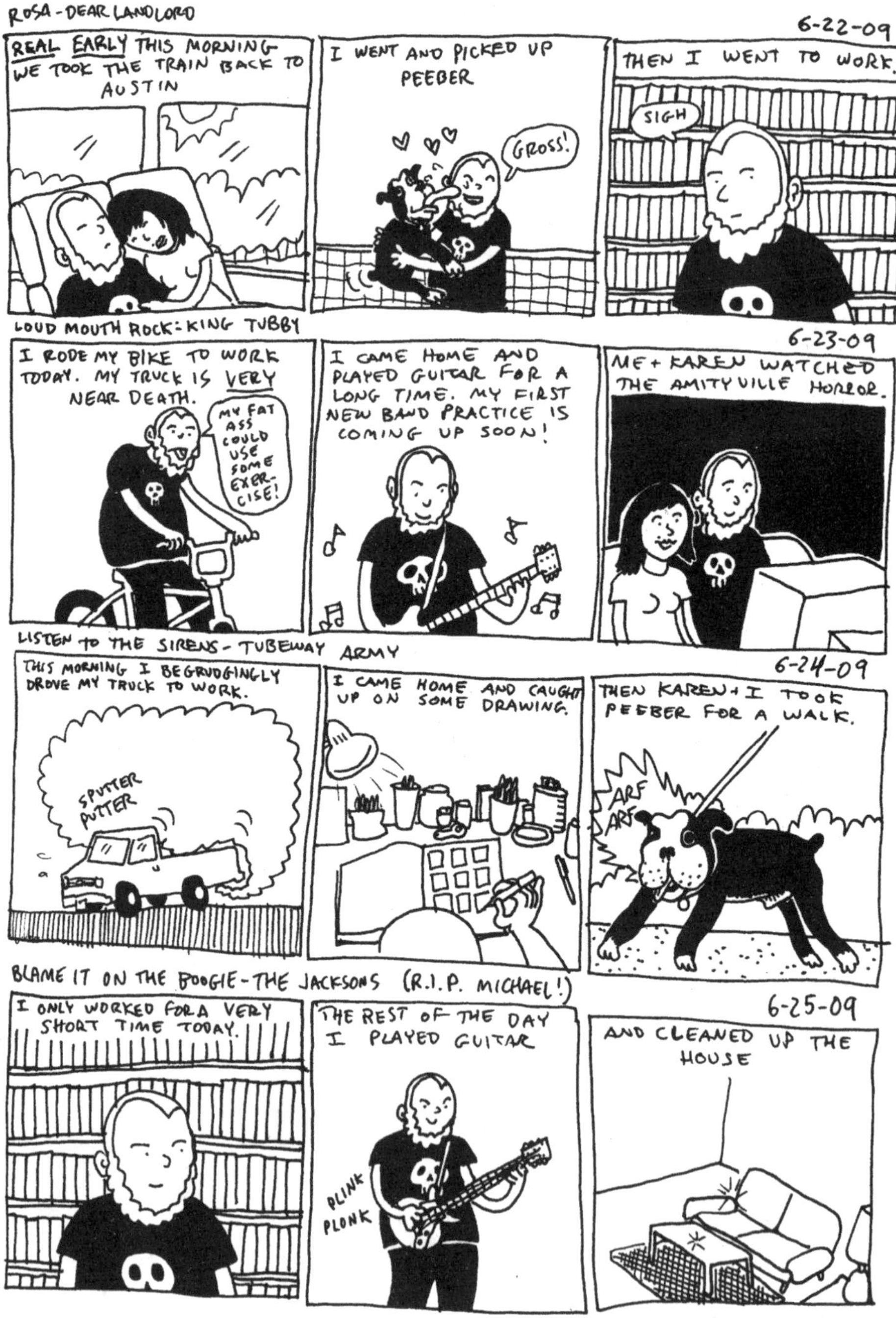
ROSA - DEAR LANDLORD
6-22-09
REAL EARLY THIS MORNING WE TOOK THE TRAIN BACK TO AUSTIN
I WENT AND PICKED UP PEEBER
GROSS!
THEN I WENT TO WORK.
SIGH
LOUD MOUTH ROCK: KING TUBBY
6-23-09
I RODE MY BIKE TO WORK TODAY. MY TRUCK IS VERY NEAR DEATH.
MY FAT ASS COULD USE SOME EXER-CISE!
I CAME HOME AND PLAYED GUITAR FOR A LONG TIME. MY FIRST NEW BAND PRACTICE IS COMING UP SOON!
ME + KAREN WATCHED THE AMITYVILLE HORROR.
LISTEN TO THE SIRENS - TUBEWAY ARMY
6-24-09
THIS MORNING I BEGRUDGINGLY DROVE MY TRUCK TO WORK.
SPUTTER PUTTER
I CAME HOME AND CAUGHT UP ON SOME DRAWING.
THEN KAREN + I TOOK PEEBER FOR A WALK.
ARF ARF
BLAME IT ON THE BOOGIE - THE JACKSONS (R.I.P. MICHAEL!)
6-25-09
I ONLY WORKED FOR A VERY SHORT TIME TODAY.
THE REST OF THE DAY I PLAYED GUITAR
PLINK PLONK
AND CLEANED UP THE HOUSE

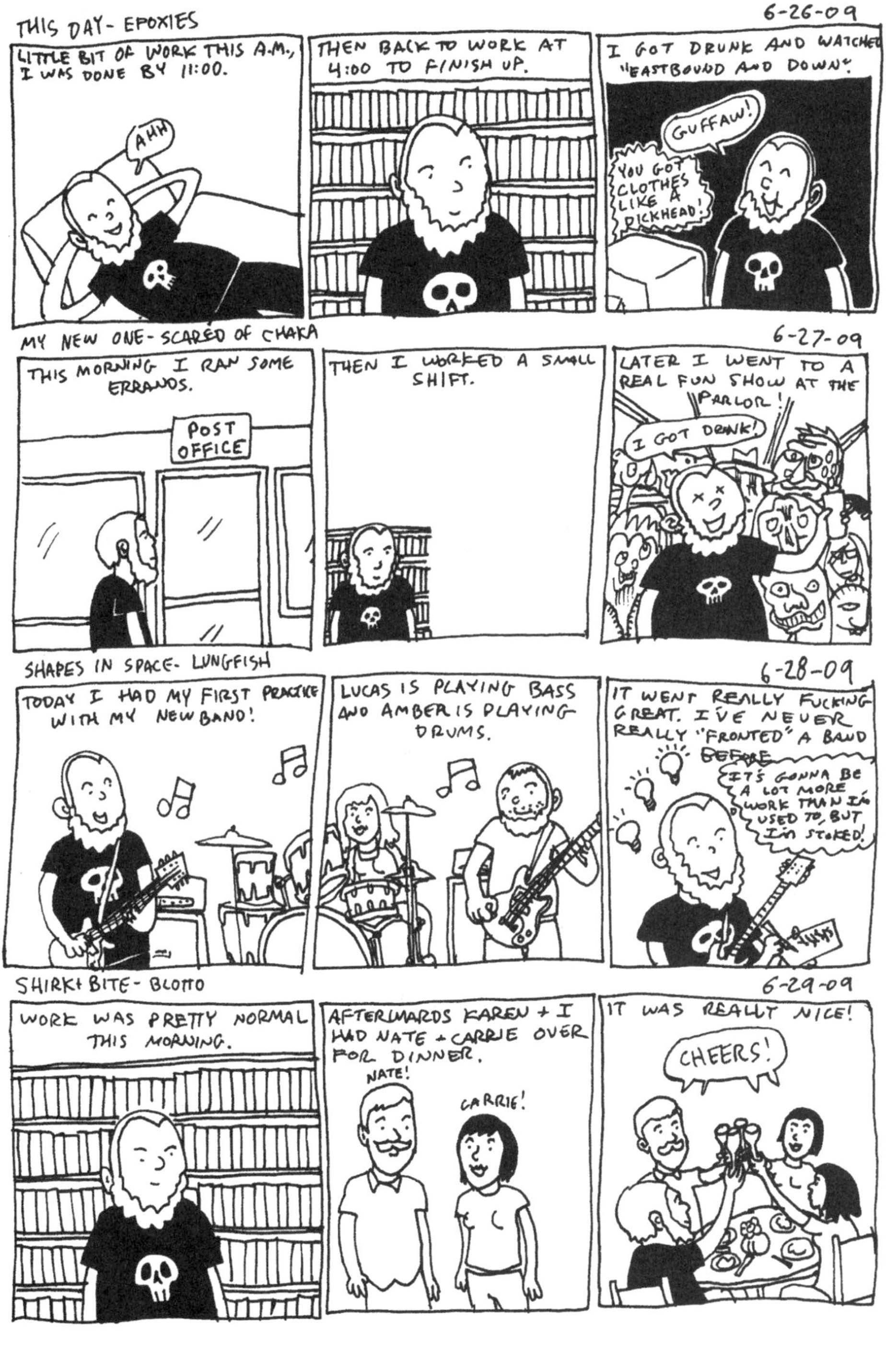
THIS DAY- EPOXIES
6-26-09
LITTLE BIT OF WORK THIS A.M., I WAS DONE BY 11:00.
AHH
THEN BACK TO WORK AT 4:00 TO FINISH UP.
I GOT DRUNK AND WATCHED "EASTBOUND AND DOWN".
GUFFAW!
YOU GOT CLOTHES LIKE A DICKHEAD!
MY NEW ONE- SCARED OF CHAKA
6-27-09
THIS MORNING I RAN SOME ERRANDS.
POST OFFICE
THEN I WORKED A SMALL SHIFT.
LATER I WENT TO A REAL FUN SHOW AT THE PARLOR!
I GOT DRUNK!
SHAPES IN SPACE- LUNGFISH
6-28-09
TODAY I HAD MY FIRST PRACTICE WITH MY NEW BAND!
LUCAS IS PLAYING BASS AND AMBER IS PLAYING DRUMS.
IT WENT REALLY FUCKING GREAT. I'VE NEVER REALLY "FRONTED" A BAND BEFORE
IT'S GONNA BE A LOT MORE WORK THAN I'M USED TO, BUT I'M STOKED!
SHIRK+BITE- BLOTTO
6-29-09
WORK WAS PRETTY NORMAL THIS MORNING.
AFTERWARDS KAREN + I HAD NATE + CARRIE OVER FOR DINNER.
NATE!
CARRIE!
IT WAS REALLY NICE!
CHEERS!

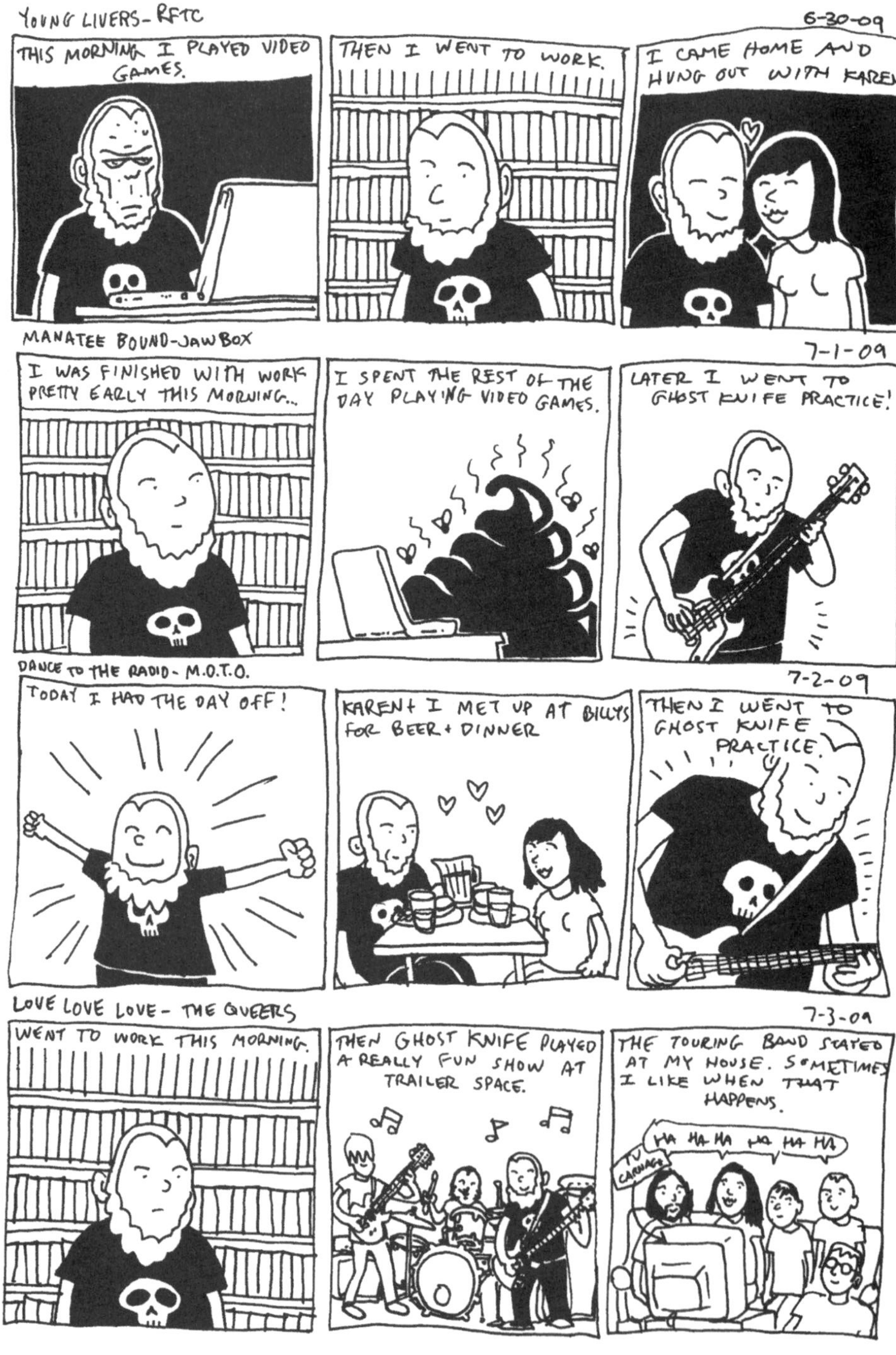
YOUNG LIVERS - RFTC
6-30-09
THIS MORNING I PLAYED VIDEO GAMES.
THEN I WENT TO WORK.
I CAME HOME AND HUNG OUT WITH KAREN!
MANATEE BOUND - JAWBOX
7-1-09
I WAS FINISHED WITH WORK PRETTY EARLY THIS MORNING...
I SPENT THE REST OF THE DAY PLAYING VIDEO GAMES.
LATER I WENT TO GHOST KNIFE PRACTICE!
DANCE TO THE RADIO - M.O.T.O.
7-2-09
TODAY I HAD THE DAY OFF!
KAREN + I MET UP AT BILLYS FOR BEER + DINNER
THEN I WENT TO GHOST KNIFE PRACTICE.
LOVE LOVE LOVE - THE QUEERS
7-3-09
WENT TO WORK THIS MORNING.
THEN GHOST KNIFE PLAYED A REALLY FUN SHOW AT TRAILER SPACE.
THE TOURING BAND STAYED AT MY HOUSE. SOMETIMES I LIKE WHEN THAT HAPPENS.
HA HA HA HA HA HA
TV CARNAGE

KILL THE POOR - DEAD KENNEDYS   7-4-09

THIS MORNING I PLAYED GUITAR.

THEN I WENT TO A BAR WITH KAREN.

THEN I HAD TO WORK TIL 3 AM!

FLORIDA - 50 MILLION   7-5-09

DAY OFF TODAY. I DIDN'T DO SHIT.

KNOCK IT OFF, STEVIE!

SIGH

IT WAS SUPER HOT OUTSIDE, I DIDN'T LEAVE THE HOUSE ALL DAY.

BORED BORED

KAREN + I WATCHED "ENCOUNTER OF THE SPOOKY KIND."

JIANG-SHI ARE COOL!

HOP HOP   HOP HOP

BOOBARELLA - QUEERS   7-6-09

KAREN FORGOT TO SET THE ALARM, SO I WAS 45 MINUTES LATE FOR WORK TODAY!

OH FUCK!

ZZZ

ON TOP OF THAT, IT WAS A CRAZY STRESSFUL BUSY DAY.

AAAAAAGGH!

WHEN I GOT HOME, I WAS OUT OF WEED.

AAAAAAAAGGH!

HEY SUBURBIA - SCREECHING WEASEL   7-7-09

I STARTED A BIG AMBITIOUS PROJECT AT WORK TODAY.

I TOOK CARE OF MY PROBLEM FROM YESTERDAY.

THAT ONE

ME + KAREN + PEEBER TOOK A NICE EVENING WALK

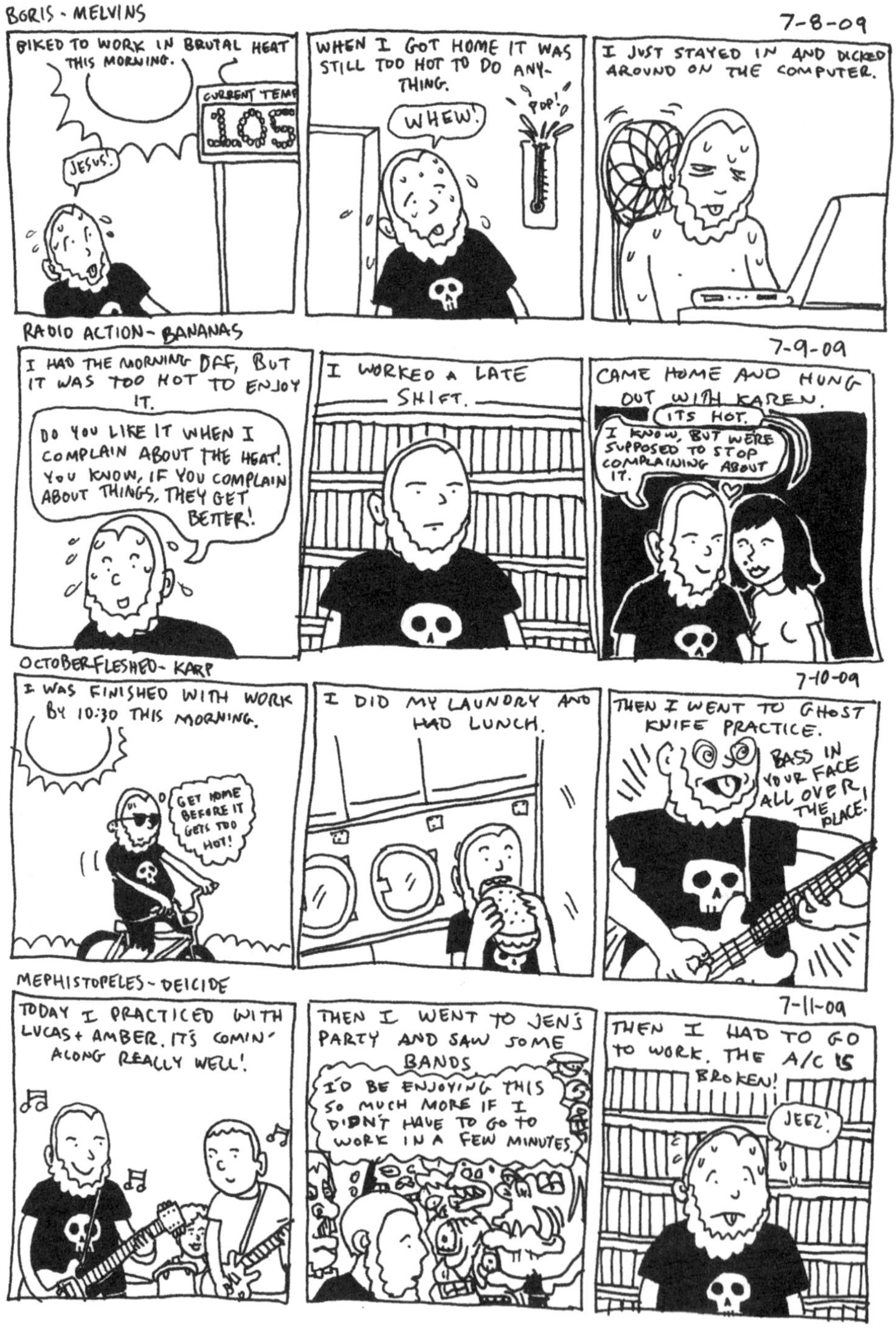

BORIS - MELVINS
7-8-09
BIKED TO WORK IN BRUTAL HEAT THIS MORNING.
CURRENT TEMP
105
JESUS!
WHEN I GOT HOME IT WAS STILL TOO HOT TO DO ANY-THING.
WHEW!
POP!
I JUST STAYED IN AND DICKED AROUND ON THE COMPUTER.
RADIO ACTION - BANANAS
7-9-09
I HAD THE MORNING OFF, BUT IT WAS TOO HOT TO ENJOY IT.
DO YOU LIKE IT WHEN I COMPLAIN ABOUT THE HEAT! YOU KNOW, IF YOU COMPLAIN ABOUT THINGS, THEY GET BETTER!
I WORKED A LATE SHIFT.
CAME HOME AND HUNG OUT WITH KAREN.
ITS HOT.
I KNOW, BUT WERE SUPPOSED TO STOP COMPLAINING ABOUT IT.
OCTOBERFLESHED - KARP
7-10-09
I WAS FINISHED WITH WORK BY 10:30 THIS MORNING.
GET HOME BEFORE IT GETS TOO HOT!
I DID MY LAUNDRY AND HAD LUNCH.
THEN I WENT TO GHOST KNIFE PRACTICE.
BASS IN YOUR FACE ALL OVER THE PLACE!
MEPHISTOPELES - DEICIDE
7-11-09
TODAY I PRACTICED WITH LUCAS + AMBER. IT'S COMIN' ALONG REALLY WELL!
THEN I WENT TO JEN'S PARTY AND SAW SOME BANDS
I'D BE ENJOYING THIS SO MUCH MORE IF I DIDN'T HAVE TO GO TO WORK IN A FEW MINUTES.
THEN I HAD TO GO TO WORK. THE A/C IS BROKEN!
JEEZ!

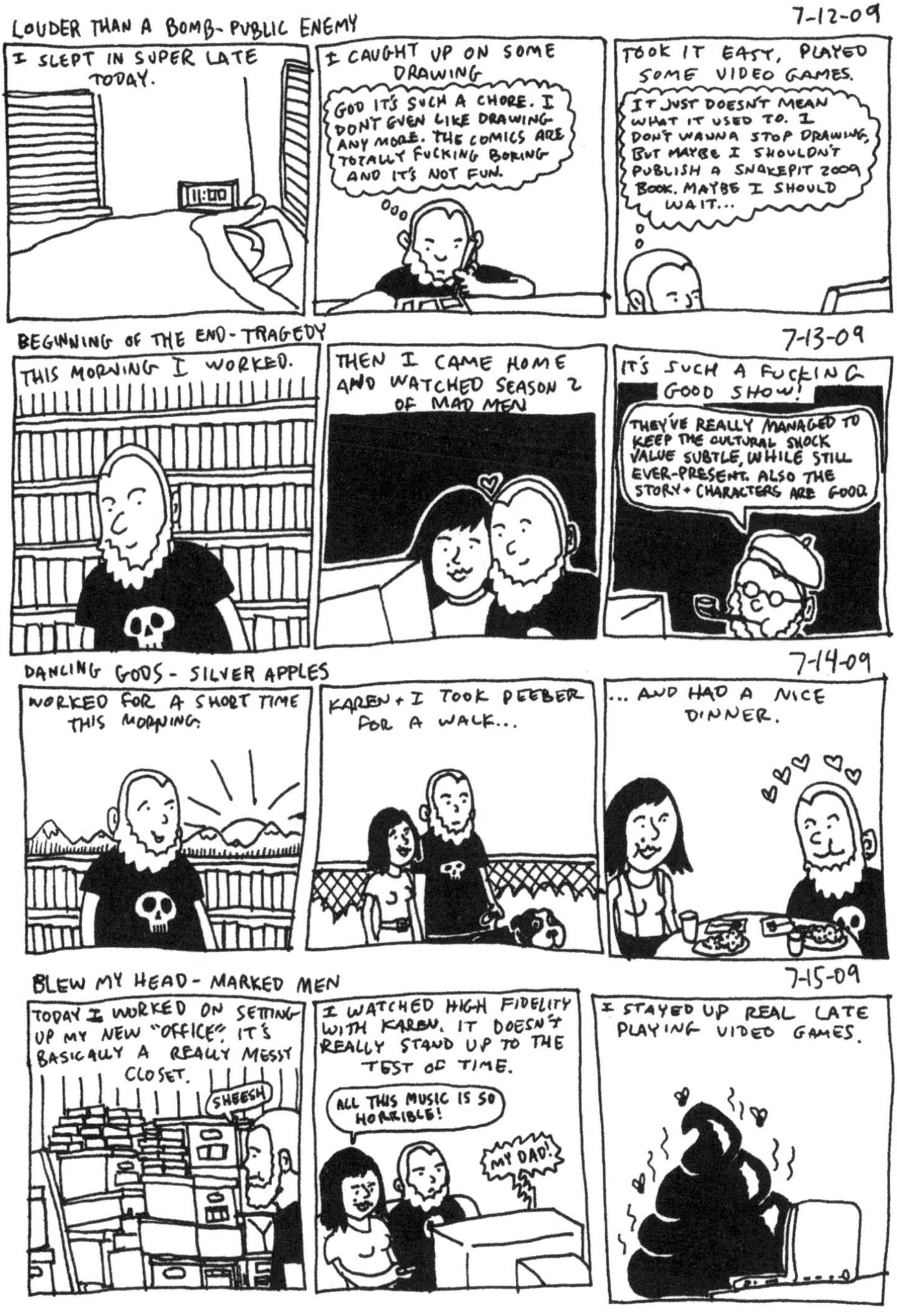
LOUDER THAN A BOMB - PUBLIC ENEMY
7-12-09
I SLEPT IN SUPER LATE TODAY.
11:00
I CAUGHT UP ON SOME DRAWING
GOD IT'S SUCH A CHORE. I DONT EVEN LIKE DRAWING ANY MORE. THE COMICS ARE TOTALLY FUCKING BORING AND IT'S NOT FUN.
TOOK IT EASY, PLAYED SOME VIDEO GAMES.
IT JUST DOESN'T MEAN WHAT IT USED TO. I DON'T WANNA STOP DRAWING, BUT MAYBE I SHOULDN'T PUBLISH A SNAKEPIT 2009 BOOK. MAYBE I SHOULD WAIT...
BEGINNING OF THE END - TRAGEDY
7-13-09
THIS MORNING I WORKED.
THEN I CAME HOME AND WATCHED SEASON 2 OF MAD MEN
IT'S SUCH A FUCKING GOOD SHOW!
THEY'VE REALLY MANAGED TO KEEP THE CULTURAL SHOCK VALUE SUBTLE, WHILE STILL EVER-PRESENT. ALSO THE STORY + CHARACTERS ARE GOOD.
DANCING GODS - SILVER APPLES
7-14-09
WORKED FOR A SHORT TIME THIS MORNING.
KAREN + I TOOK PEEBER FOR A WALK...
... AND HAD A NICE DINNER.
BLEW MY HEAD - MARKED MEN
7-15-09
TODAY I WORKED ON SETTING UP MY NEW "OFFICE". IT'S BASICALLY A REALLY MESSY CLOSET.
SHEESH
I WATCHED HIGH FIDELITY WITH KAREN. IT DOESN'T REALLY STAND UP TO THE TEST OF TIME.
ALL THIS MUSIC IS SO HORRIBLE!
MY DAD!
I STAYED UP REAL LATE PLAYING VIDEO GAMES.

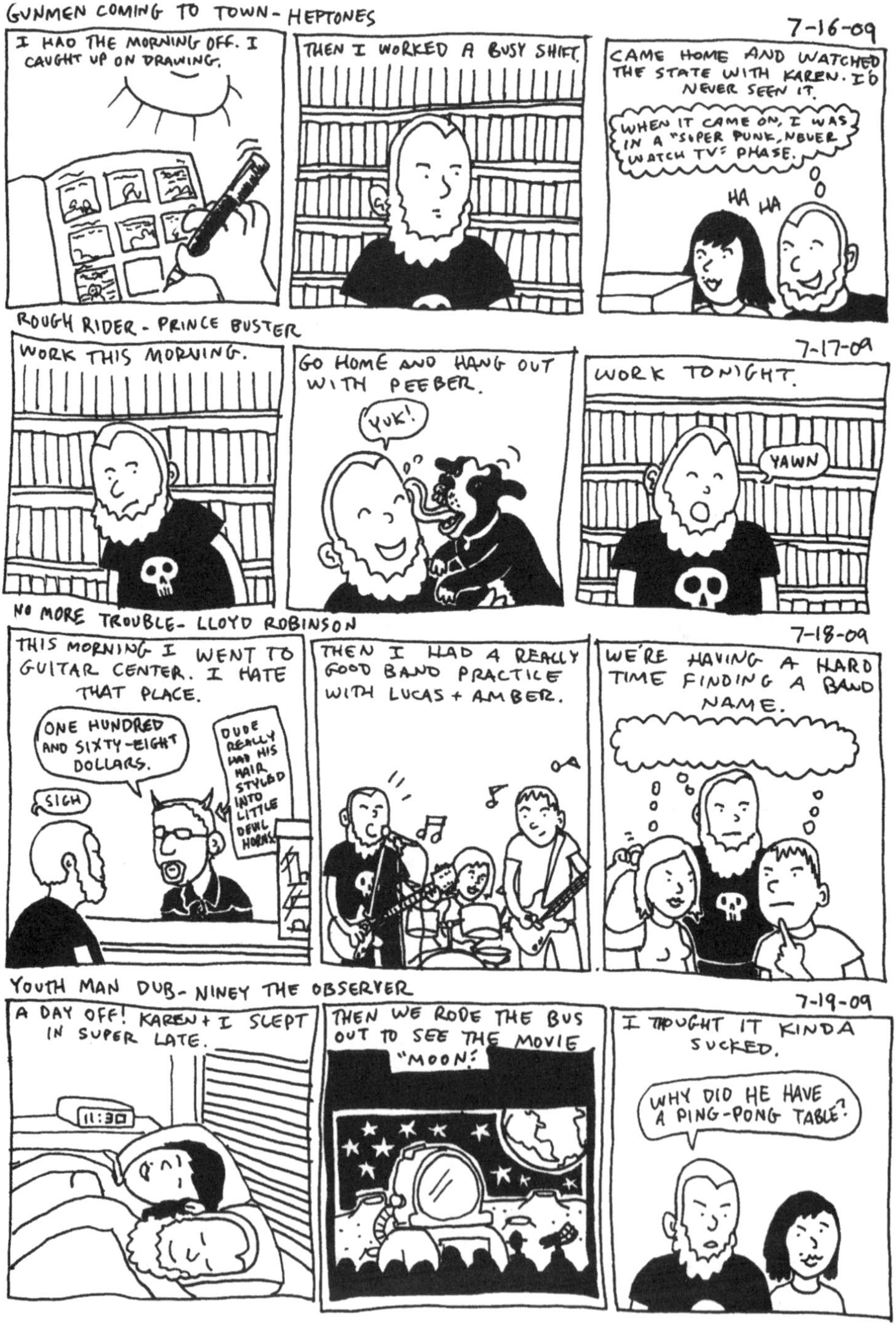

GUNMEN COMING TO TOWN - HEPTONES
7-16-09
I HAD THE MORNING OFF. I CAUGHT UP ON DRAWING.
THEN I WORKED A BUSY SHIFT.
CAME HOME AND WATCHED THE STATE WITH KAREN. I'D NEVER SEEN IT.
WHEN IT CAME ON, I WAS IN A "SUPER PUNK, NEVER WATCH TV" PHASE.
HA HA
ROUGH RIDER - PRINCE BUSTER
7-17-09
WORK THIS MORNING.
GO HOME AND HANG OUT WITH PEEBER.
YUK!
WORK TONIGHT.
YAWN
NO MORE TROUBLE - LLOYD ROBINSON
7-18-09
THIS MORNING I WENT TO GUITAR CENTER. I HATE THAT PLACE.
ONE HUNDRED AND SIXTY-EIGHT DOLLARS.
SIGH
DUDE REALLY HAD HIS HAIR STYLED INTO LITTLE DEVIL HORNS!
THEN I HAD A REALLY GOOD BAND PRACTICE WITH LUCAS + AMBER.
WE'RE HAVING A HARD TIME FINDING A BAND NAME.
YOUTH MAN DUB - NINEY THE OBSERVER
7-19-09
A DAY OFF! KAREN + I SLEPT IN SUPER LATE.
11:30
THEN WE RODE THE BUS OUT TO SEE THE MOVIE "MOON."
I THOUGHT IT KINDA SUCKED.
WHY DID HE HAVE A PING-PONG TABLE?

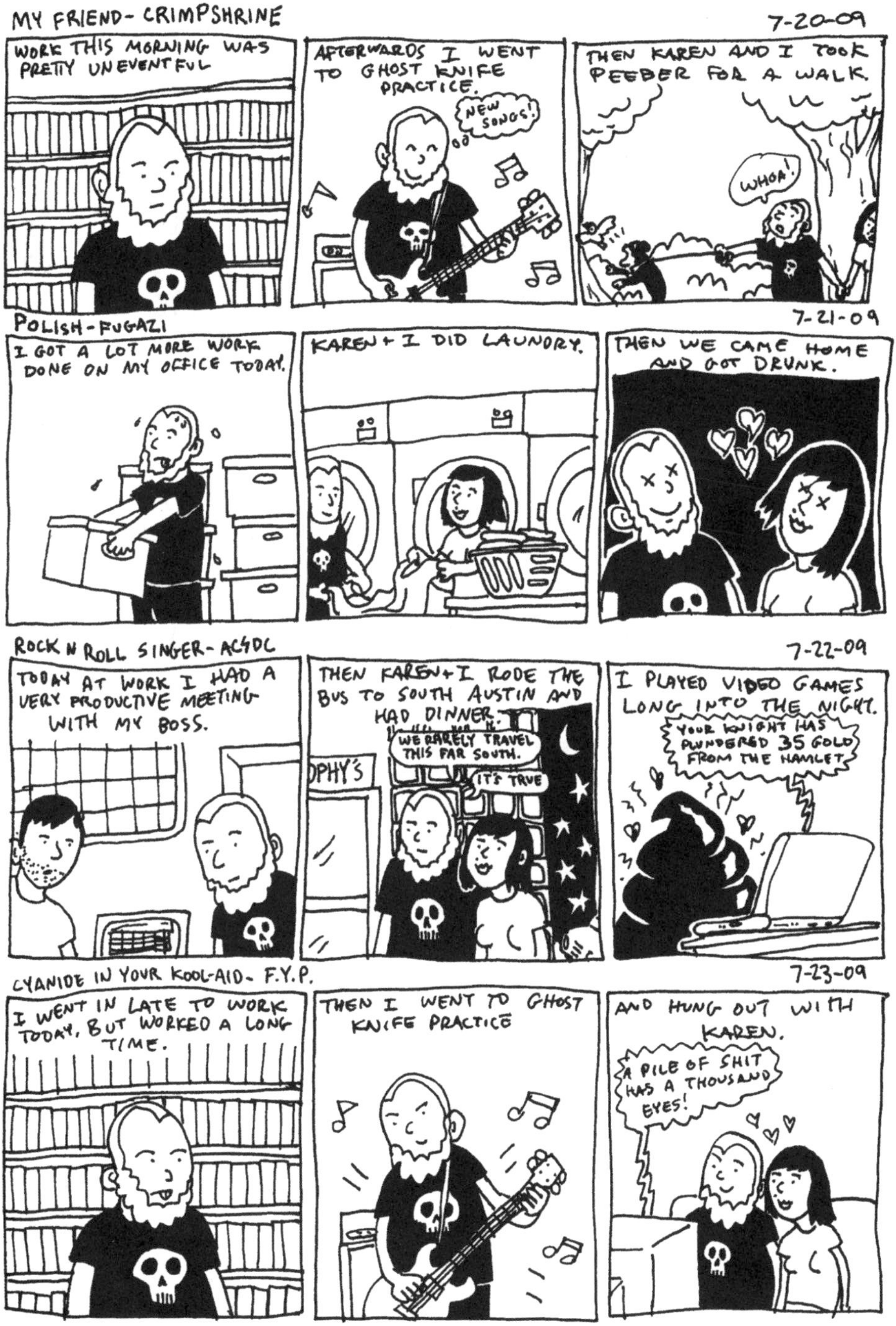
MY FRIEND- CRIMPSHRINE
7-20-09
WORK THIS MORNING WAS PRETTY UNEVENTFUL
AFTERWARDS I WENT TO GHOST KNIFE PRACTICE.
NEW SONGS!
THEN KAREN AND I TOOK PEEBER FOR A WALK.
WHOA!
POLISH-FUGAZI
7-21-09
I GOT A LOT MORE WORK DONE ON MY OFFICE TODAY.
KAREN + I DID LAUNDRY.
THEN WE CAME HOME AND GOT DRUNK.
ROCK N ROLL SINGER- AC/DC
7-22-09
TODAY AT WORK I HAD A VERY PRODUCTIVE MEETING WITH MY BOSS.
THEN KAREN + I RODE THE BUS TO SOUTH AUSTIN AND HAD DINNER.
WE RARELY TRAVEL THIS FAR SOUTH.
IT'S TRUE
I PLAYED VIDEO GAMES LONG INTO THE NIGHT.
YOUR KNIGHT HAS PLUNDERED 35 GOLD FROM THE HAMLET.
CYANIDE IN YOUR KOOL-AID- F.Y.P.
7-23-09
I WENT IN LATE TO WORK TODAY, BUT WORKED A LONG TIME.
THEN I WENT TO GHOST KNIFE PRACTICE
AND HUNG OUT WITH KAREN.
A PILE OF SHIT HAS A THOUSAND EYES!

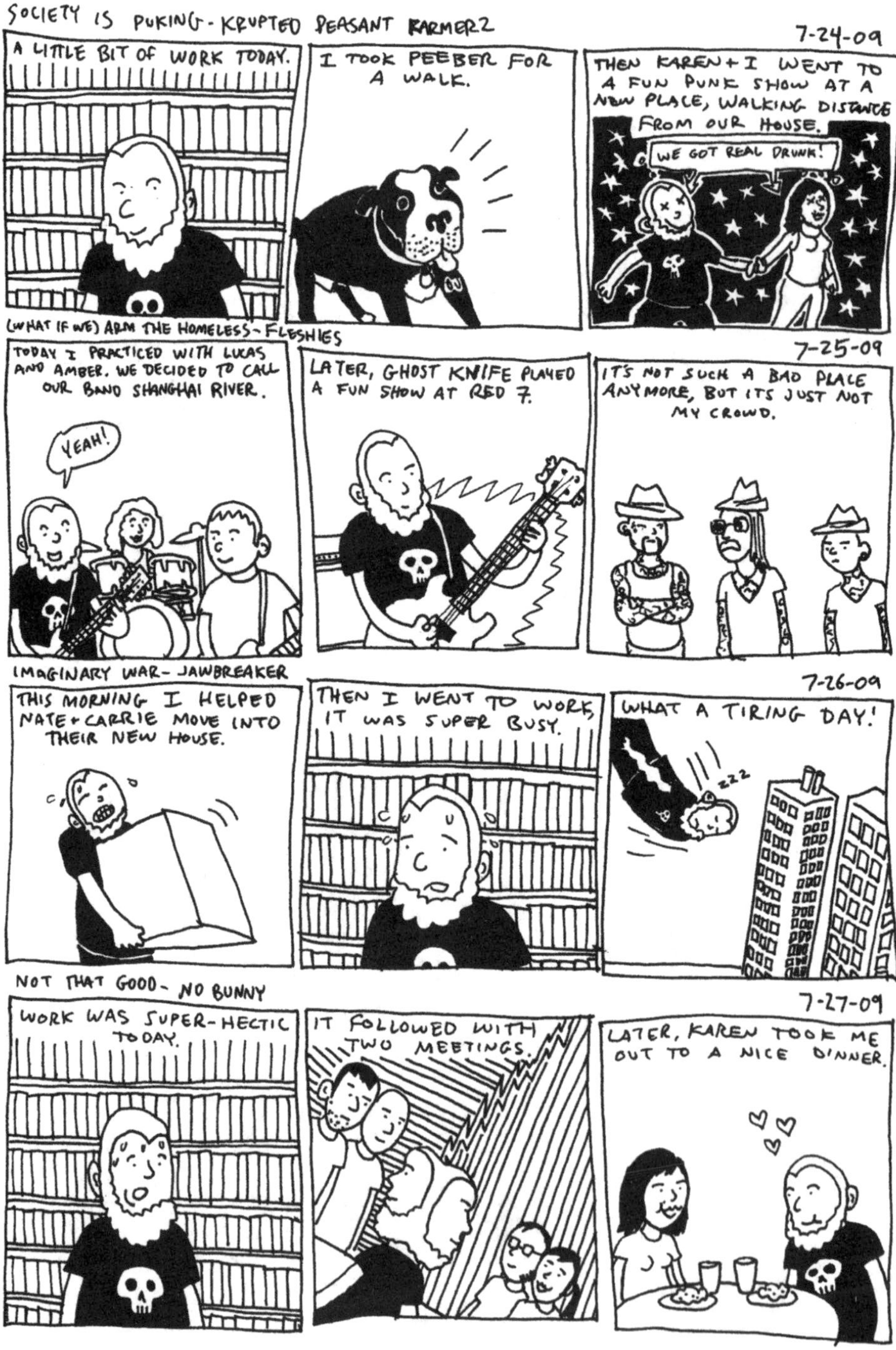

SOCIETY IS PUKING - KRUPTED PEASANT FARMERZ
7-24-09
A LITTLE BIT OF WORK TODAY.
I TOOK PEEBER FOR A WALK.
THEN KAREN + I WENT TO A FUN PUNK SHOW AT A NEW PLACE, WALKING DISTANCE FROM OUR HOUSE.
WE GOT REAL DRUNK!
(WHAT IF WE) ARM THE HOMELESS - FLESHIES
7-25-09
TODAY I PRACTICED WITH LUCAS AND AMBER. WE DECIDED TO CALL OUR BAND SHANGHAI RIVER.
YEAH!
LATER, GHOST KNIFE PLAYED A FUN SHOW AT RED 7.
IT'S NOT SUCH A BAD PLACE ANYMORE, BUT ITS JUST NOT MY CROWD.
IMAGINARY WAR - JAWBREAKER
7-26-09
THIS MORNING I HELPED NATE + CARRIE MOVE INTO THEIR NEW HOUSE.
THEN I WENT TO WORK, IT WAS SUPER BUSY.
WHAT A TIRING DAY!
ZZZ
NOT THAT GOOD - NO BUNNY
7-27-09
WORK WAS SUPER-HECTIC TODAY.
IT FOLLOWED WITH TWO MEETINGS.
LATER, KAREN TOOK ME OUT TO A NICE DINNER.

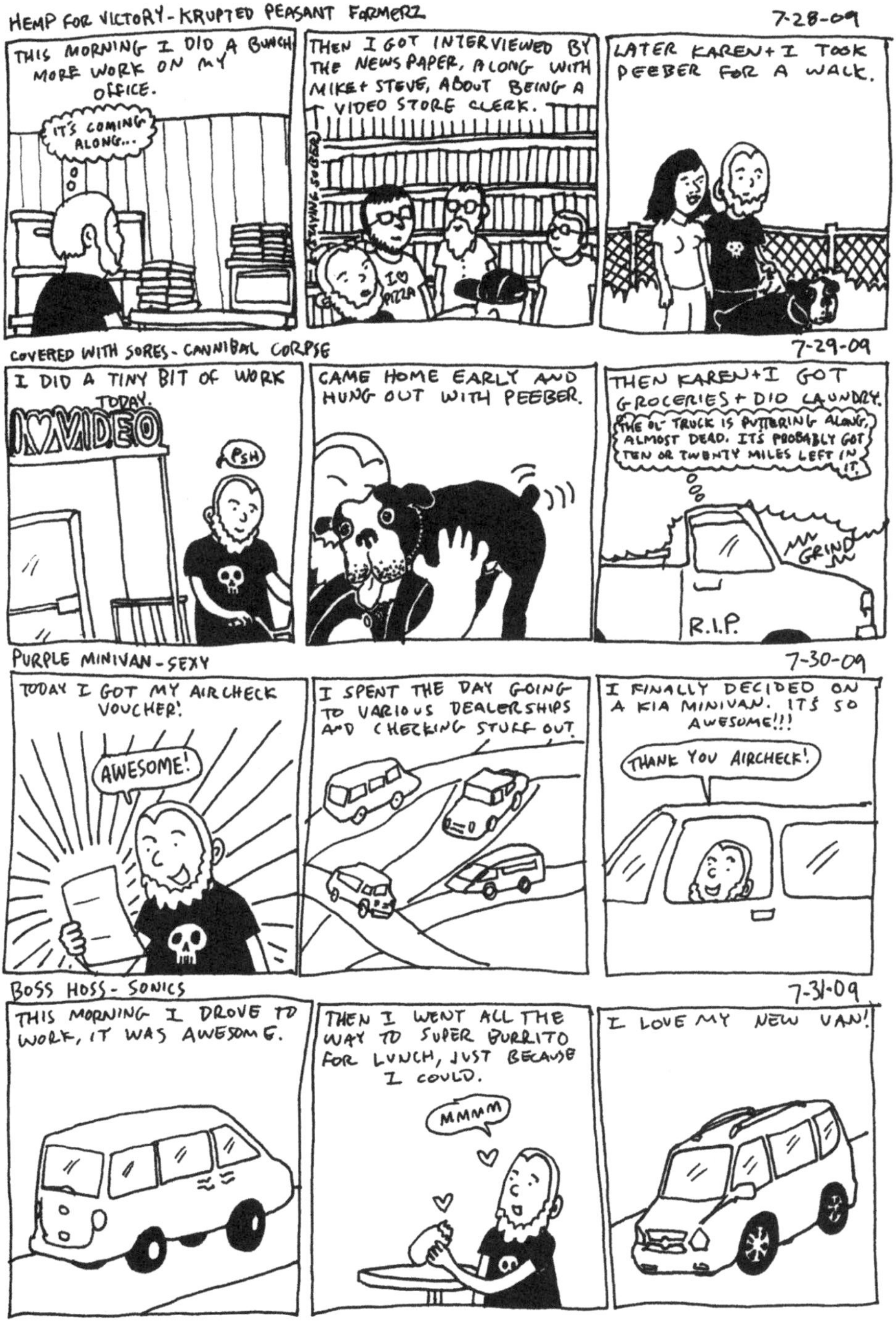
HEMP FOR VICTORY - KRUPTED PEASANT FARMERZ
7-28-09
THIS MORNING I DID A BUNCH MORE WORK ON MY OFFICE.
IT'S COMING ALONG...
THEN I GOT INTERVIEWED BY THE NEWSPAPER, ALONG WITH MIKE + STEVE, ABOUT BEING A VIDEO STORE CLERK.
I ♥ PIZZA
LATER KAREN + I TOOK PEEBER FOR A WALK.
COVERED WITH SORES - CANNIBAL CORPSE
7-29-09
I DID A TINY BIT OF WORK TODAY.
I ♥ VIDEO
PSH
CAME HOME EARLY AND HUNG OUT WITH PEEBER.
THEN KAREN + I GOT GROCERIES + DID LAUNDRY.
THE OL' TRUCK IS PUTTERING ALONG, ALMOST DEAD. IT'S PROBABLY GOT TEN OR TWENTY MILES LEFT IN IT.
GRIND
R.I.P.
PURPLE MINIVAN - SEXY
7-30-09
TODAY I GOT MY AIRCHECK VOUCHER!
AWESOME!
I SPENT THE DAY GOING TO VARIOUS DEALERSHIPS AND CHECKING STUFF OUT.
I FINALLY DECIDED ON A KIA MINIVAN. IT'S SO AWESOME!!!
THANK YOU AIRCHECK!
BOSS HOSS - SONICS
7-31-09
THIS MORNING I DROVE TO WORK, IT WAS AWESOME.
THEN I WENT ALL THE WAY TO SUPER BURRITO FOR LUNCH, JUST BECAUSE I COULD.
MMMM
I LOVE MY NEW VAN!

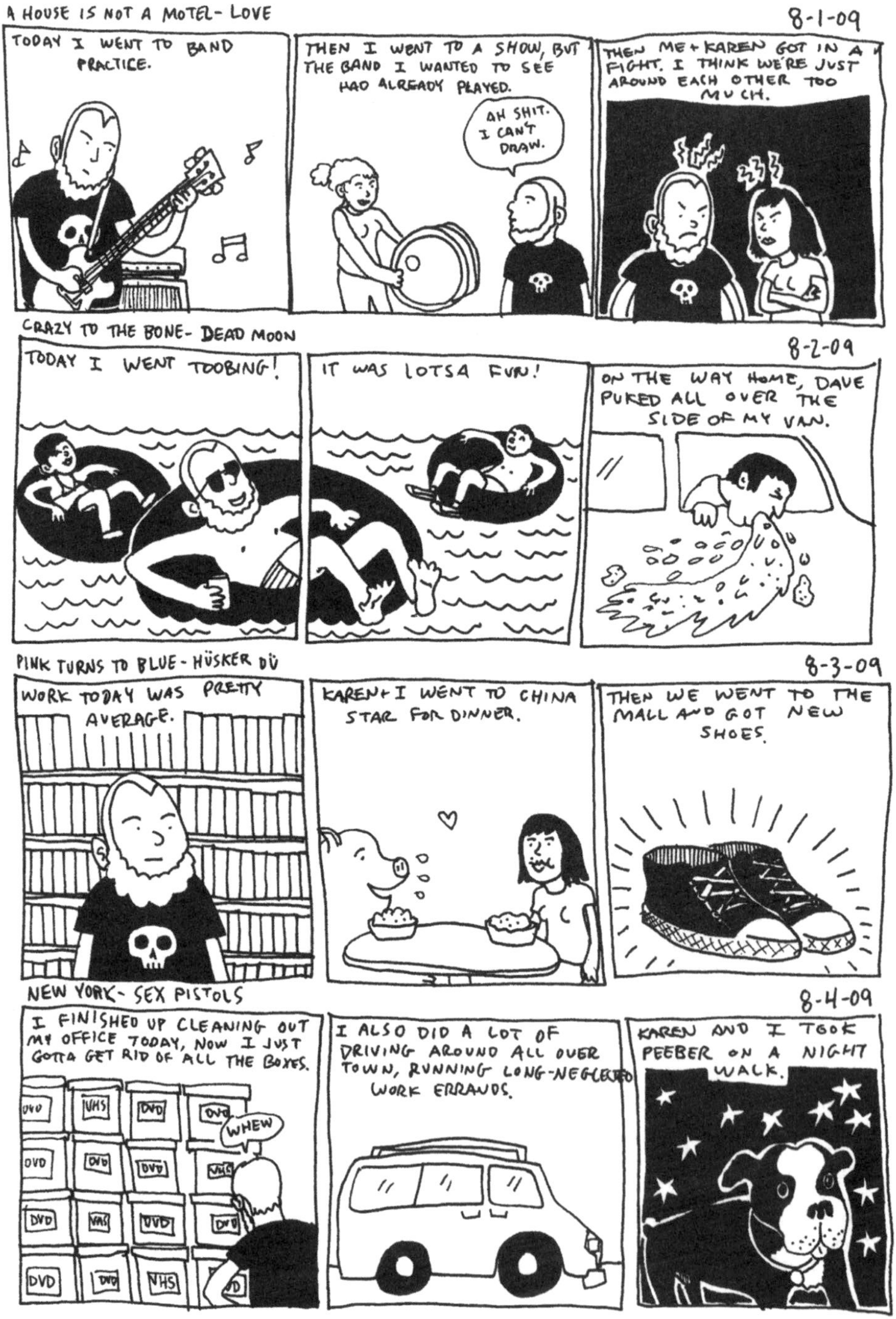
A HOUSE IS NOT A MOTEL- LOVE
8-1-09
TODAY I WENT TO BAND PRACTICE.
THEN I WENT TO A SHOW, BUT THE BAND I WANTED TO SEE HAD ALREADY PLAYED.
AH SHIT. I CAN'T DRAW.
THEN ME + KAREN GOT IN A FIGHT. I THINK WE'RE JUST AROUND EACH OTHER TOO MUCH.
CRAZY TO THE BONE- DEAD MOON
8-2-09
TODAY I WENT TOOBING!
IT WAS LOTSA FUN!
ON THE WAY HOME, DAVE PUKED ALL OVER THE SIDE OF MY VAN.
PINK TURNS TO BLUE- HÜSKER DÜ
8-3-09
WORK TODAY WAS PRETTY AVERAGE.
KAREN + I WENT TO CHINA STAR FOR DINNER.
THEN WE WENT TO THE MALL AND GOT NEW SHOES.
NEW YORK- SEX PISTOLS
8-4-09
I FINISHED UP CLEANING OUT MY OFFICE TODAY, NOW I JUST GOTTA GET RID OF ALL THE BOXES.
DVD
VHS
WHEW
I ALSO DID A LOT OF DRIVING AROUND ALL OVER TOWN, RUNNING LONG-NEGLECTED WORK ERRANDS.
KAREN AND I TOOK PEEBER ON A NIGHT WALK.

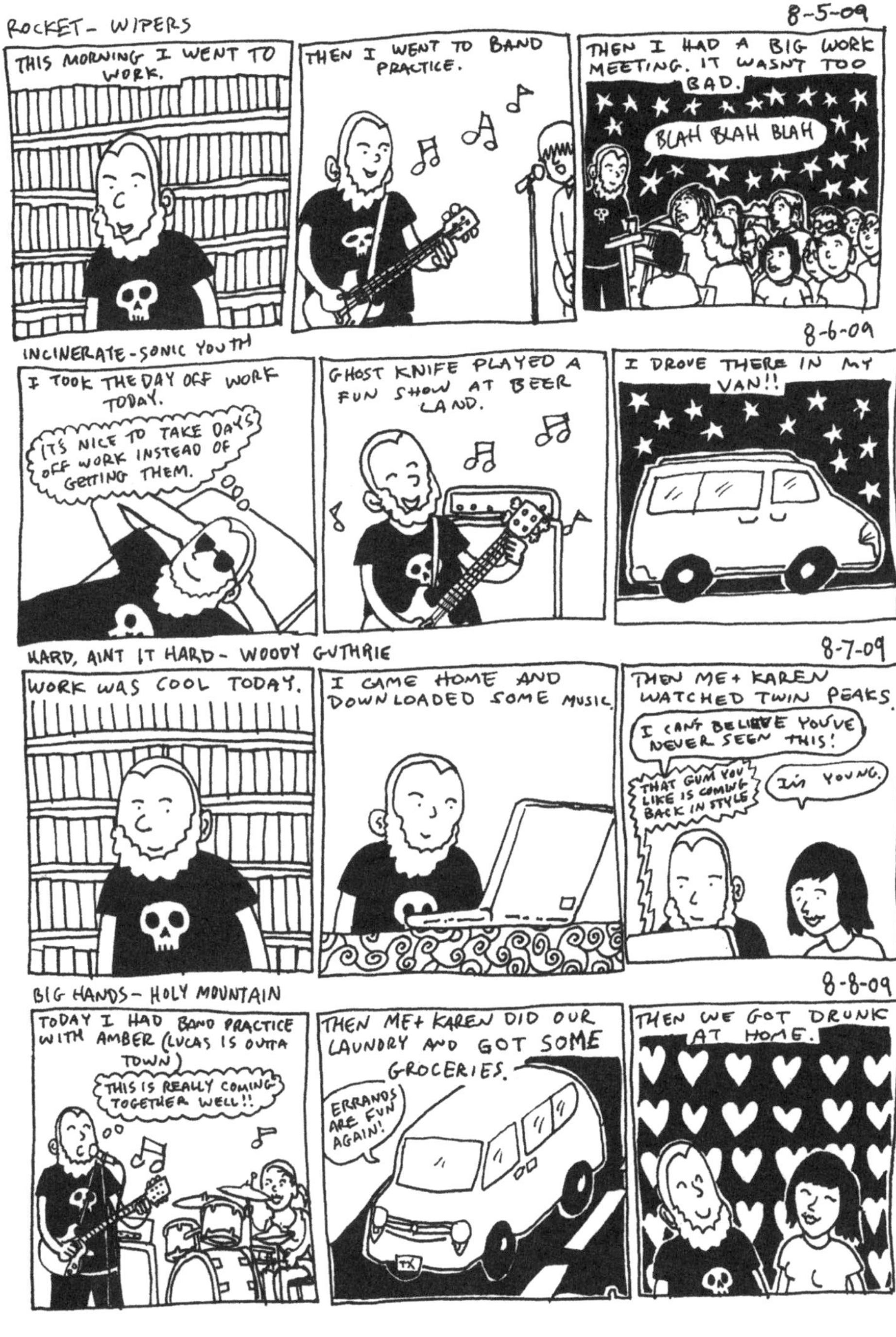
ROCKET- WIPERS
8-5-09
THIS MORNING I WENT TO WORK.
THEN I WENT TO BAND PRACTICE.
THEN I HAD A BIG WORK MEETING. IT WASNT TOO BAD.
BLAH BLAH BLAH
INCINERATE-SONIC YOUTH
8-6-09
I TOOK THE DAY OFF WORK TODAY.
IT'S NICE TO TAKE DAYS OFF WORK INSTEAD OF GETTING THEM.
GHOST KNIFE PLAYED A FUN SHOW AT BEER LAND.
I DROVE THERE IN MY VAN!!
HARD, AINT IT HARD- WOODY GUTHRIE
8-7-09
WORK WAS COOL TODAY.
I CAME HOME AND DOWNLOADED SOME MUSIC.
THEN ME + KAREN WATCHED TWIN PEAKS.
I CAN'T BELIEVE YOU'VE NEVER SEEN THIS!
THAT GUM YOU LIKE IS COMING BACK IN STYLE
I'M YOUNG.
BIG HANDS- HOLY MOUNTAIN
8-8-09
TODAY I HAD BAND PRACTICE WITH AMBER (LUCAS IS OUTTA TOWN)
THIS IS REALLY COMING TOGETHER WELL!!
THEN ME + KAREN DID OUR LAUNDRY AND GOT SOME GROCERIES.
ERRANDS ARE FUN AGAIN!
TX
THEN WE GOT DRUNK AT HOME.

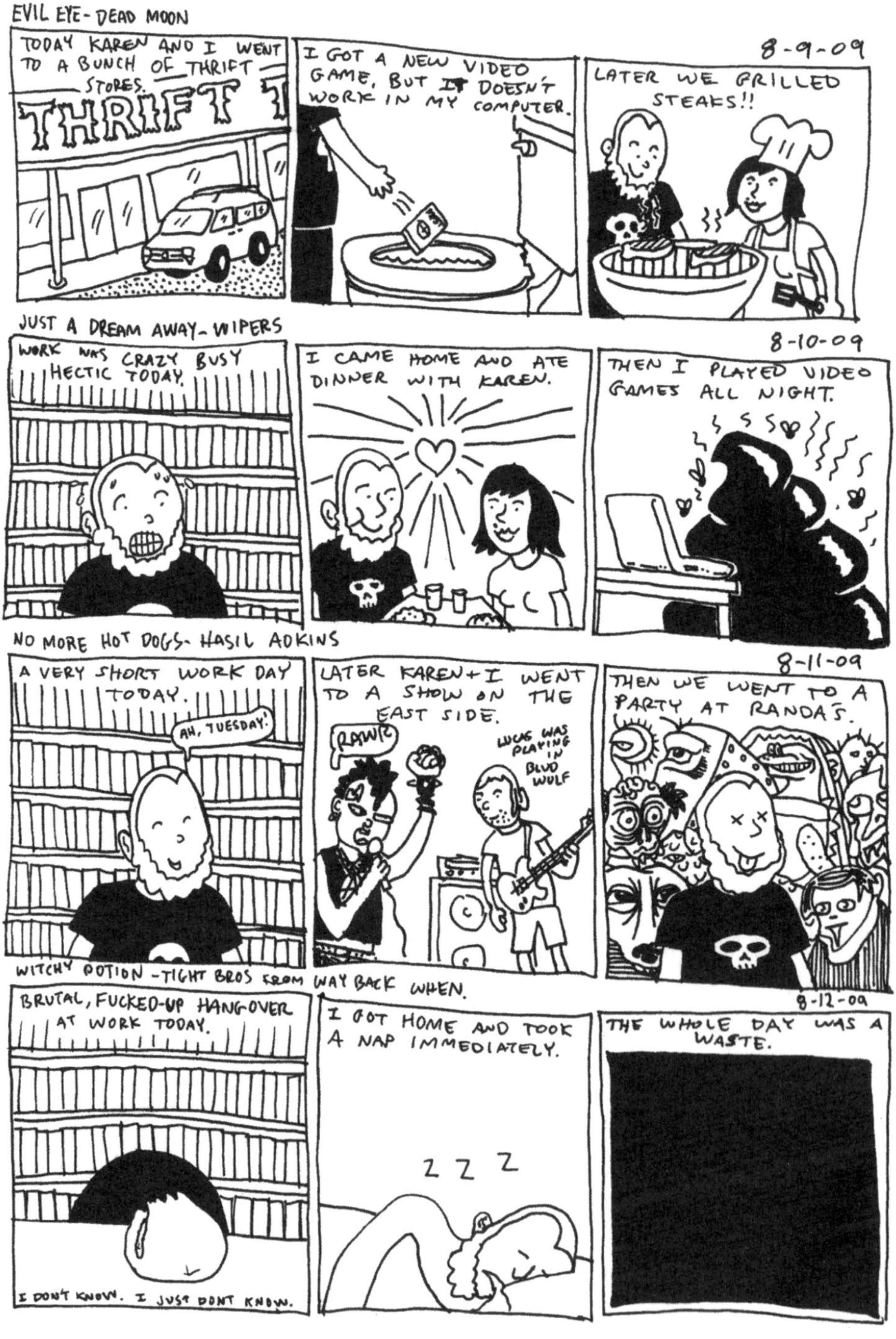
EVIL EYE - DEAD MOON
8-9-09
TODAY KAREN AND I WENT TO A BUNCH OF THRIFT STORES.
THRIFT
I GOT A NEW VIDEO GAME, BUT IT DOESN'T WORK IN MY COMPUTER.
LATER WE GRILLED STEAKS!!
JUST A DREAM AWAY - WIPERS
8-10-09
WORK WAS CRAZY BUSY HECTIC TODAY.
I CAME HOME AND ATE DINNER WITH KAREN.
THEN I PLAYED VIDEO GAMES ALL NIGHT.
NO MORE HOT DOGS - HASIL ADKINS
8-11-09
A VERY SHORT WORK DAY TODAY.
AH, TUESDAY!
LATER KAREN + I WENT TO A SHOW ON THE EAST SIDE.
RAWR
LUCAS WAS PLAYING IN BLVD WULF
THEN WE WENT TO A PARTY AT RANDA'S.
WITCHY POTION - TIGHT BROS FROM WAY BACK WHEN.
8-12-09
BRUTAL, FUCKED-UP HANGOVER AT WORK TODAY.
I DON'T KNOW. I JUST DONT KNOW.
I GOT HOME AND TOOK A NAP IMMEDIATELY.
Z Z Z
THE WHOLE DAY WAS A WASTE.

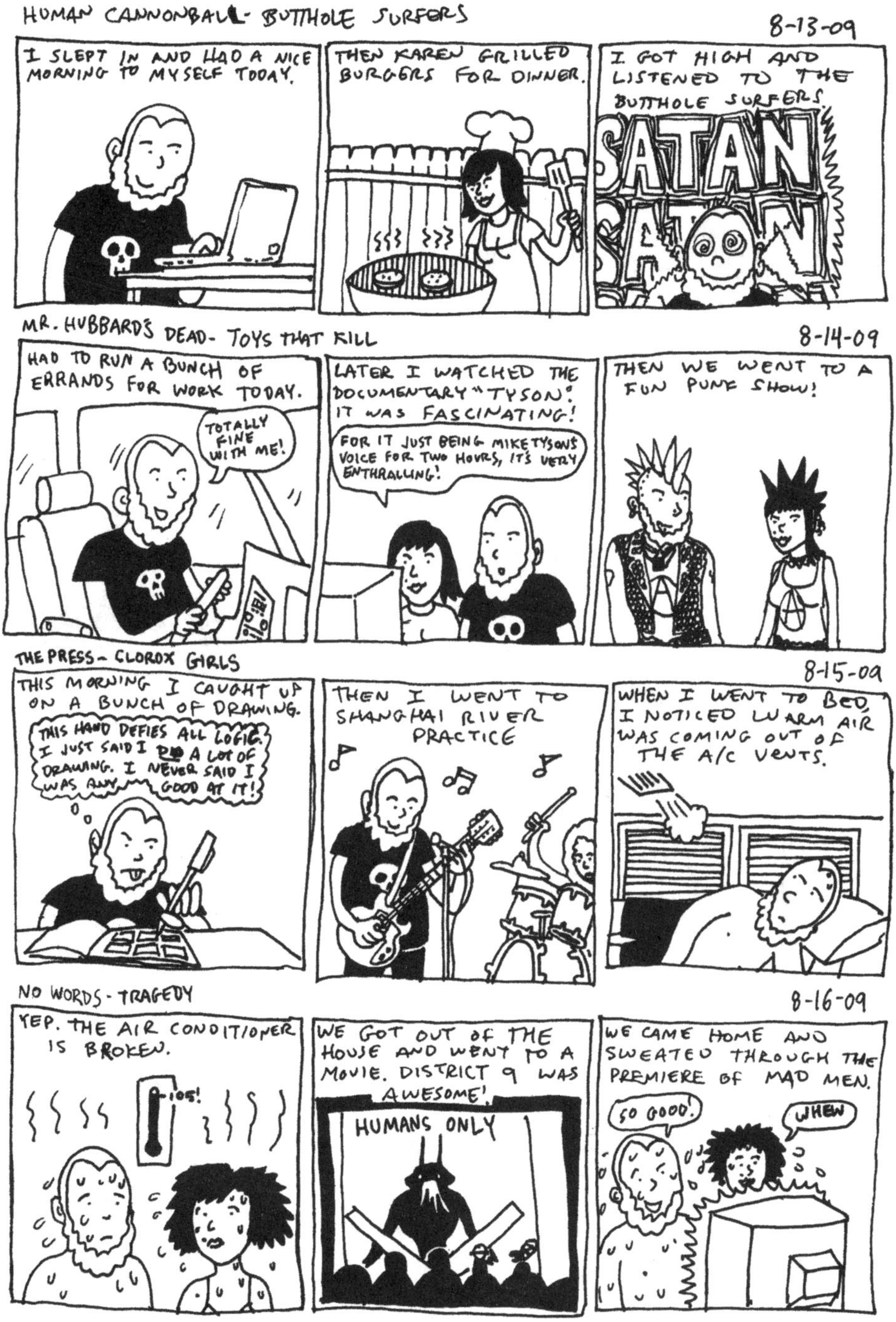
HUMAN CANNONBALL - BUTTHOLE SURFERS
8-13-09
I SLEPT IN AND HAD A NICE MORNING TO MYSELF TODAY.
THEN KAREN GRILLED BURGERS FOR DINNER.
I GOT HIGH AND LISTENED TO THE BUTTHOLE SURFERS.
SATAN
SATAN
MR. HUBBARD'S DEAD - TOYS THAT KILL
8-14-09
HAD TO RUN A BUNCH OF ERRANDS FOR WORK TODAY.
TOTALLY FINE WITH ME!
LATER I WATCHED THE DOCUMENTARY "TYSON". IT WAS FASCINATING!
FOR IT JUST BEING MIKE TYSON'S VOICE FOR TWO HOURS, IT'S VERY ENTHRALLING!
THEN WE WENT TO A FUN PUNK SHOW!
THE PRESS - CLOROX GIRLS
8-15-09
THIS MORNING I CAUGHT UP ON A BUNCH OF DRAWING.
THIS HAND DEFIES ALL LOGIC. I JUST SAID I DID A LOT OF DRAWING. I NEVER SAID I WAS ANY GOOD AT IT!
THEN I WENT TO SHANGHAI RIVER PRACTICE
WHEN I WENT TO BED, I NOTICED WARM AIR WAS COMING OUT OF THE A/C VENTS.
NO WORDS - TRAGEDY
8-16-09
YEP. THE AIR CONDITIONER IS BROKEN.
105!
WE GOT OUT OF THE HOUSE AND WENT TO A MOVIE. DISTRICT 9 WAS AWESOME!
HUMANS ONLY
WE CAME HOME AND SWEATED THROUGH THE PREMIERE OF MAD MEN.
SO GOOD!
WHEW

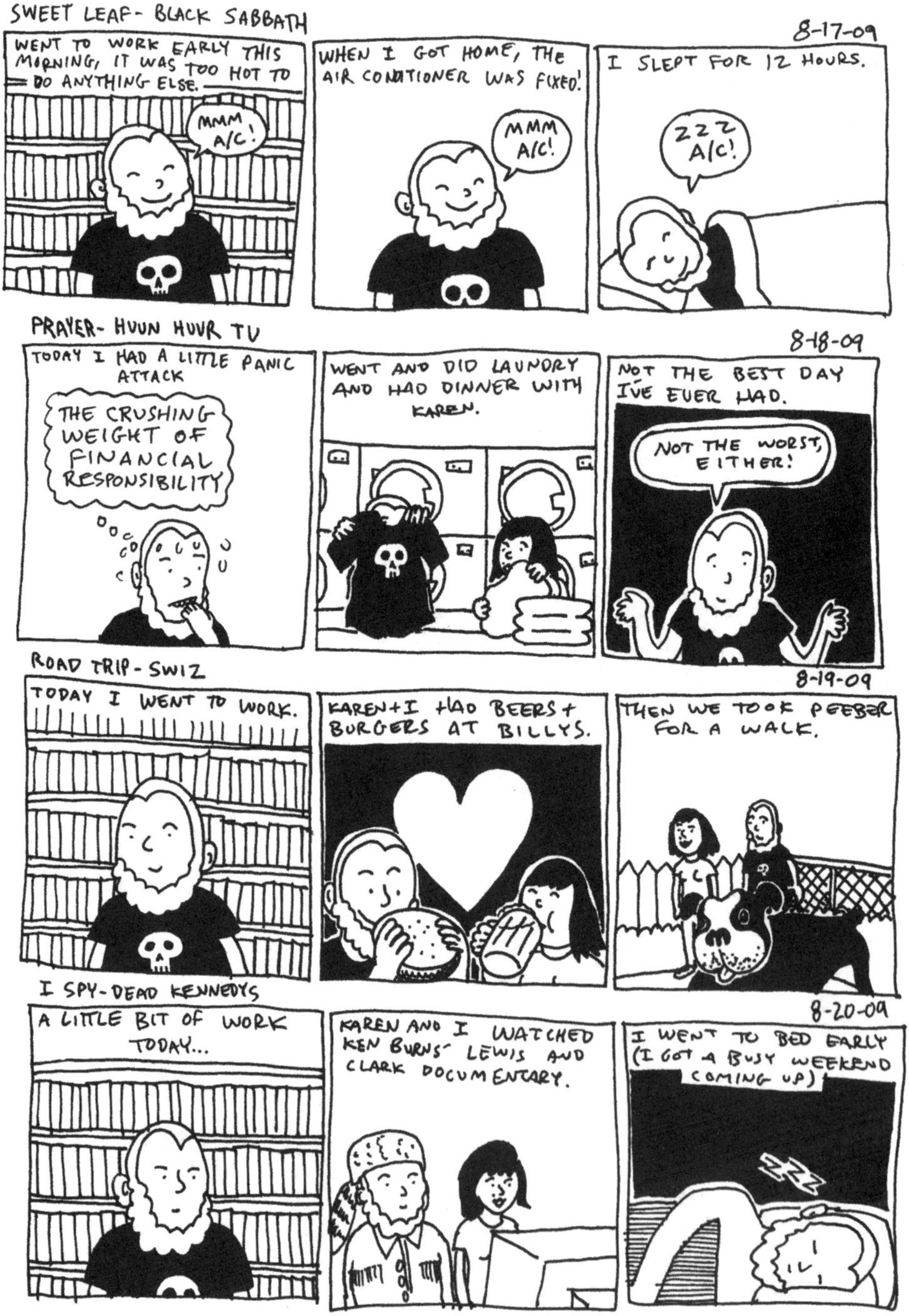

SWEET LEAF- BLACK SABBATH
8-17-09
WENT TO WORK EARLY THIS MORNING, IT WAS TOO HOT TO DO ANYTHING ELSE.
MMM A/C!
WHEN I GOT HOME, THE AIR CONDITIONER WAS FIXED!
MMM A/C!
I SLEPT FOR 12 HOURS.
ZZZ A/C!
PRAYER- HUUN HUUR TU
8-18-09
TODAY I HAD A LITTLE PANIC ATTACK
THE CRUSHING WEIGHT OF FINANCIAL RESPONSIBILITY
WENT AND DID LAUNDRY AND HAD DINNER WITH KAREN.
NOT THE BEST DAY I'VE EVER HAD.
NOT THE WORST, EITHER!
ROAD TRIP- SWIZ
8-19-09
TODAY I WENT TO WORK.
KAREN+I HAD BEERS+ BURGERS AT BILLYS.
THEN WE TOOK PEEBER FOR A WALK.
I SPY- DEAD KENNEDYS
8-20-09
A LITTLE BIT OF WORK TODAY...
KAREN AND I WATCHED KEN BURNS' LEWIS AND CLARK DOCUMENTARY.
I WENT TO BED EARLY (I GOT A BUSY WEEKEND COMING UP)

HISTORY LESSON PT. II - MINUTEMEN

8-21-09

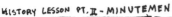

I HAD A BUSY WORK DAY TODAY, GETTING READY FOR THE BIG SALE TOMORROW.

ME + CHRIS LOADED 81 BOXES OF VIDEOS INTO A VAN

I HAD A COUPLE BEERS AND WENT TO BED EARLY.

BIG DAY TOMORROW...!

WHAT'S GOING ON - HUSKER DU

CLOCKED IN AT 8AM AND GOT BUSY.

THE SALE WAS HUGELY SUCCESSFUL.

I ACCOMPLISHED MY PERSONAL SALES GOAL.

↑ THAT IS ABSOLUTELY THE LEAST PUNK THING I'VE EVER SAID IN MY LIFE.

8-22-09

AND I WAS HUGELY TIRED!

LITTLE DARLING PAL OF MINE - CARTER FAMILY

8-23-09

TODAY KAREN & I TOOK PEEBER TO THE DOG PARK.

ARF ARF ARF ARF ARF ARF

THEN SHE BAKED ME A STRAWBERRY + RHUBARB PIE!

WE RELAXED AND WATCHED THE NEW EPISODE OF MAD MEN.

DRILLING FOR BRAINS - MORTICIAN

8-24-09

BACK AT WORK TODAY LIKE NOTHING EVEN HAPPENED.

I CAME HOME AND PLAYED SOME VIDEO GAMES FOR A WHILE.

ME + KAREN WATCHED A MOVIE.

SERIAL MOM

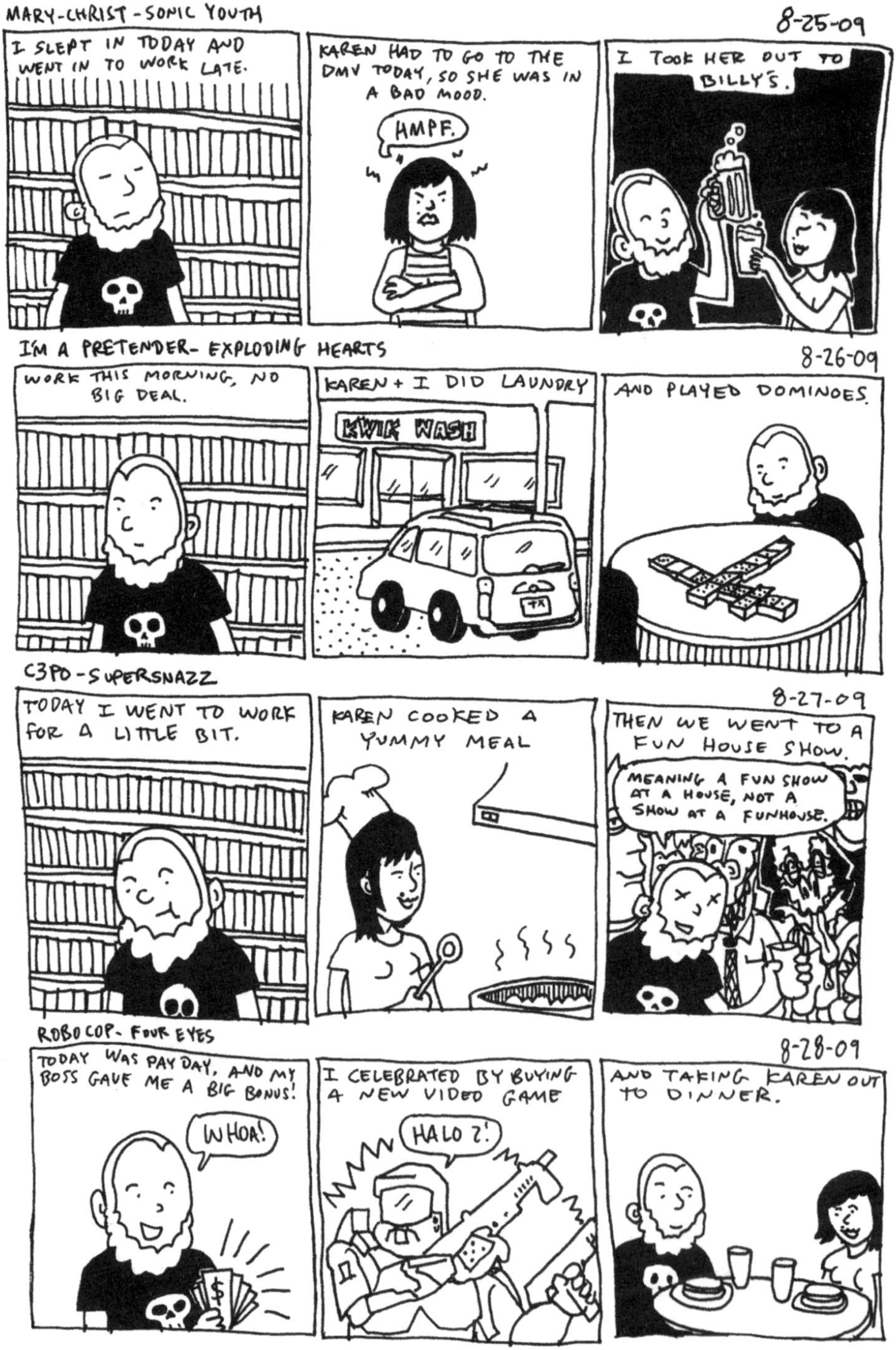
MARY-CHRIST - SONIC YOUTH
8-25-09
I SLEPT IN TODAY AND WENT IN TO WORK LATE.
KAREN HAD TO GO TO THE DMV TODAY, SO SHE WAS IN A BAD MOOD.
HMPF.
I TOOK HER OUT TO BILLY'S.
I'M A PRETENDER - EXPLODING HEARTS
8-26-09
WORK THIS MORNING, NO BIG DEAL.
KAREN + I DID LAUNDRY
KWIK WASH
TX
AND PLAYED DOMINOES.
C3PO - SUPERSNAZZ
8-27-09
TODAY I WENT TO WORK FOR A LITTLE BIT.
KAREN COOKED A YUMMY MEAL
THEN WE WENT TO A FUN HOUSE SHOW.
MEANING A FUN SHOW AT A HOUSE, NOT A SHOW AT A FUNHOUSE.
ROBOCOP - FOUR EYES
8-28-09
TODAY WAS PAY DAY, AND MY BOSS GAVE ME A BIG BONUS!
WHOA!
$
I CELEBRATED BY BUYING A NEW VIDEO GAME
HALO 2!
AND TAKING KAREN OUT TO DINNER.

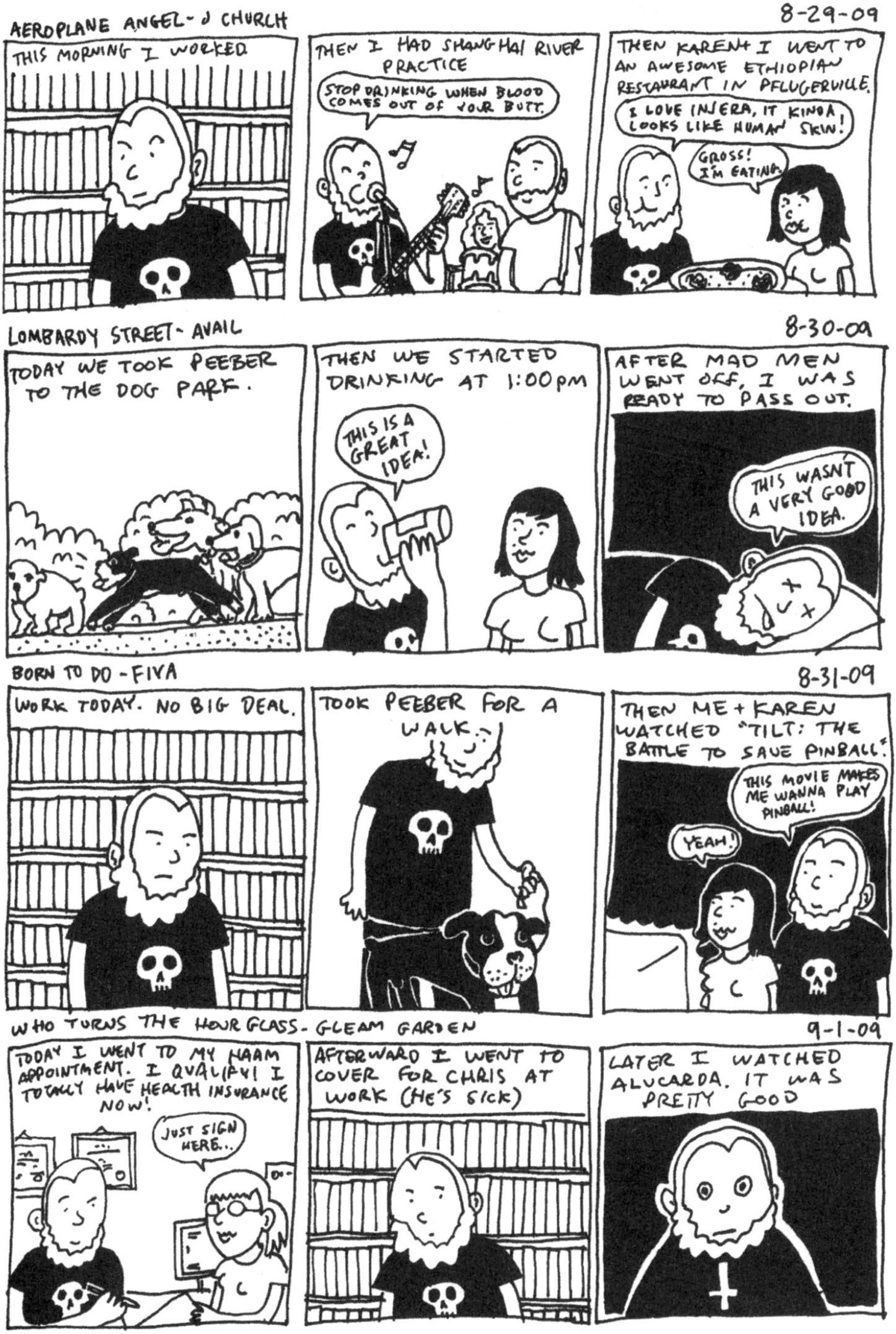
AEROPLANE ANGEL - J CHURCH
8-29-09
THIS MORNING I WORKED
THEN I HAD SHANGHAI RIVER PRACTICE
STOP DRINKING WHEN BLOOD COMES OUT OF YOUR BUTT.
THEN KAREN + I WENT TO AN AWESOME ETHIOPIAN RESTAURANT IN PFLUGERVILLE.
I LOVE INJERA, IT KINDA LOOKS LIKE HUMAN SKIN!
GROSS! I'M EATING.
LOMBARDY STREET - AVAIL
8-30-09
TODAY WE TOOK PEEBER TO THE DOG PARK.
THEN WE STARTED DRINKING AT 1:00pm
THIS IS A GREAT IDEA!
AFTER MAD MEN WENT OFF, I WAS READY TO PASS OUT.
THIS WASN'T A VERY GOOD IDEA.
BORN TO DO - FIVA
8-31-09
WORK TODAY. NO BIG DEAL.
TOOK PEEBER FOR A WALK.
THEN ME + KAREN WATCHED "TILT: THE BATTLE TO SAVE PINBALL"
THIS MOVIE MAKES ME WANNA PLAY PINBALL!
YEAH!
WHO TURNS THE HOUR GLASS - GLEAM GARDEN
9-1-09
TODAY I WENT TO MY HAAM APPOINTMENT. I QUALIFY! I TOTALLY HAVE HEALTH INSURANCE NOW!
JUST SIGN HERE...
AFTERWARD I WENT TO COVER FOR CHRIS AT WORK (HE'S SICK)
LATER I WATCHED ALUCARDA. IT WAS PRETTY GOOD

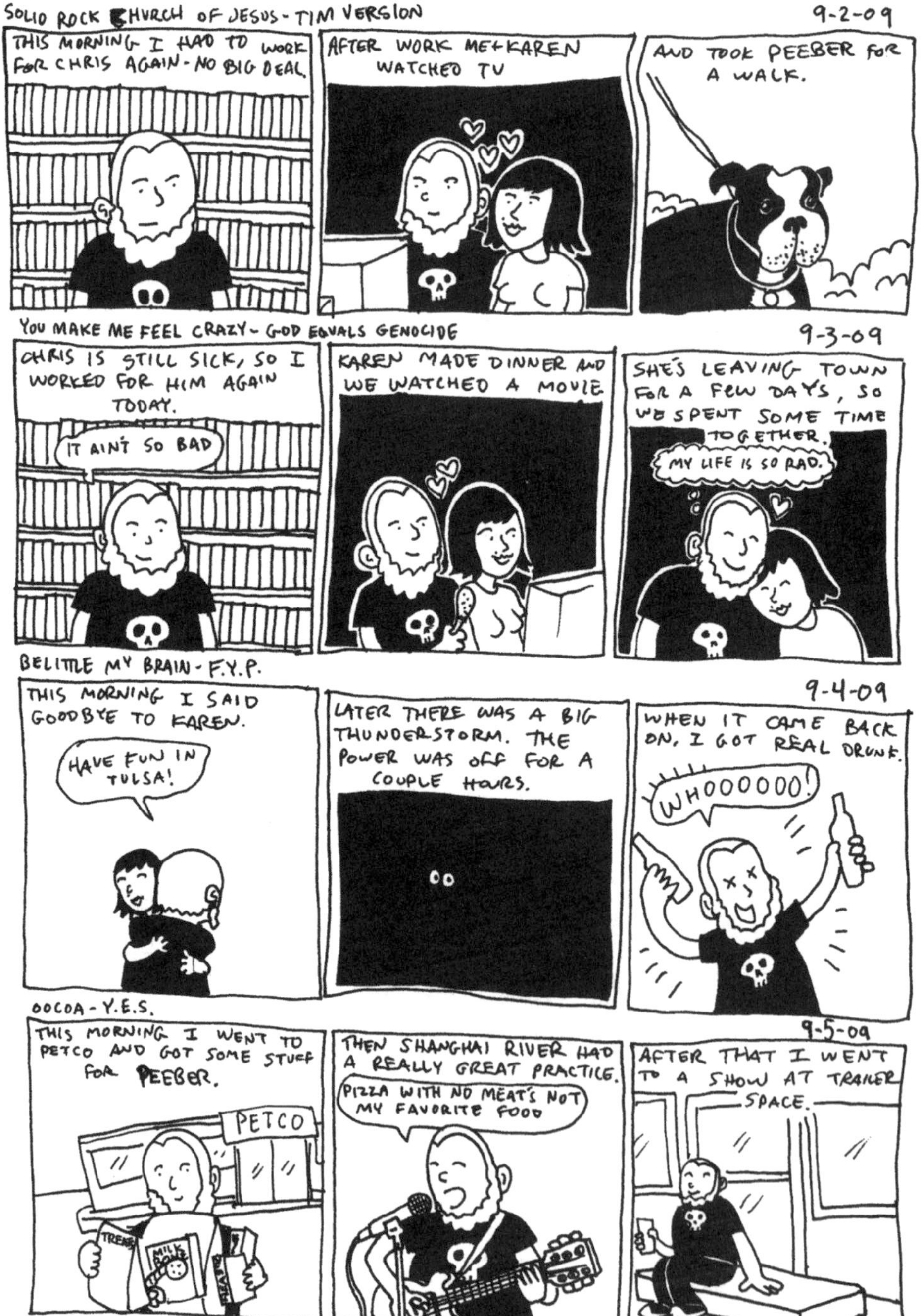
SOLID ROCK CHURCH OF JESUS - TIM VERSION
9-2-09
THIS MORNING I HAD TO WORK FOR CHRIS AGAIN - NO BIG DEAL
AFTER WORK ME+KAREN WATCHED TV
AND TOOK PEEBER FOR A WALK.
YOU MAKE ME FEEL CRAZY - GOD EQUALS GENOCIDE
9-3-09
CHRIS IS STILL SICK, SO I WORKED FOR HIM AGAIN TODAY.
IT AIN'T SO BAD
KAREN MADE DINNER AND WE WATCHED A MOVIE.
SHE'S LEAVING TOWN FOR A FEW DAYS, SO WE SPENT SOME TIME TOGETHER.
MY LIFE IS SO RAD.
BELITTLE MY BRAIN - F.Y.P.
9-4-09
THIS MORNING I SAID GOODBYE TO KAREN.
HAVE FUN IN TULSA!
LATER THERE WAS A BIG THUNDERSTORM. THE POWER WAS OFF FOR A COUPLE HOURS.
WHEN IT CAME BACK ON, I GOT REAL DRUNK.
WHOOOOOO!
OOCDA - Y.E.S.
9-5-09
THIS MORNING I WENT TO PETCO AND GOT SOME STUFF FOR PEEBER.
PETCO
TREAT
MILK BONE
THEN SHANGHAI RIVER HAD A REALLY GREAT PRACTICE.
PIZZA WITH NO MEAT'S NOT MY FAVORITE FOOD
AFTER THAT I WENT TO A SHOW AT TRAILER SPACE.

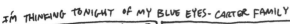
I'M THINKING TONIGHT OF MY BLUE EYES- CARTER FAMILY

9-6-09

THIS MORNING I SAT AROUND AND WATCHED T.V.

THEN I WENT TO A BBQ AT TOM+JEN'S.

I GOT DRUNK AND PLAYED LADDER GOLF.

TWIST OF CAIN- SAMHAIN

9-7-09

THIS MORNING I WENT TO WORK.

I CAME HOME AND CLEANED THE HOUSE, EAGERLY AWAITING KAREN'S RETURN.

I WAS SO HAPPY WHEN SHE GOT HOME!

EVERYTHING FALLS APART- HUSKER DU

9-8-09

WORK WAS PRODUCTIVE BUT HECTIC TODAY.

I DID LAUNDRY AFTER.
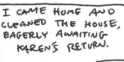

THEN ME+KAREN WATCHED THE OFFICE

I AM A GREAT ARTIST.

SNAKE PIT RADIO THEME SONG- SEX ADVICE

-9-9-9-

LATELY I'VE BEEN THINKING A LOT ABOUT WHETHER OR NOT I WANT TO KEEP DRAWING THESE COMICS

ITS COMING UP ON TEN YEARS, WHICH MIGHT BE A GOOD STOPPING PLACE.

I JUST DON'T HAVE THE SAME PASSION FOR DRAWING THEM AS I USED TO. I DON'T FEEL LIKE I'M GETTING ANYTHING OUT OF THEM ANYMORE

YET I'M PUTTING THE SAME ENERGY INTO THEM THAT I ALWAYS HAVE.

IF I DO DECIDE TO STOP, THE LAST ONE WILL BE ON 12-31-10, SO I'VE STILL GOT A LITTLE WHILE TO MAKE UP MY MIND.

THAT WILL MAKE EXACTLY TEN YEARS.

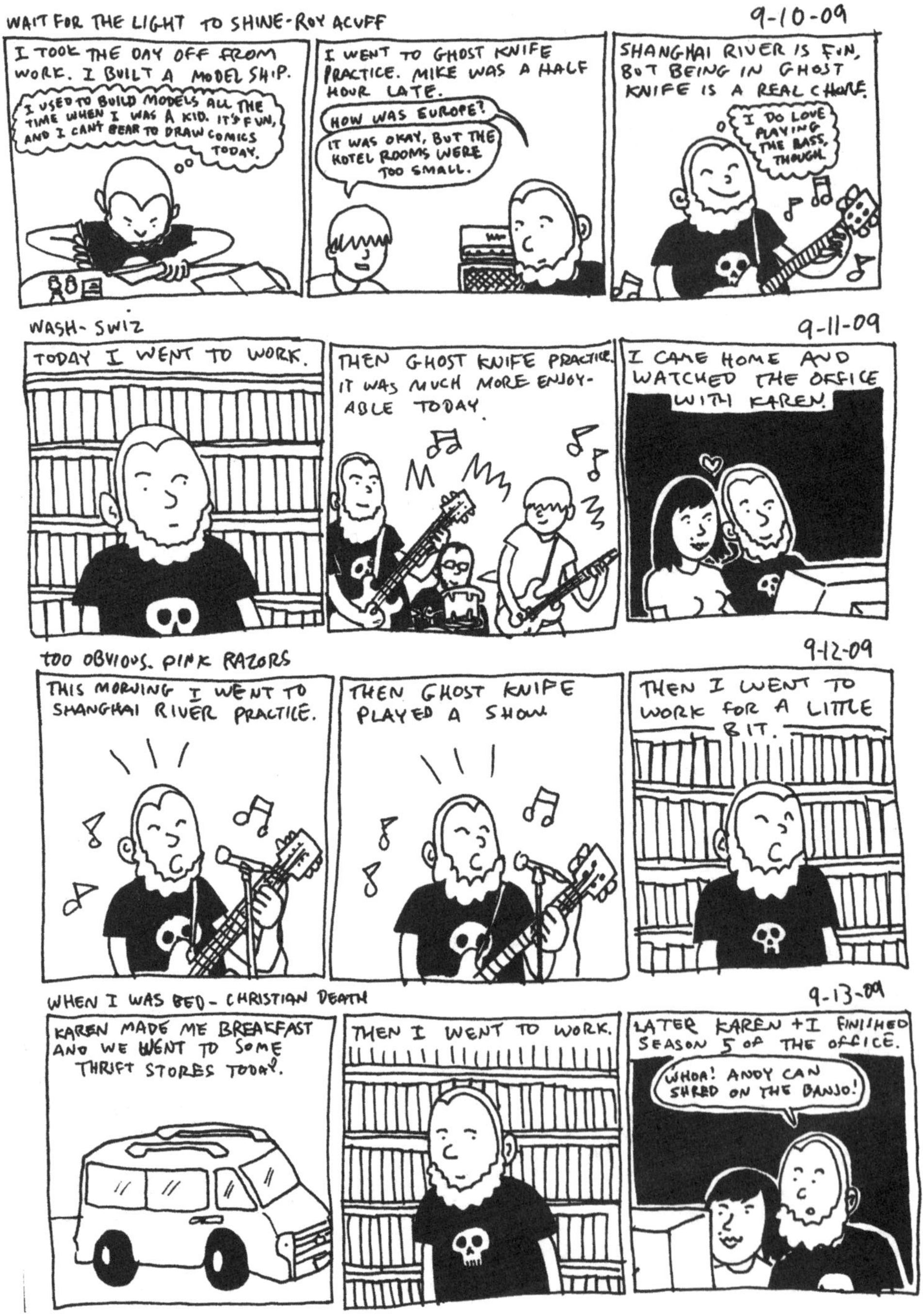
WAIT FOR THE LIGHT TO SHINE-ROY ACUFF
9-10-09
I TOOK THE DAY OFF FROM WORK. I BUILT A MODEL SHIP.
I USED TO BUILD MODELS ALL THE TIME WHEN I WAS A KID. IT'S FUN, AND I CAN'T BEAR TO DRAW COMICS TODAY.
I WENT TO GHOST KNIFE PRACTICE. MIKE WAS A HALF HOUR LATE.
HOW WAS EUROPE?
IT WAS OKAY, BUT THE HOTEL ROOMS WERE TOO SMALL.
SHANGHAI RIVER IS FUN, BUT BEING IN GHOST KNIFE IS A REAL CHORE.
I DO LOVE PLAYING THE BASS, THOUGH.
WASH-SWIZ
9-11-09
TODAY I WENT TO WORK.
THEN GHOST KNIFE PRACTICE. IT WAS MUCH MORE ENJOY-ABLE TODAY.
I CAME HOME AND WATCHED THE OFFICE WITH KAREN.
TOO OBVIOUS. PINK RAZORS
9-12-09
THIS MORNING I WENT TO SHANGHAI RIVER PRACTICE.
THEN GHOST KNIFE PLAYED A SHOW
THEN I WENT TO WORK FOR A LITTLE BIT.
WHEN I WAS BED- CHRISTIAN DEATH
9-13-09
KAREN MADE ME BREAKFAST AND WE WENT TO SOME THRIFT STORES TODAY.
THEN I WENT TO WORK.
LATER KAREN + I FINISHED SEASON 5 OF THE OFFICE.
WHOA! ANDY CAN SHRED ON THE BANJO!

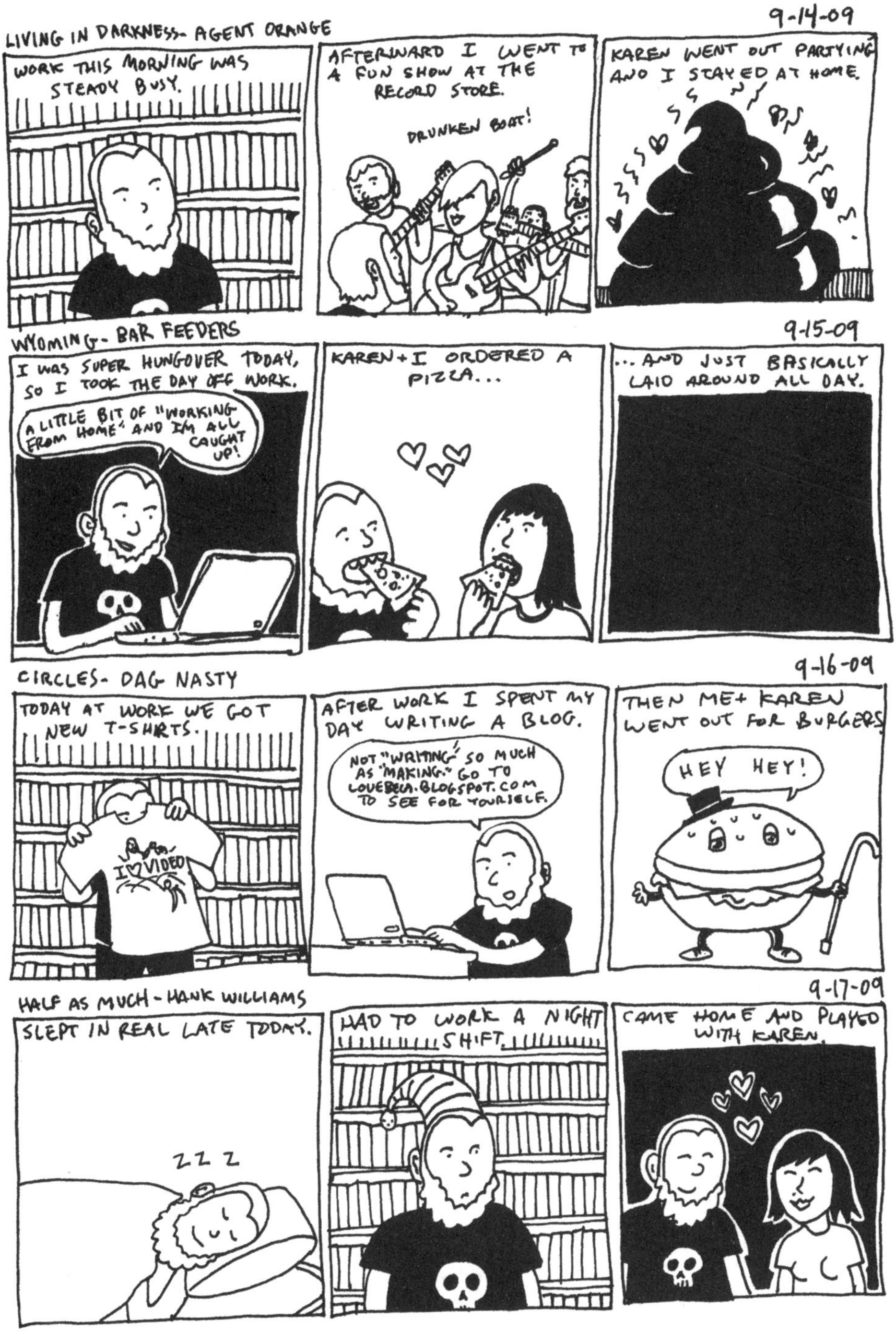
LIVING IN DARKNESS - AGENT ORANGE
9-14-09
WORK THIS MORNING WAS STEADY BUSY.
AFTERWARD I WENT TO A FUN SHOW AT THE RECORD STORE.
DRUNKEN BOAT!
KAREN WENT OUT PARTYING AND I STAYED AT HOME.
WYOMING - BAR FEEDERS
9-15-09
I WAS SUPER HUNGOVER TODAY, SO I TOOK THE DAY OFF WORK.
A LITTLE BIT OF "WORKING FROM HOME" AND I'M ALL CAUGHT UP!
KAREN + I ORDERED A PIZZA...
...AND JUST BASICALLY LAID AROUND ALL DAY.
CIRCLES - DAG NASTY
9-16-09
TODAY AT WORK WE GOT NEW T-SHIRTS.
I ♡ VIDEO
AFTER WORK I SPENT MY DAY WRITING A BLOG.
NOT "WRITING" SO MUCH AS "MAKING." GO TO LOVEBEKA.BLOGSPOT.COM TO SEE FOR YOURSELF.
THEN ME + KAREN WENT OUT FOR BURGERS.
HEY HEY!
HALF AS MUCH - HANK WILLIAMS
9-17-09
SLEPT IN REAL LATE TODAY.
ZZZ
HAD TO WORK A NIGHT SHIFT.
CAME HOME AND PLAYED WITH KAREN.

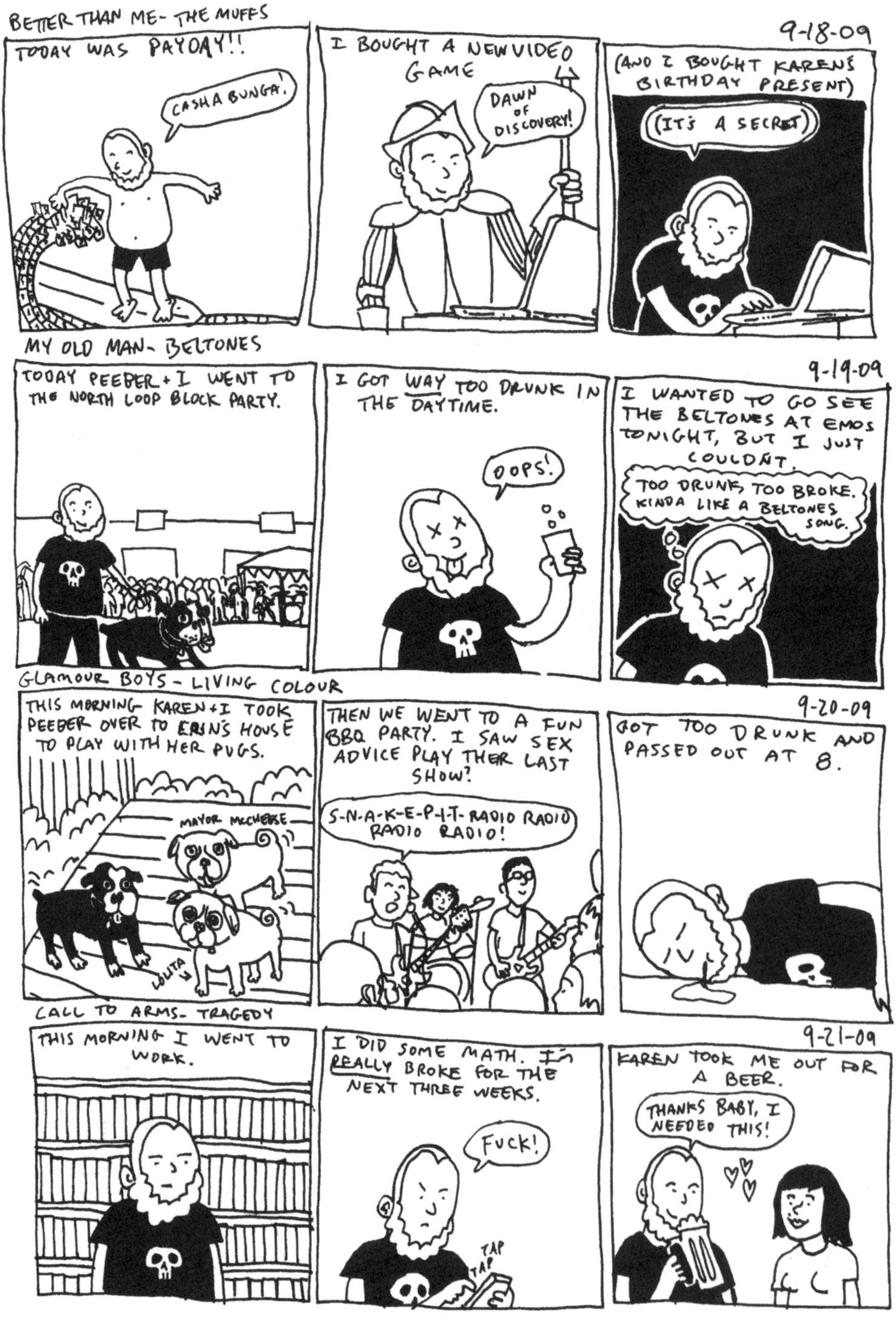
BETTER THAN ME - THE MUFFS
9-18-09
TODAY WAS PAYDAY!!
CASHABUNGA!
I BOUGHT A NEW VIDEO GAME
DAWN OF DISCOVERY!
(AND I BOUGHT KAREN'S BIRTHDAY PRESENT)
(IT'S A SECRET)
MY OLD MAN - BELTONES
9-19-09
TODAY PEEBER + I WENT TO THE NORTH LOOP BLOCK PARTY.
I GOT WAY TOO DRUNK IN THE DAYTIME.
OOPS!
I WANTED TO GO SEE THE BELTONES AT EMOS TONIGHT, BUT I JUST COULDN'T.
TOO DRUNK, TOO BROKE. KINDA LIKE A BELTONES SONG.
GLAMOUR BOYS - LIVING COLOUR
9-20-09
THIS MORNING KAREN + I TOOK PEEBER OVER TO ERIN'S HOUSE TO PLAY WITH HER PUGS.
MAYOR MCCHEESE
LOLITA
THEN WE WENT TO A FUN BBQ PARTY. I SAW SEX ADVICE PLAY THEIR LAST SHOW?
S-N-A-K-E-P-I-T- RADIO RADIO RADIO RADIO!
GOT TOO DRUNK AND PASSED OUT AT 8.
CALL TO ARMS - TRAGEDY
9-21-09
THIS MORNING I WENT TO WORK.
I DID SOME MATH. I'M REALLY BROKE FOR THE NEXT THREE WEEKS.
FUCK!
TAP TAP
KAREN TOOK ME OUT FOR A BEER.
THANKS BABY, I NEEDED THIS!

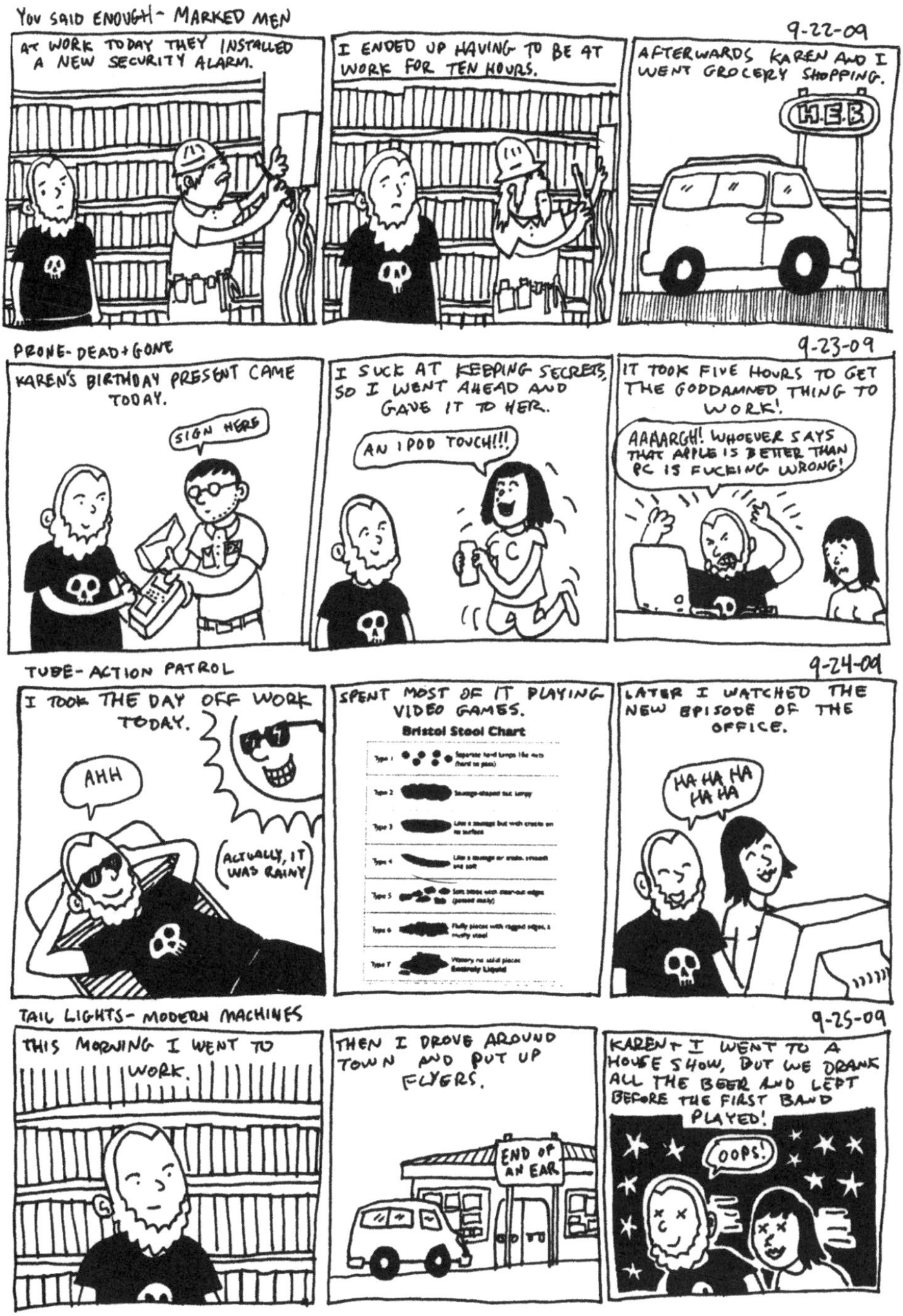
YOU SAID ENOUGH - MARKED MEN
9-22-09
AT WORK TODAY THEY INSTALLED A NEW SECURITY ALARM.
I ENDED UP HAVING TO BE AT WORK FOR TEN HOURS.
AFTERWARDS KAREN AND I WENT GROCERY SHOPPING.
H.E.B
PRONE - DEAD + GONE
9-23-09
KAREN'S BIRTHDAY PRESENT CAME TODAY.
SIGN HERE
I SUCK AT KEEPING SECRETS, SO I WENT AHEAD AND GAVE IT TO HER.
AN IPOD TOUCH!!!
IT TOOK FIVE HOURS TO GET THE GODDAMNED THING TO WORK!
AAAARGH! WHOEVER SAYS THAT APPLE IS BETTER THAN PC IS FUCKING WRONG!
TUBE - ACTION PATROL
9-24-09
I TOOK THE DAY OFF WORK TODAY.
AHH
(ACTUALLY, IT WAS RAINY)
SPENT MOST OF IT PLAYING VIDEO GAMES.
Bristol Stool Chart
LATER I WATCHED THE NEW EPISODE OF THE OFFICE.
HA HA HA HA HA
TAIL LIGHTS - MODERN MACHINES
9-25-09
THIS MORNING I WENT TO WORK.
THEN I DROVE AROUND TOWN AND PUT UP FLYERS.
END OF AN EAR
KAREN + I WENT TO A HOUSE SHOW, BUT WE DRANK ALL THE BEER AND LEFT BEFORE THE FIRST BAND PLAYED!
OOPS!

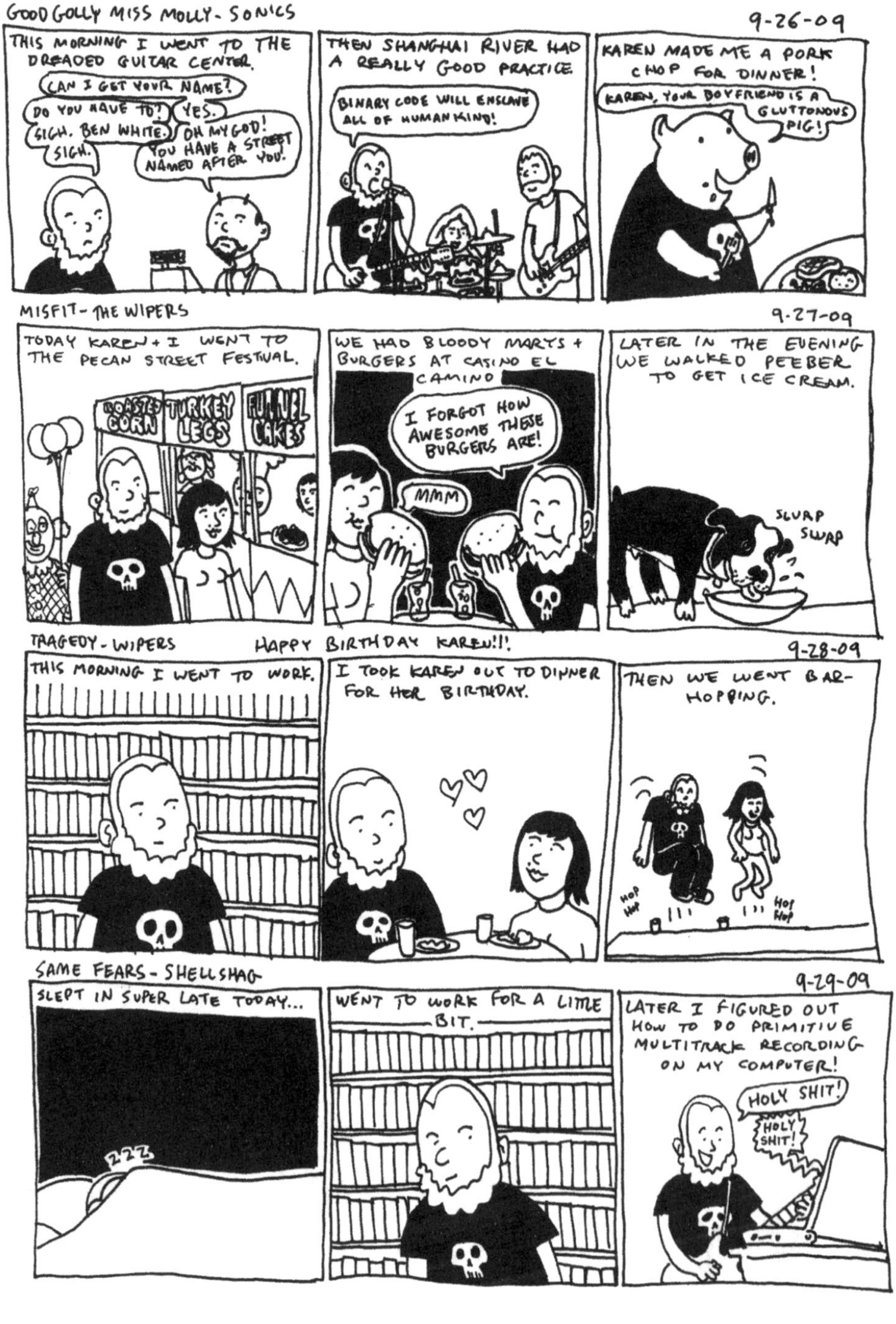
GOOD GOLLY MISS MOLLY - SONICS
9-26-09
THIS MORNING I WENT TO THE DREADED GUITAR CENTER.
CAN I GET YOUR NAME?
DO YOU HAVE TO?
YES.
SIGH. BEN WHITE.
SIGH.
OH MY GOD! YOU HAVE A STREET NAMED AFTER YOU!
THEN SHANGHAI RIVER HAD A REALLY GOOD PRACTICE.
BINARY CODE WILL ENSLAVE ALL OF HUMANKIND!
KAREN MADE ME A PORK CHOP FOR DINNER!
KAREN, YOUR BOYFRIEND IS A GLUTTONOUS PIG!
MISFIT - THE WIPERS
9-27-09
TODAY KAREN + I WENT TO THE PECAN STREET FESTIVAL.
ROASTED CORN
TURKEY LEGS
FUNNEL CAKES
WE HAD BLOODY MARYS + BURGERS AT CASINO EL CAMINO
I FORGOT HOW AWESOME THESE BURGERS ARE!
MMM
LATER IN THE EVENING WE WALKED PEEBER TO GET ICE CREAM.
SLURP SLURP
TRAGEDY - WIPERS
HAPPY BIRTHDAY KAREN!!!
9-28-09
THIS MORNING I WENT TO WORK.
I TOOK KAREN OUT TO DINNER FOR HER BIRTHDAY.
THEN WE WENT BAR-HOPPING.
HOP HOP
HOP HOP
SAME FEARS - SHELLSHAG
9-29-09
SLEPT IN SUPER LATE TODAY...
ZZZ
WENT TO WORK FOR A LITTLE BIT.
LATER I FIGURED OUT HOW TO DO PRIMITIVE MULTITRACK RECORDING ON MY COMPUTER!
HOLY SHIT!
HOLY SHIT!

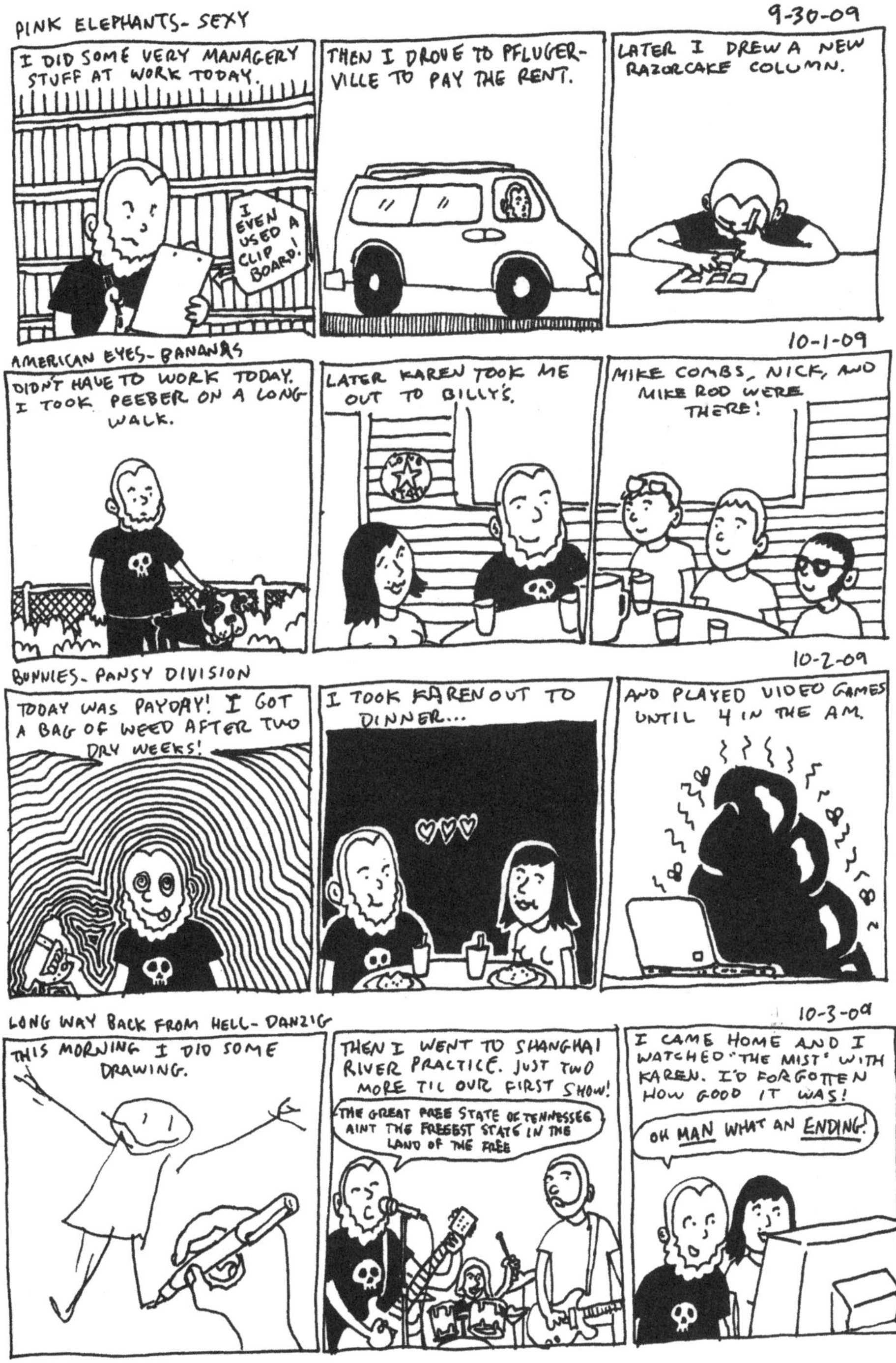
PINK ELEPHANTS- SEXY
9-30-09
I DID SOME VERY MANAGERY STUFF AT WORK TODAY.
I EVEN USED A CLIP BOARD!
THEN I DROVE TO PFLUGERVILLE TO PAY THE RENT.
LATER I DREW A NEW RAZORCAKE COLUMN.
AMERICAN EYES- BANANAS
10-1-09
DIDN'T HAVE TO WORK TODAY. I TOOK PEEBER ON A LONG WALK.
LATER KAREN TOOK ME OUT TO BILLY'S.
LONE STAR
MIKE COMBS, NICK, AND MIKE ROD WERE THERE!
BUNNIES- PANSY DIVISION
10-2-09
TODAY WAS PAYDAY! I GOT A BAG OF WEED AFTER TWO DRY WEEKS!
I TOOK KAREN OUT TO DINNER...
AND PLAYED VIDEO GAMES UNTIL 4 IN THE AM.
LONG WAY BACK FROM HELL- DANZIG
10-3-09
THIS MORNING I DID SOME DRAWING.
THEN I WENT TO SHANGHAI RIVER PRACTICE. JUST TWO MORE TIL OUR FIRST SHOW!
THE GREAT FREE STATE OF TENNESSEE AINT THE FREEST STATE IN THE LAND OF THE FREE
I CAME HOME AND I WATCHED "THE MIST" WITH KAREN. I'D FORGOTTEN HOW GOOD IT WAS!
OH MAN WHAT AN ENDING!

WHEN I'M OLD - FASTBACKS

Panel 1: TODAY KAREN AND I WENT TO SUPER BURRITO!

Panel 2: THEN I WENT TO GHOST KNIFE PRACTICE.
YEEK! I'M RUSTY!
FLUB FLUB FLUB

Panel 3: AFTER THAT KAREN + I WATCHED A DOUBLE FEATURE OF COCKTAIL AND COYOTE UGLY.
THESE ARE BOTH PRACTICALLY THE SAME MOVIE!

WHY ARE YOU WEIRD? - SCARED OF CHAKA

Panel 1: TODAY I WENT TO WORK.
YOU LOOK FAMILIAR. DO I KNOW YOU FROM AA MEETINGS?
NOT YET.

Panel 2: KAREN + I WATCHED "ANVIL: THE STORY OF ANVIL"
THIS IS JUST LIKE A J CHURCH TOUR.

Panel 3: LATER I DICKED AROUND ON THE INTERNET.
MY APOLOGIES.

COUNTRY GIRL - BLACK SABBATH

Panel 1: HAD AN EARLY LUNCH WITH KAREN + PEEBERAT THUNDERBIRD.

Panel 2: THEN I WENT TO WORK AND GOT STOOD UP FOR TWO MEETINGS.
SIGH

Panel 3: LATER I HUNG OUT WITH KAREN AND LISTENED TO RECORDS.

SOUTH BOUND 95 - AVAIL

Panel 1: TODAY I WENT TO WORK.

Panel 2: HAD A MEETING WITH MY BOSS, WE BOTH GOT A LITTLE DRUNK.

Panel 3: KAREN + I WENT TO A LITTLE PARTY AT DEEON'S.

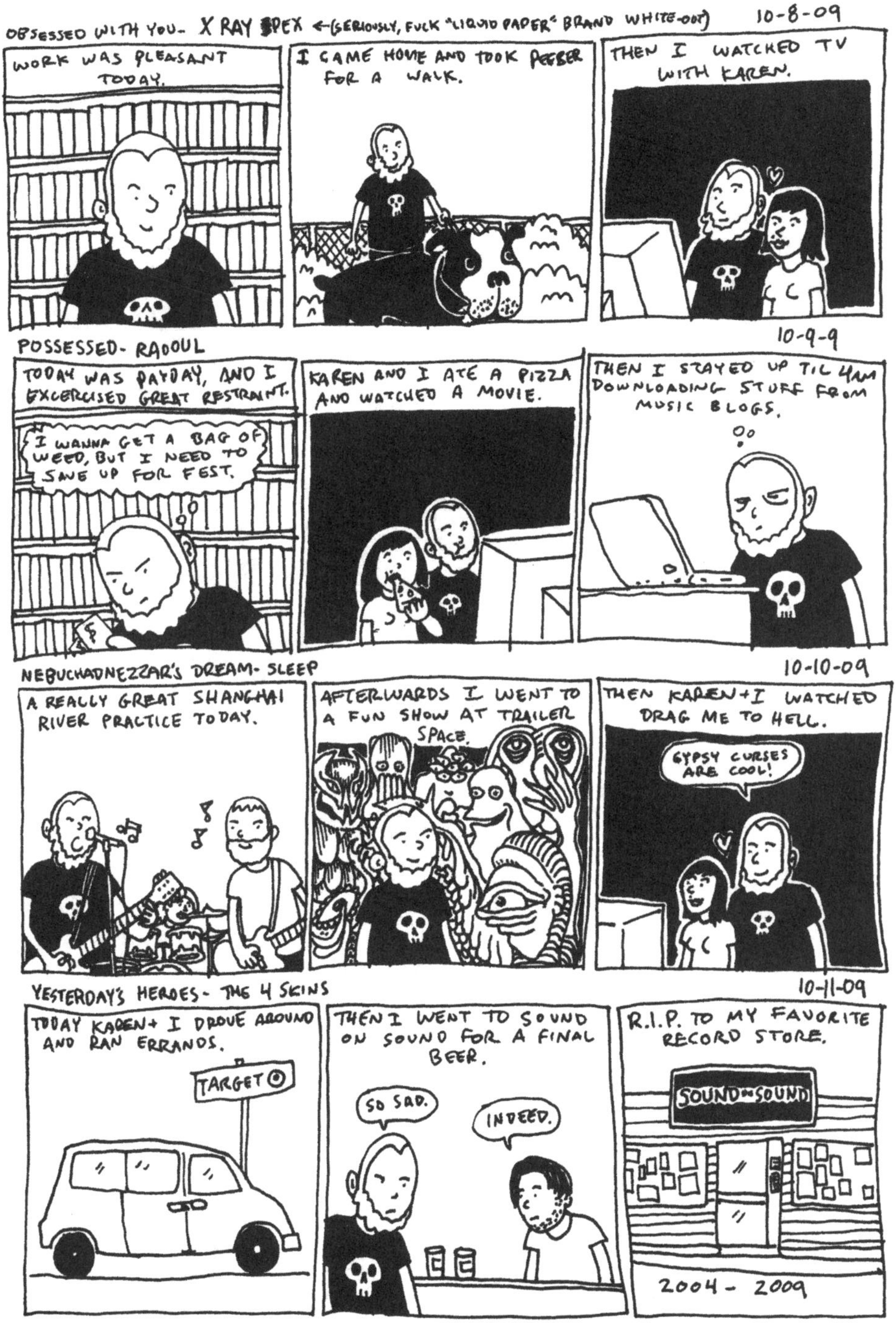
OBSESSED WITH YOU - X RAY SPEX ← (SERIOUSLY, FUCK "LIQUID PAPER" BRAND WHITE-OUT)
10-8-09
WORK WAS PLEASANT TODAY.
I CAME HOME AND TOOK PEEBER FOR A WALK.
THEN I WATCHED TV WITH KAREN.
POSSESSED - RADOUL
10-9-9
TODAY WAS PAYDAY, AND I EXCERCISED GREAT RESTRAINT.
I WANNA GET A BAG OF WEED, BUT I NEED TO SAVE UP FOR FEST.
KAREN AND I ATE A PIZZA AND WATCHED A MOVIE.
THEN I STAYED UP TIL 4AM DOWNLOADING STUFF FROM MUSIC BLOGS.
NEBUCHADNEZZAR'S DREAM - SLEEP
10-10-09
A REALLY GREAT SHANGHAI RIVER PRACTICE TODAY.
AFTERWARDS I WENT TO A FUN SHOW AT TRAILER SPACE.
THEN KAREN + I WATCHED DRAG ME TO HELL.
GYPSY CURSES ARE COOL!
YESTERDAY'S HEROES - THE 4 SKINS
10-11-09
TODAY KAREN + I DROVE AROUND AND RAN ERRANDS.
TARGET
THEN I WENT TO SOUND ON SOUND FOR A FINAL BEER.
SO SAD.
INDEED.
R.I.P. TO MY FAVORITE RECORD STORE.
SOUND ON SOUND
2004 - 2009

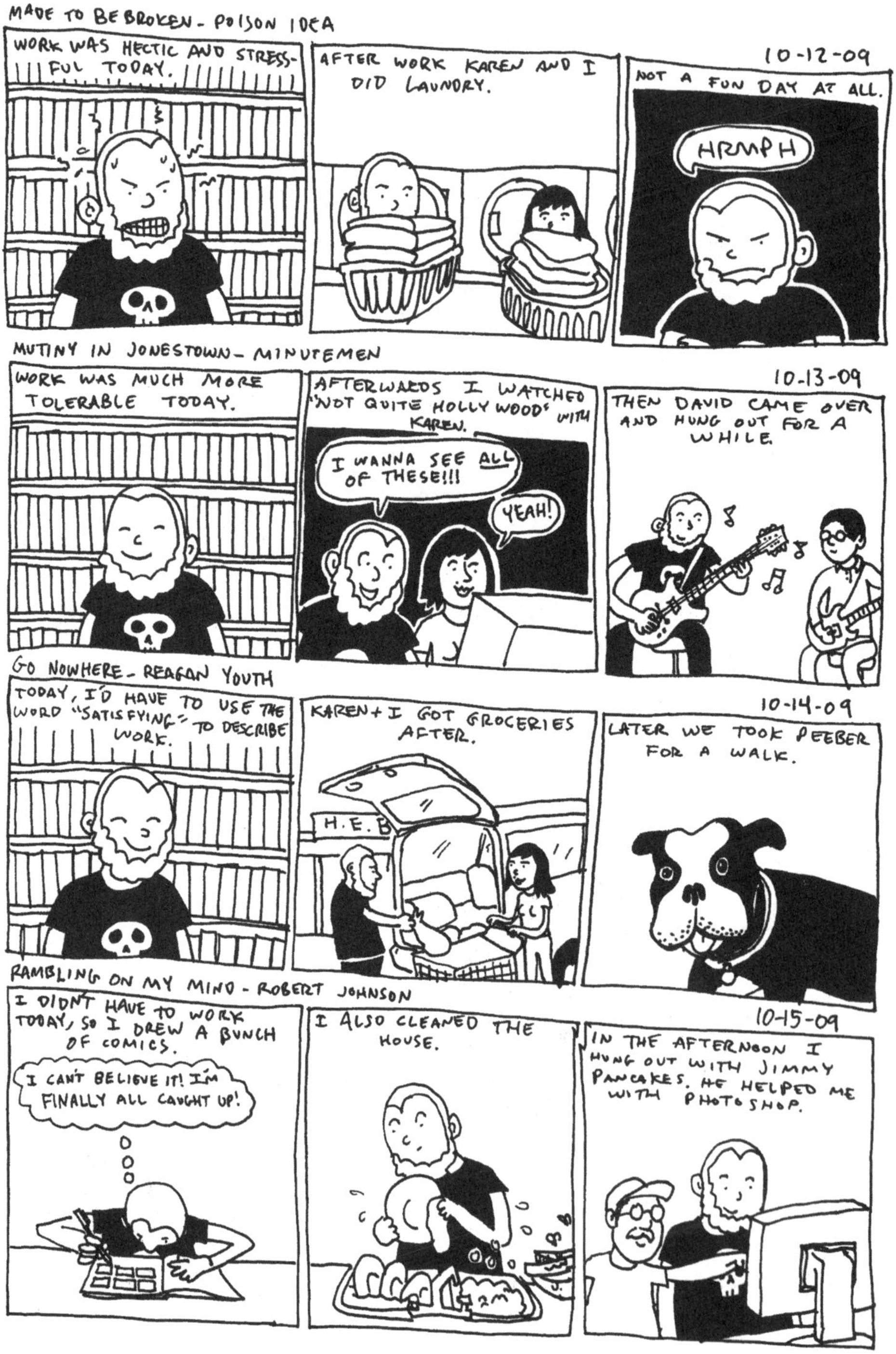
MADE TO BE BROKEN - POISON IDEA
10-12-09
WORK WAS HECTIC AND STRESS-FUL TODAY.
AFTER WORK KAREN AND I DID LAUNDRY.
NOT A FUN DAY AT ALL.
HRMPH
MUTINY IN JONESTOWN - MINUTEMEN
10-13-09
WORK WAS MUCH MORE TOLERABLE TODAY.
AFTERWARDS I WATCHED 'NOT QUITE HOLLYWOOD' WITH KAREN.
I WANNA SEE ALL OF THESE!!!
YEAH!
THEN DAVID CAME OVER AND HUNG OUT FOR A WHILE.
GO NOWHERE - REAGAN YOUTH
10-14-09
TODAY, I'D HAVE TO USE THE WORD "SATISFYING" TO DESCRIBE WORK.
KAREN + I GOT GROCERIES AFTER.
H.E.B
LATER WE TOOK PEEBER FOR A WALK.
RAMBLING ON MY MIND - ROBERT JOHNSON
10-15-09
I DIDN'T HAVE TO WORK TODAY, SO I DREW A BUNCH OF COMICS.
I CAN'T BELIEVE IT! I'M FINALLY ALL CAUGHT UP!
I ALSO CLEANED THE HOUSE.
IN THE AFTERNOON I HUNG OUT WITH JIMMY PANCAKES. HE HELPED ME WITH PHOTOSHOP.

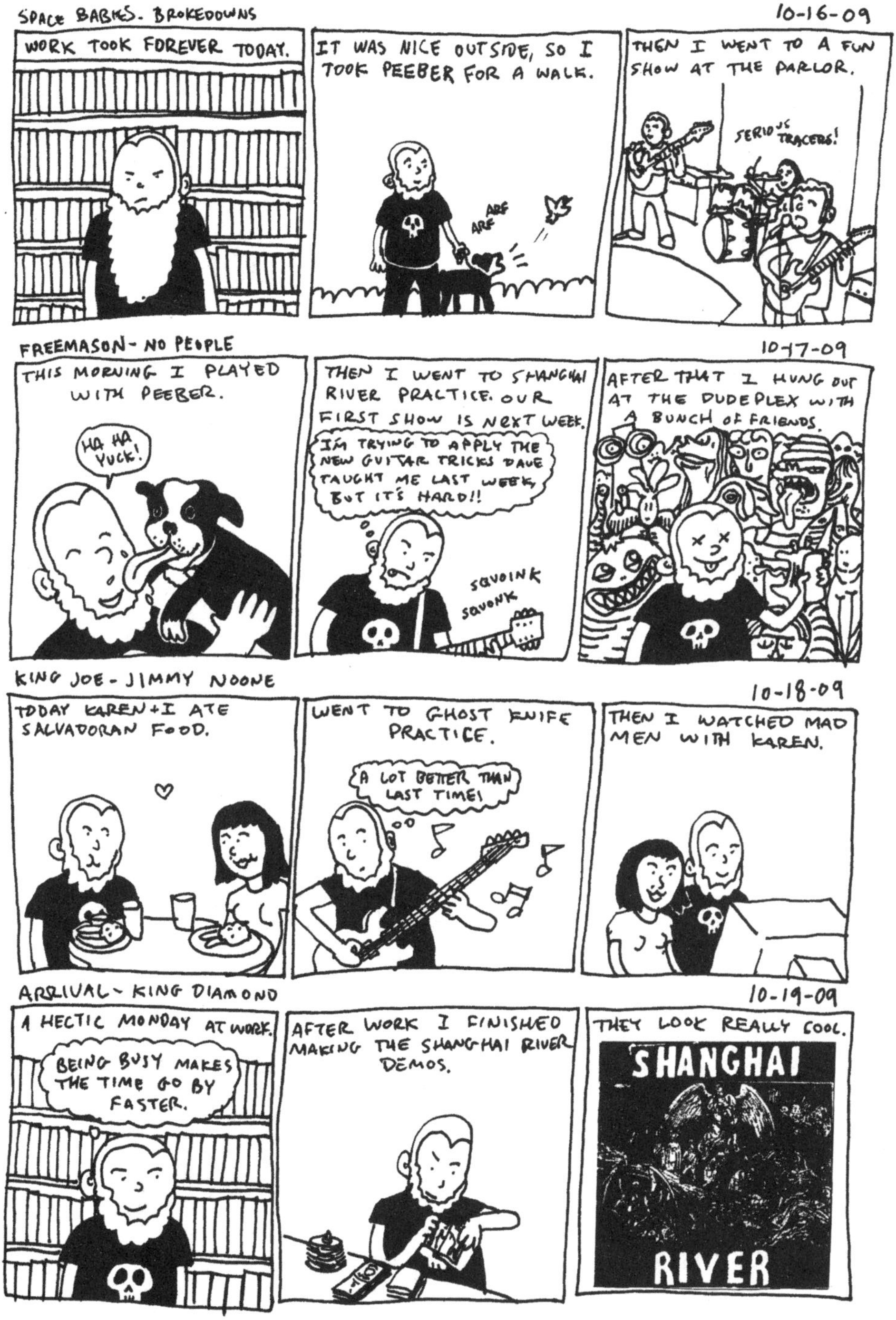
SPACE BABIES. BROKEDOWNS
10-16-09
WORK TOOK FOREVER TODAY.
IT WAS NICE OUTSIDE, SO I TOOK PEEBER FOR A WALK.
ARF
ARF
THEN I WENT TO A FUN SHOW AT THE PARLOR.
SERIOUS TRACERS!
FREEMASON - NO PEOPLE
10-17-09
THIS MORNING I PLAYED WITH PEEBER.
HA HA YUCK!
THEN I WENT TO SHANGHAI RIVER PRACTICE. OUR FIRST SHOW IS NEXT WEEK.
I'M TRYING TO APPLY THE NEW GUITAR TRICKS DAVE TAUGHT ME LAST WEEK, BUT IT'S HARD!!
SQUOINK
SQUONK
AFTER THAT I HUNG OUT AT THE DUDEPLEX WITH A BUNCH OF FRIENDS.
KING JOE - JIMMY NOONE
10-18-09
TODAY KAREN + I ATE SALVADORAN FOOD.
WENT TO GHOST KNIFE PRACTICE.
A LOT BETTER THAN LAST TIME!
THEN I WATCHED MAD MEN WITH KAREN.
ARRIVAL - KING DIAMOND
10-19-09
A HECTIC MONDAY AT WORK.
BEING BUSY MAKES THE TIME GO BY FASTER.
AFTER WORK I FINISHED MAKING THE SHANGHAI RIVER DEMOS.
THEY LOOK REALLY COOL.
SHANGHAI
RIVER

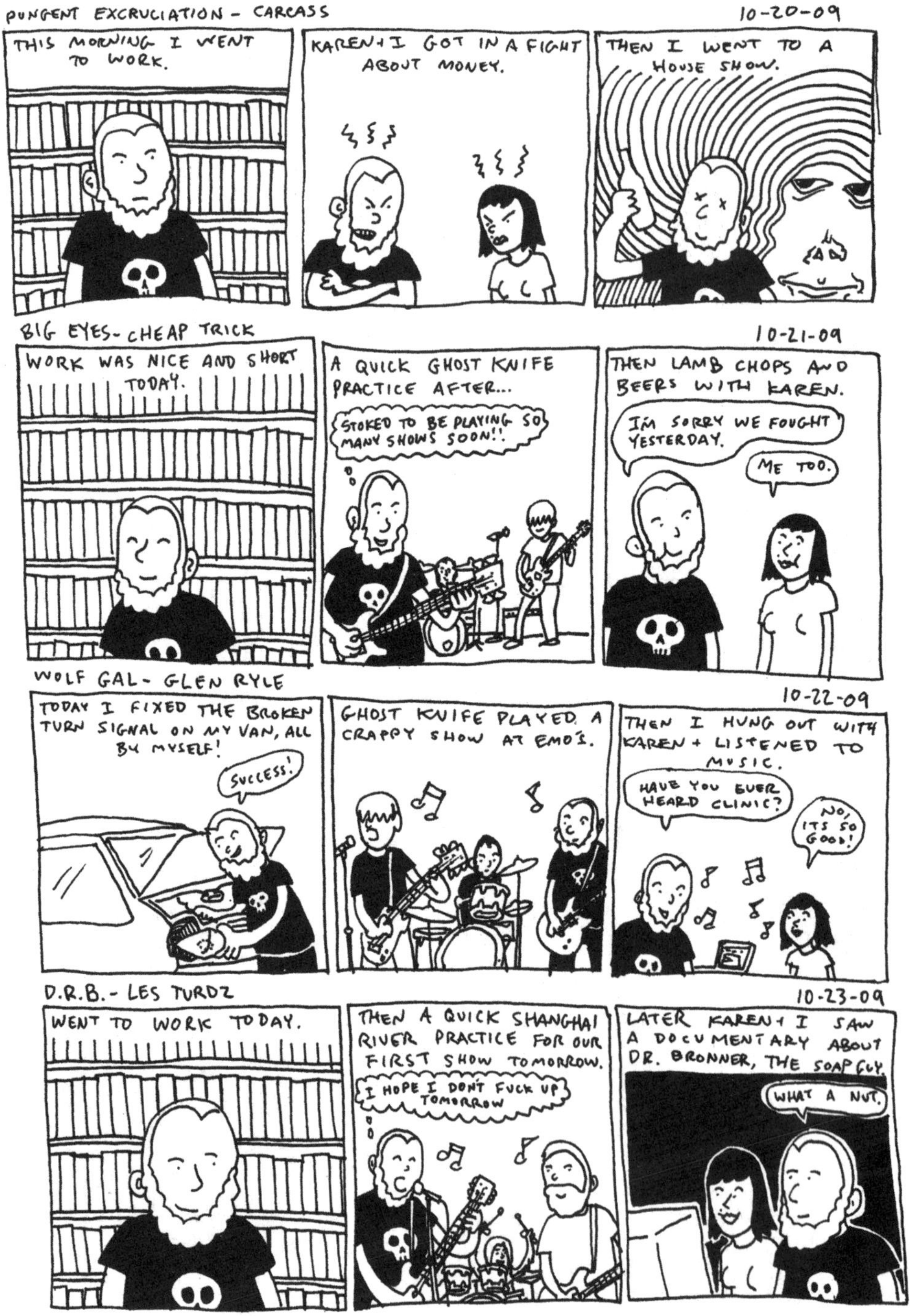
PUNGENT EXCRUCIATION - CARCASS
10-20-09
THIS MORNING I WENT TO WORK.
KAREN + I GOT IN A FIGHT ABOUT MONEY.
THEN I WENT TO A HOUSE SHOW.
BIG EYES - CHEAP TRICK
10-21-09
WORK WAS NICE AND SHORT TODAY.
A QUICK GHOST KNIFE PRACTICE AFTER...
STOKED TO BE PLAYING SO MANY SHOWS SOON!!
THEN LAMB CHOPS AND BEERS WITH KAREN.
I'M SORRY WE FOUGHT YESTERDAY.
ME TOO.
WOLF GAL - GLEN RYLE
10-22-09
TODAY I FIXED THE BROKEN TURN SIGNAL ON MY VAN, ALL BY MYSELF!
SUCCESS!
GHOST KNIFE PLAYED A CRAPPY SHOW AT EMO'S.
THEN I HUNG OUT WITH KAREN + LISTENED TO MUSIC.
HAVE YOU EVER HEARD CLINIC?
NO, ITS SO GOOD!
D.R.B. - LES TURDZ
10-23-09
WENT TO WORK TODAY.
THEN A QUICK SHANGHAI RIVER PRACTICE FOR OUR FIRST SHOW TOMORROW.
I HOPE I DON'T FUCK UP TOMORROW
LATER KAREN + I SAW A DOCUMENTARY ABOUT DR. BRONNER, THE SOAP GUY.
WHAT A NUT.

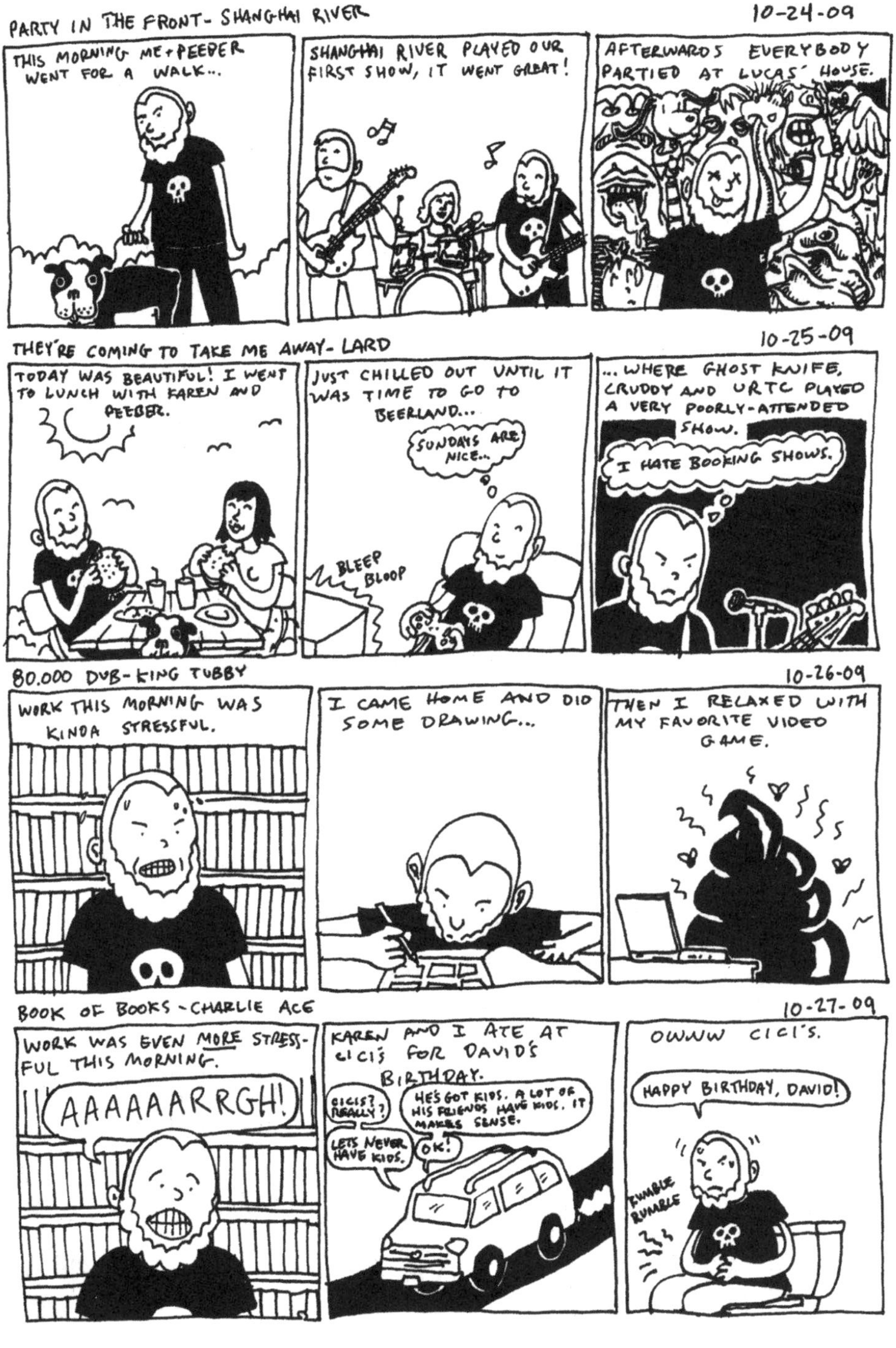
PARTY IN THE FRONT - SHANGHAI RIVER
10-24-09
THIS MORNING ME + PEEBER WENT FOR A WALK...
SHANGHAI RIVER PLAYED OUR FIRST SHOW, IT WENT GREAT!
AFTERWARDS EVERYBODY PARTIED AT LUCAS' HOUSE.
THEY'RE COMING TO TAKE ME AWAY - LARD
10-25-09
TODAY WAS BEAUTIFUL! I WENT TO LUNCH WITH KAREN AND PEEBER.
JUST CHILLED OUT UNTIL IT WAS TIME TO GO TO BEERLAND...
SUNDAYS ARE NICE...
BLEEP BLOOP
...WHERE GHOST KNIFE, CRUDDY AND URTC PLAYED A VERY POORLY-ATTENDED SHOW.
I HATE BOOKING SHOWS.
80.000 DUB - KING TUBBY
10-26-09
WORK THIS MORNING WAS KINDA STRESSFUL.
I CAME HOME AND DID SOME DRAWING...
THEN I RELAXED WITH MY FAVORITE VIDEO GAME.
BOOK OF BOOKS - CHARLIE ACE
10-27-09
WORK WAS EVEN MORE STRESSFUL THIS MORNING.
AAAAAARRGH!
KAREN AND I ATE AT CICI'S FOR DAVID'S BIRTHDAY.
CICIS? REALLY?
HE'S GOT KIDS. A LOT OF HIS FRIENDS HAVE KIDS. IT MAKES SENSE.
LETS NEVER HAVE KIDS.
OK!
OWWW CICI'S.
HAPPY BIRTHDAY, DAVID!
RUMBLE RUMBLE

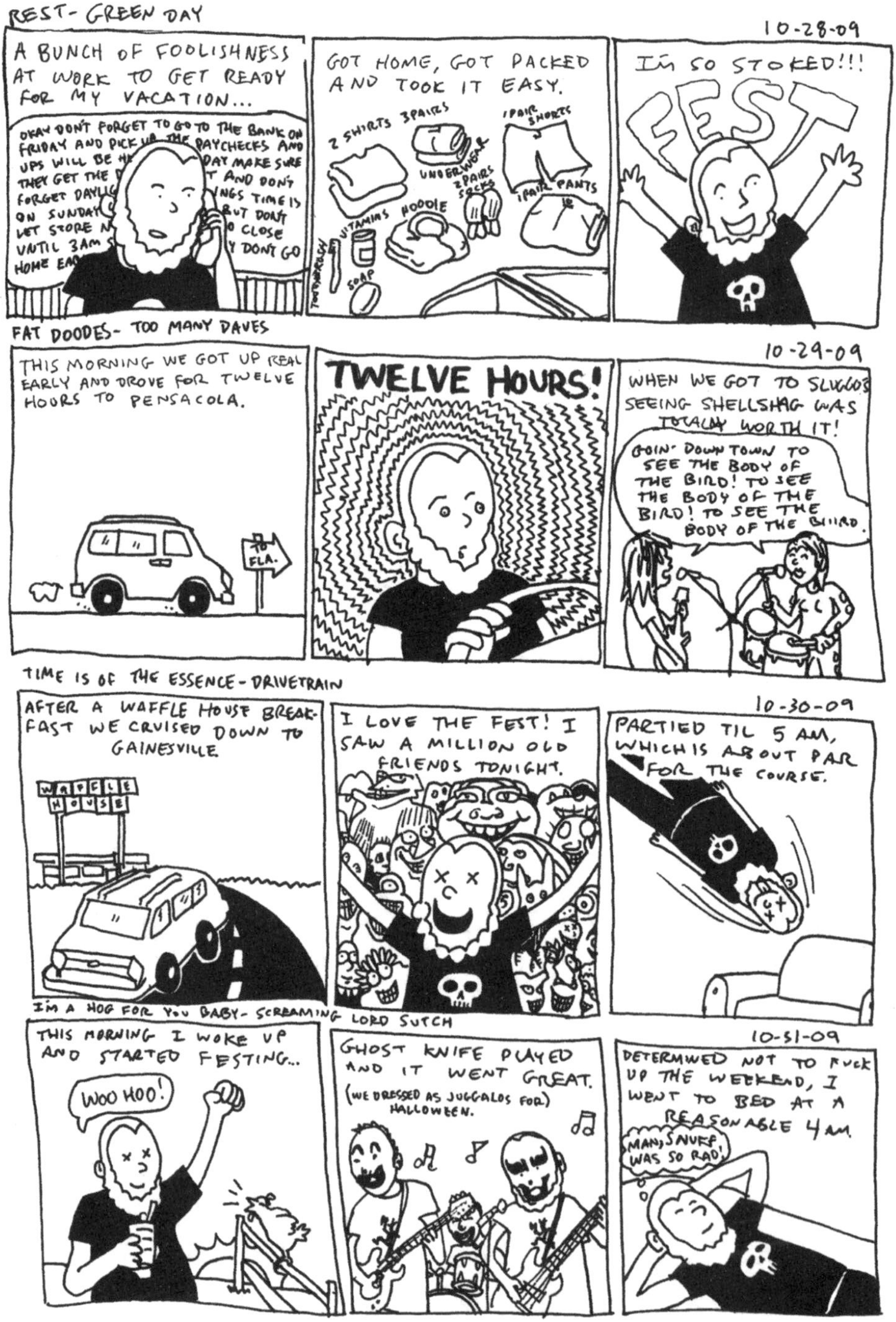
REST- GREEN DAY
10-28-09
A BUNCH OF FOOLISHNESS AT WORK TO GET READY FOR MY VACATION...
OKAY DON'T FORGET TO GO TO THE BANK ON FRIDAY AND PICK UP THE PAYCHECKS AND UPS WILL BE H DAY MAKE SURE THEY GET THE T AND DON'T FORGET DAYLI NGS TIME IS ON SUNDAY BUT DON'T LET STORE N O CLOSE UNTIL 3AM Y DON'T GO HOME EA
GOT HOME, GOT PACKED AND TOOK IT EASY.
2 SHIRTS
3 PAIRS UNDERWEAR
1 PAIR SHORTS
2 PAIRS SOCKS
1 PAIR PANTS
VITAMINS
HOODIE
TOOTHBRUSH
SOAP
I'M SO STOKED!!!
FEST
FAT DOODES- TOO MANY DAVES
10-29-09
THIS MORNING WE GOT UP REAL EARLY AND DROVE FOR TWELVE HOURS TO PENSACOLA.
TO FLA.
TWELVE HOURS!
WHEN WE GOT TO SLUGGO'S SEEING SHELLSHAG WAS TOTALLY WORTH IT!
GOIN' DOWNTOWN TO SEE THE BODY OF THE BIRD! TO SEE THE BODY OF THE BIRD! TO SEE THE BODY OF THE BIIRD.
TIME IS OF THE ESSENCE- DRIVETRAIN
10-30-09
AFTER A WAFFLE HOUSE BREAKFAST WE CRUISED DOWN TO GAINESVILLE.
WAFFLE HOUSE
I LOVE THE FEST! I SAW A MILLION OLD FRIENDS TONIGHT.
PARTIED TIL 5 AM, WHICH IS ABOUT PAR FOR THE COURSE.
I'M A HOG FOR YOU BABY- SCREAMING LORD SUTCH
10-31-09
THIS MORNING I WOKE UP AND STARTED FESTING...
WOO HOO!
GHOST KNIFE PLAYED AND IT WENT GREAT.
(WE DRESSED AS JUGGALOS FOR HALLOWEEN.)
DETERMINED NOT TO FUCK UP THE WEEKEND, I WENT TO BED AT A REASONABLE 4AM.
MAN, SNUFF WAS SO RAD!

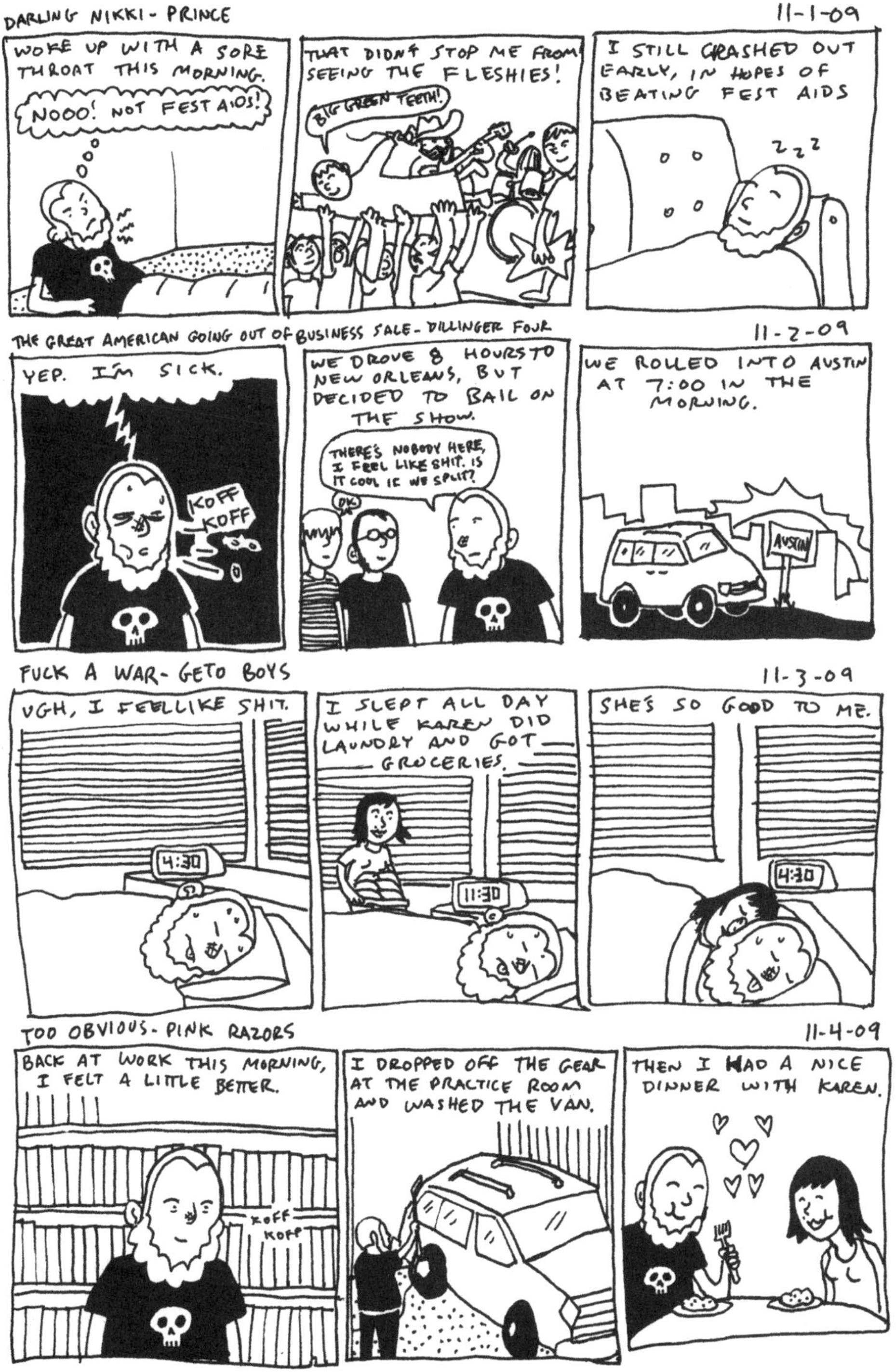
DARLING NIKKI - PRINCE
11-1-09
WOKE UP WITH A SORE THROAT THIS MORNING.
NOOO! NOT FEST AIDS!
THAT DIDN'T STOP ME FROM SEEING THE FLESHIES!
BIG GREEN TEETH!
I STILL CRASHED OUT EARLY, IN HOPES OF BEATING FEST AIDS
Z Z Z
THE GREAT AMERICAN GOING OUT OF BUSINESS SALE - DILLINGER FOUR
11-2-09
YEP. I'M SICK.
KOFF KOFF
WE DROVE 8 HOURS TO NEW ORLEANS, BUT DECIDED TO BAIL ON THE SHOW.
THERE'S NOBODY HERE, I FEEL LIKE SHIT. IS IT COOL IF WE SPLIT?
OK
WE ROLLED INTO AUSTIN AT 7:00 IN THE MORNING.
AUSTIN
FUCK A WAR - GETO BOYS
11-3-09
UGH, I FEEL LIKE SHIT.
4:30
I SLEPT ALL DAY WHILE KAREN DID LAUNDRY AND GOT GROCERIES.
11:30
SHE'S SO GOOD TO ME.
4:30
TOO OBVIOUS - PINK RAZORS
11-4-09
BACK AT WORK THIS MORNING, I FELT A LITTLE BETTER.
KOFF KOFF
I DROPPED OFF THE GEAR AT THE PRACTICE ROOM AND WASHED THE VAN.
THEN I HAD A NICE DINNER WITH KAREN.

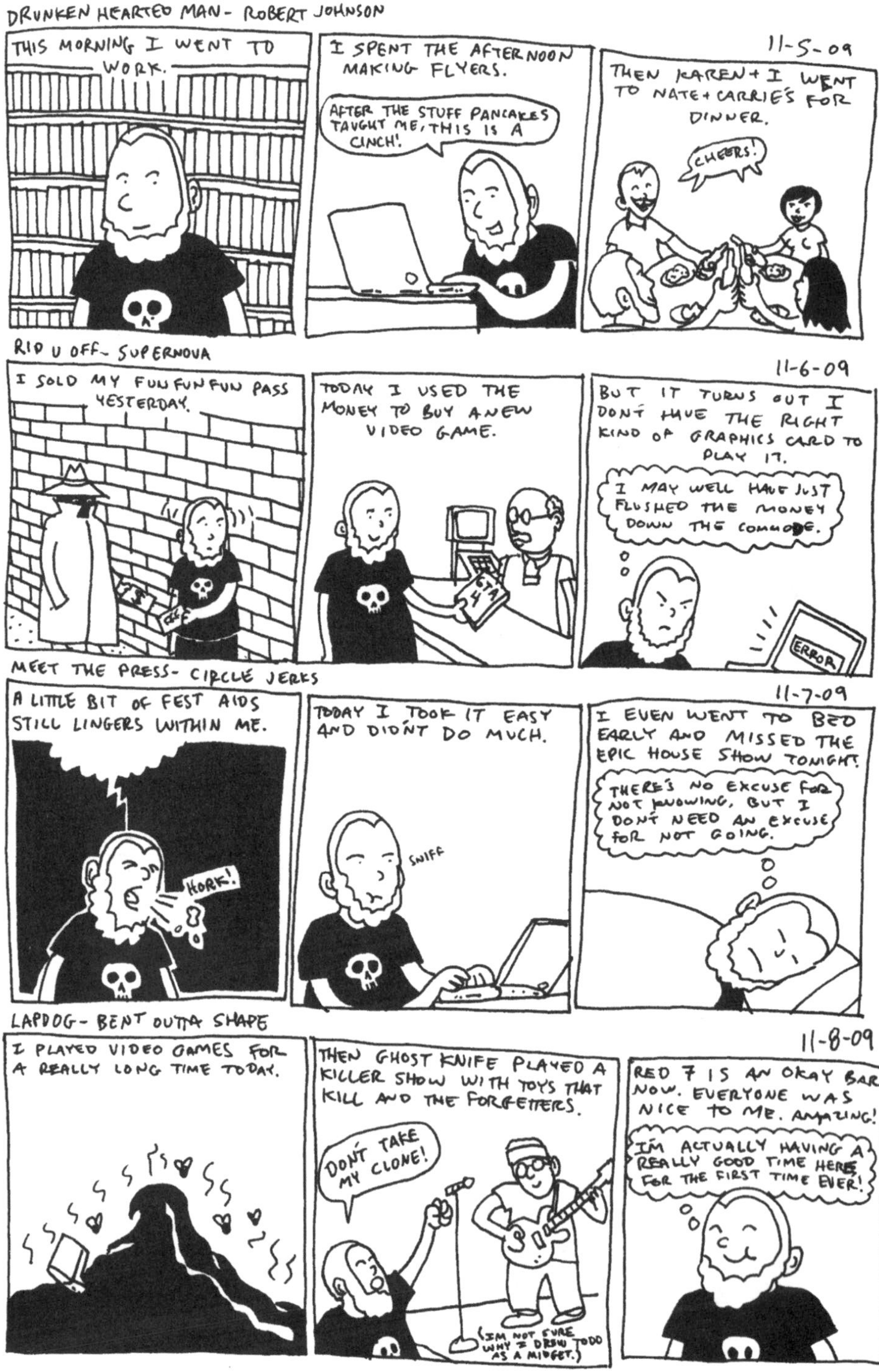
DRUNKEN HEARTED MAN - ROBERT JOHNSON
11-5-09
THIS MORNING I WENT TO WORK.
I SPENT THE AFTERNOON MAKING FLYERS.
AFTER THE STUFF PANCAKES TAUGHT ME, THIS IS A CINCH!
THEN KAREN + I WENT TO NATE + CARRIE'S FOR DINNER.
CHEERS!
RID U OFF - SUPERNOVA
11-6-09
I SOLD MY FUN FUN FUN PASS YESTERDAY.
TODAY I USED THE MONEY TO BUY A NEW VIDEO GAME.
GTA 4
BUT IT TURNS OUT I DON'T HAVE THE RIGHT KIND OF GRAPHICS CARD TO PLAY IT.
I MAY WELL HAVE JUST FLUSHED THE MONEY DOWN THE COMMODE.
ERROR
MEET THE PRESS - CIRCLE JERKS
11-7-09
A LITTLE BIT OF FEST AIDS STILL LINGERS WITHIN ME.
HORK!
TODAY I TOOK IT EASY AND DIDN'T DO MUCH.
SNIFF
I EVEN WENT TO BED EARLY AND MISSED THE EPIC HOUSE SHOW TONIGHT.
THERE'S NO EXCUSE FOR NOT KNOWING, BUT I DON'T NEED AN EXCUSE FOR NOT GOING.
LAPDOG - BENT OUTTA SHAPE
11-8-09
I PLAYED VIDEO GAMES FOR A REALLY LONG TIME TODAY.
THEN GHOST KNIFE PLAYED A KILLER SHOW WITH TOYS THAT KILL AND THE FORGETTERS.
DON'T TAKE MY CLONE!
(I'M NOT SURE WHY I DREW TODD AS A MIDGET.)
RED 7 IS AN OKAY BAR NOW. EVERYONE WAS NICE TO ME. AMAZING!
I'M ACTUALLY HAVING A REALLY GOOD TIME HERE FOR THE FIRST TIME EVER!

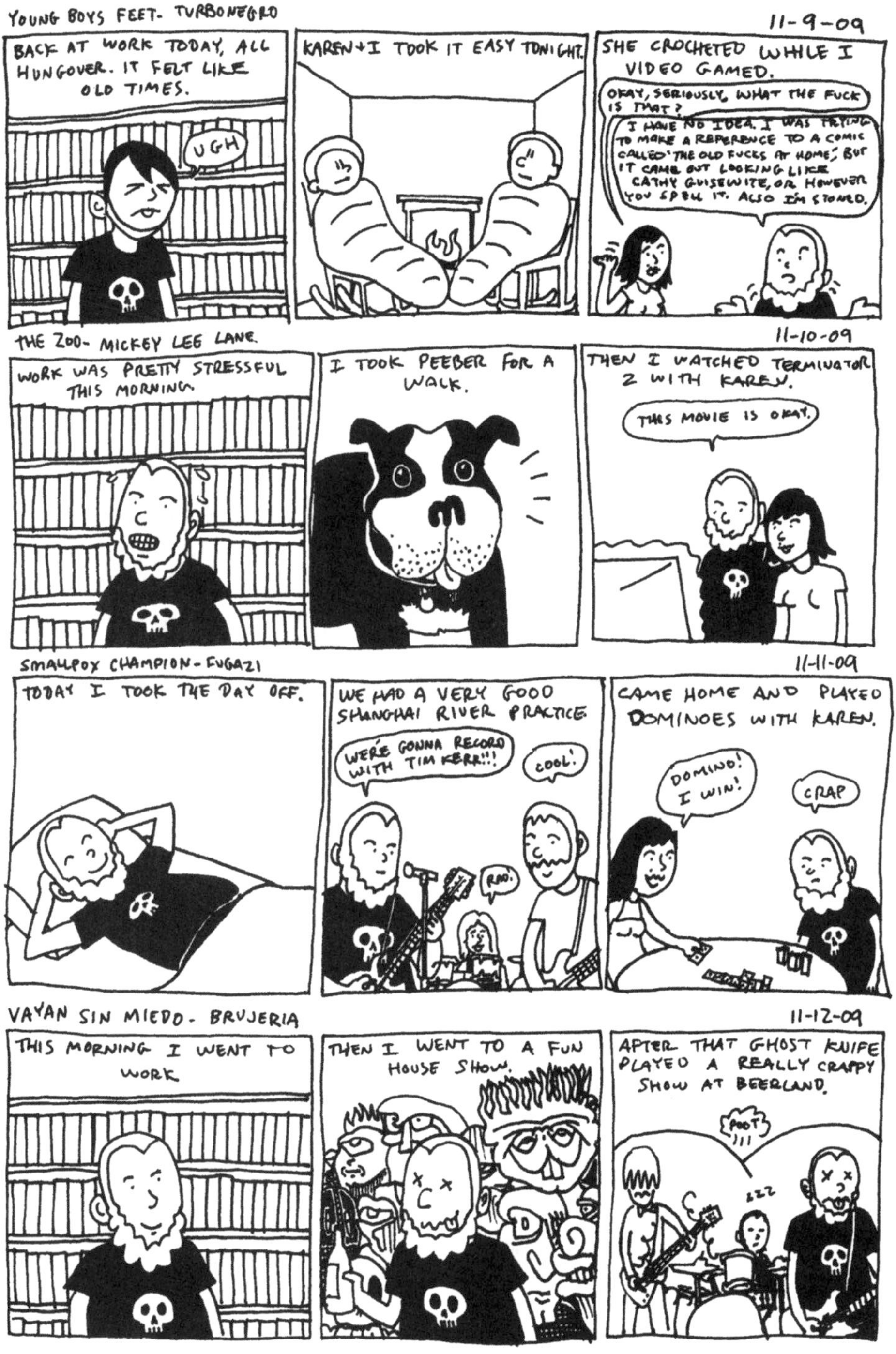
YOUNG BOYS FEET- TURBONEGRO
11-9-09
BACK AT WORK TODAY, ALL HUNGOVER. IT FELT LIKE OLD TIMES.
UGH
KAREN + I TOOK IT EASY TONIGHT.
SHE CROCHETED WHILE I VIDEO GAMED.
OKAY, SERIOUSLY, WHAT THE FUCK IS THAT?
I HAVE NO IDEA. I WAS TRYING TO MAKE A REFERENCE TO A COMIC CALLED 'THE OLD FUCKS AT HOME,' BUT IT CAME OUT LOOKING LIKE CATHY GUISEWITE, OR HOWEVER YOU SPELL IT. ALSO I'M STONED.
THE ZOO- MICKEY LEE LANE
11-10-09
WORK WAS PRETTY STRESSFUL THIS MORNING.
I TOOK PEEBER FOR A WALK.
THEN I WATCHED TERMINATOR 2 WITH KAREN.
THIS MOVIE IS OKAY.
SMALLPOX CHAMPION- FUGAZI
11-11-09
TODAY I TOOK THE DAY OFF.
WE HAD A VERY GOOD SHANGHAI RIVER PRACTICE.
WE'RE GONNA RECORD WITH TIM KERR!!!
COOL!
RAD.
CAME HOME AND PLAYED DOMINOES WITH KAREN.
DOMINO! I WIN!
CRAP
VAYAN SIN MIEDO- BRUJERIA
11-12-09
THIS MORNING I WENT TO WORK
THEN I WENT TO A FUN HOUSE SHOW.
AFTER THAT GHOST KNIFE PLAYED A REALLY CRAPPY SHOW AT BEERLAND.
POOT
ZZZ

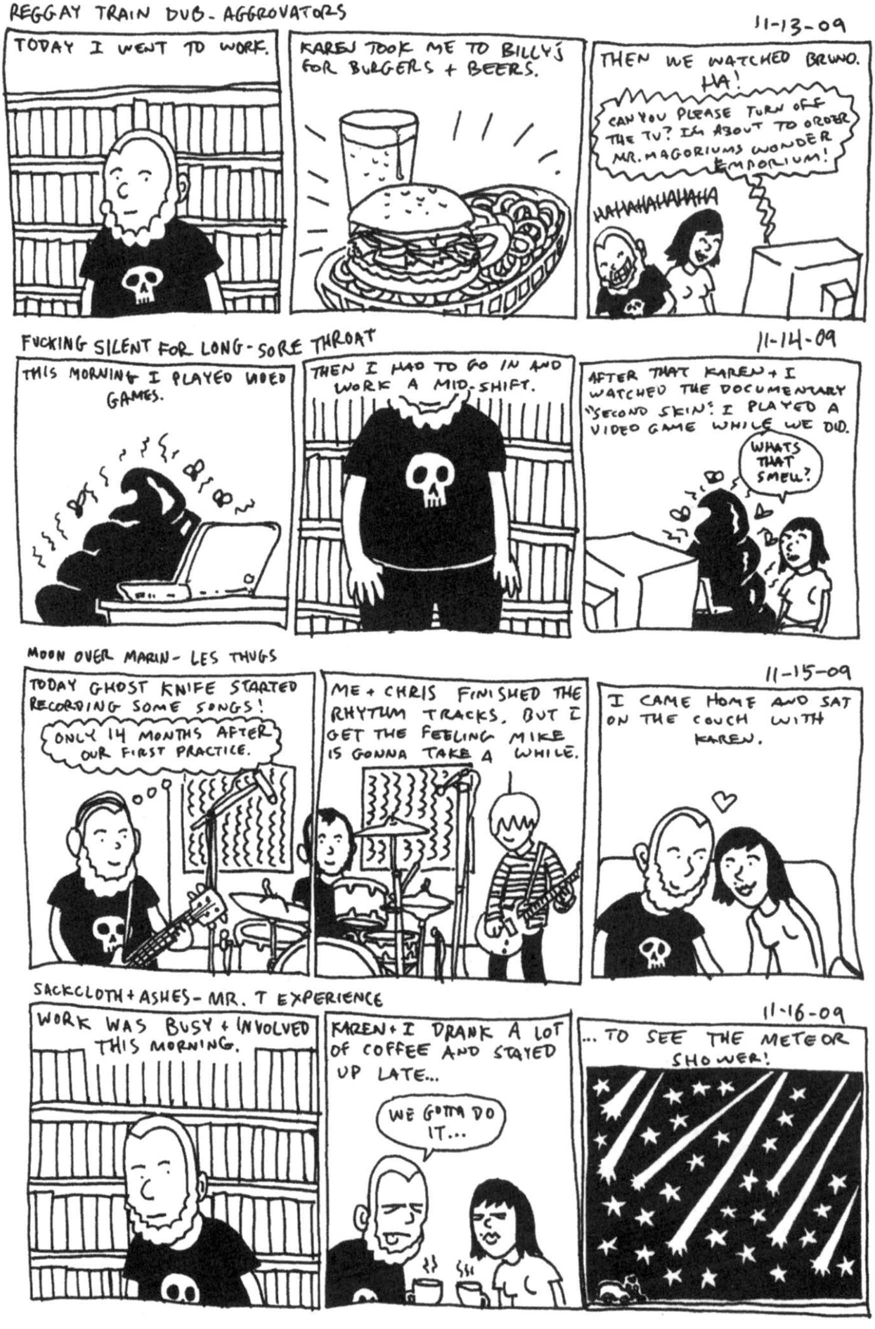
REGGAY TRAIN DUB - AGGROVATORS
11-13-09
TODAY I WENT TO WORK.
KAREN TOOK ME TO BILLY'S FOR BURGERS + BEERS.
THEN WE WATCHED BRUNO.
HA!
CAN YOU PLEASE TURN OFF THE TV? I'M ABOUT TO ORDER MR. MAGORIUMS WONDER EMPORIUM!
HAHAHAHAHAHA
FUCKING SILENT FOR LONG - SORE THROAT
11-14-09
THIS MORNING I PLAYED VIDEO GAMES.
THEN I HAD TO GO IN AND WORK A MID-SHIFT.
AFTER THAT KAREN + I WATCHED THE DOCUMENTARY "SECOND SKIN". I PLAYED A VIDEO GAME WHILE WE DID.
WHATS THAT SMELL?
MOON OVER MARIN - LES THUGS
11-15-09
TODAY GHOST KNIFE STARTED RECORDING SOME SONGS!
ONLY 14 MONTHS AFTER OUR FIRST PRACTICE.
ME + CHRIS FINISHED THE RHYTHM TRACKS, BUT I GET THE FEELING MIKE IS GONNA TAKE A WHILE.
I CAME HOME AND SAT ON THE COUCH WITH KAREN.
SACKCLOTH + ASHES - MR. T EXPERIENCE
11-16-09
WORK WAS BUSY + INVOLVED THIS MORNING.
KAREN + I DRANK A LOT OF COFFEE AND STAYED UP LATE...
WE GOTTA DO IT...
... TO SEE THE METEOR SHOWER!

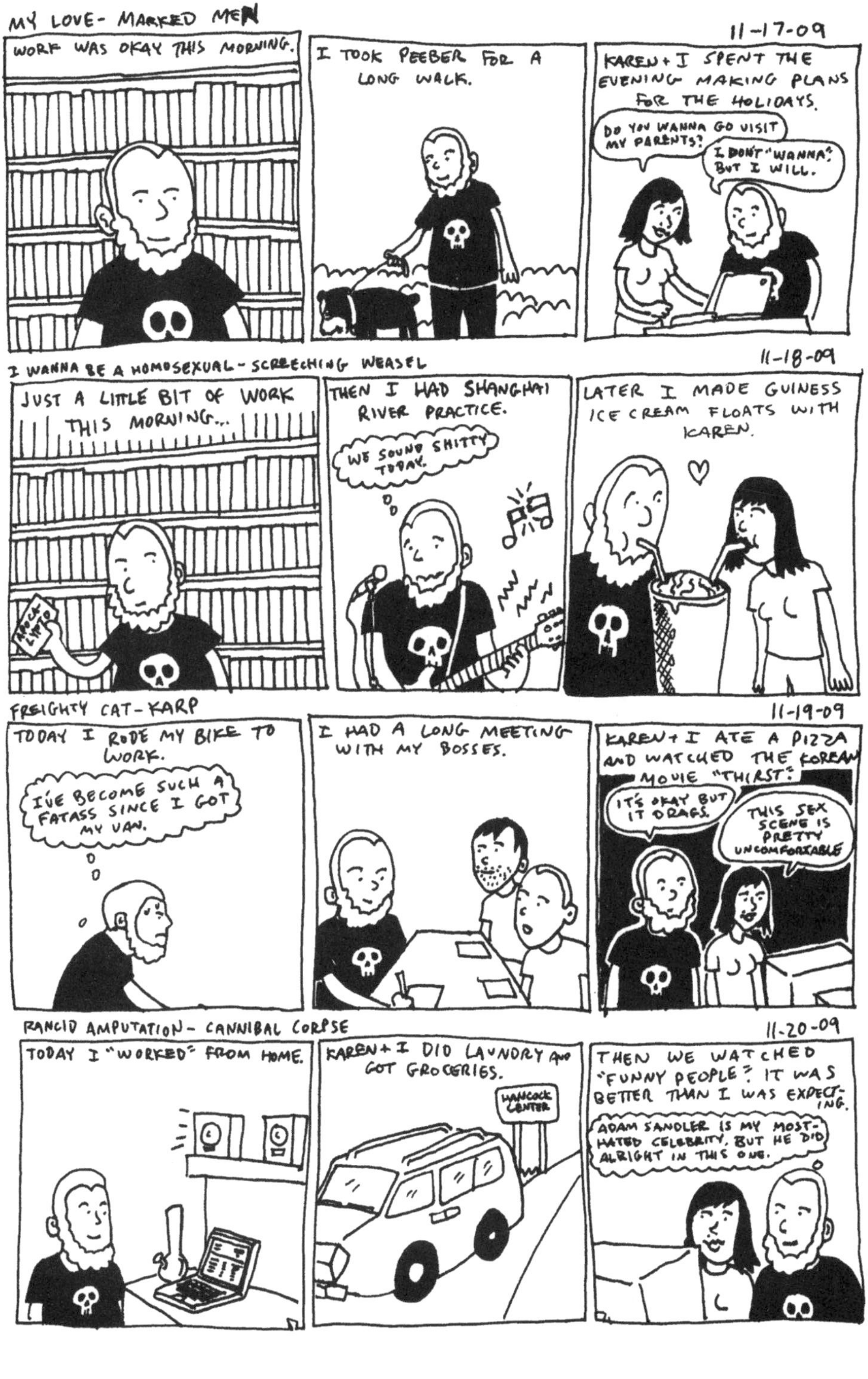
MY LOVE - MARKED MEN
11-17-09
WORK WAS OKAY THIS MORNING.
I TOOK PEEBER FOR A LONG WALK.
KAREN + I SPENT THE EVENING MAKING PLANS FOR THE HOLIDAYS.
DO YOU WANNA GO VISIT MY PARENTS?
I DON'T "WANNA" BUT I WILL.
I WANNA BE A HOMOSEXUAL - SCREECHING WEASEL
11-18-09
JUST A LITTLE BIT OF WORK THIS MORNING...
APOCALYPTO
THEN I HAD SHANGHAI RIVER PRACTICE.
WE SOUND SHITTY TODAY.
LATER I MADE GUINESS ICE CREAM FLOATS WITH KAREN.
FREIGHTY CAT - KARP
11-19-09
TODAY I RODE MY BIKE TO WORK.
I'VE BECOME SUCH A FATASS SINCE I GOT MY VAN.
I HAD A LONG MEETING WITH MY BOSSES.
KAREN + I ATE A PIZZA AND WATCHED THE KOREAN MOVIE "THIRST".
IT'S OKAY BUT IT DRAGS.
THIS SEX SCENE IS PRETTY UNCOMFORTABLE
RANCID AMPUTATION - CANNIBAL CORPSE
11-20-09
TODAY I "WORKED" FROM HOME.
KAREN + I DID LAUNDRY AND GOT GROCERIES.
HANCOCK CENTER
THEN WE WATCHED "FUNNY PEOPLE". IT WAS BETTER THAN I WAS EXPECTING.
ADAM SANDLER IS MY MOST-HATED CELEBRITY, BUT HE DID ALRIGHT IN THIS ONE.

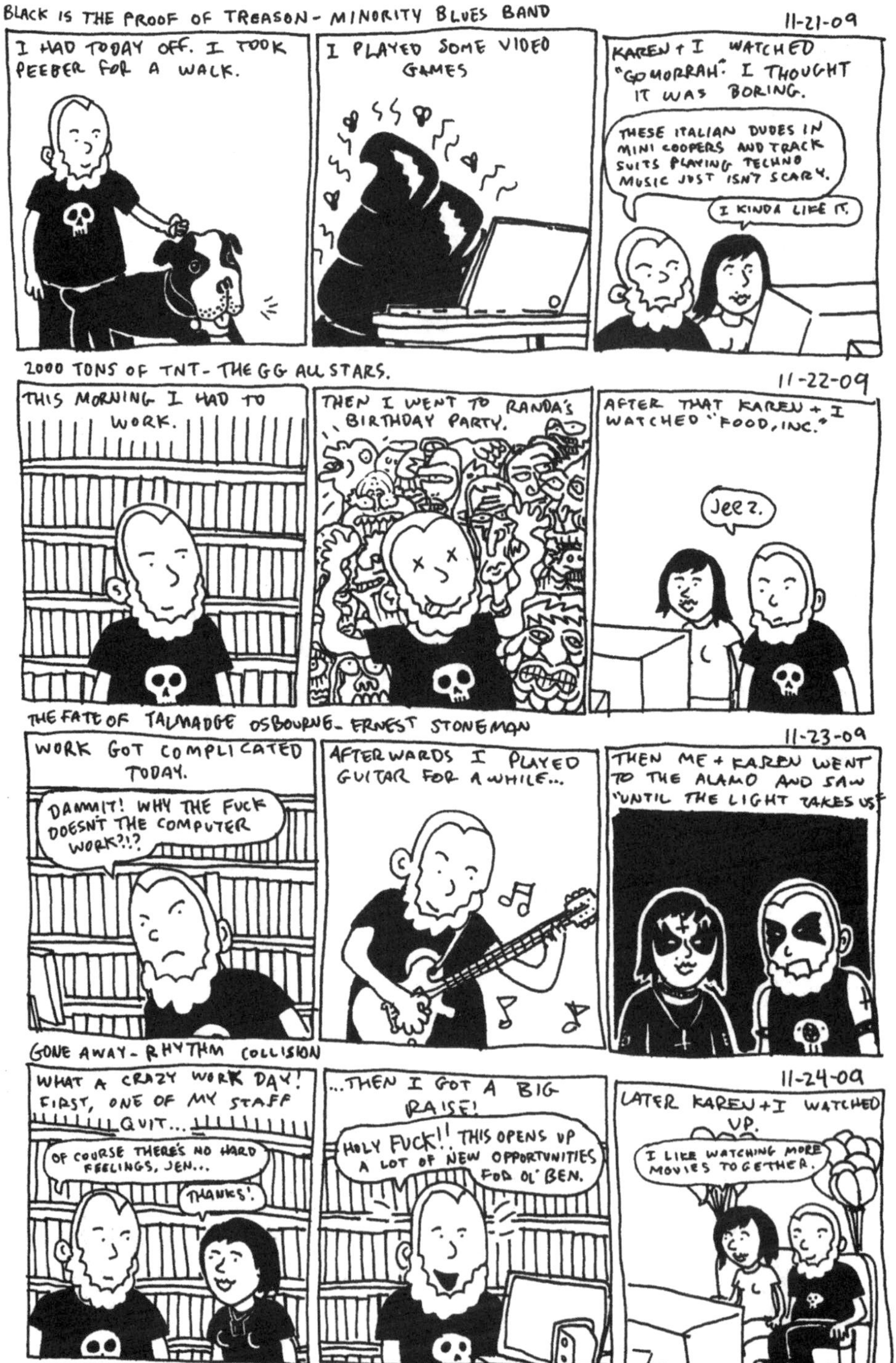
BLACK IS THE PROOF OF TREASON - MINORITY BLUES BAND
11-21-09
I HAD TODAY OFF. I TOOK PEEBER FOR A WALK.
I PLAYED SOME VIDEO GAMES
KAREN + I WATCHED "GOMORRAH." I THOUGHT IT WAS BORING.
THESE ITALIAN DUDES IN MINI COOPERS AND TRACK SUITS PLAYING TECHNO MUSIC JUST ISN'T SCARY.
I KINDA LIKE IT.
2000 TONS OF TNT - THE GG ALLSTARS.
11-22-09
THIS MORNING I HAD TO WORK.
THEN I WENT TO RANDA'S BIRTHDAY PARTY.
AFTER THAT KAREN + I WATCHED "FOOD, INC."
Jeez.
THE FATE OF TALMADGE OSBOURNE - ERNEST STONEMAN
11-23-09
WORK GOT COMPLICATED TODAY.
DAMMIT! WHY THE FUCK DOESN'T THE COMPUTER WORK?!?
AFTERWARDS I PLAYED GUITAR FOR A WHILE...
THEN ME + KAREN WENT TO THE ALAMO AND SAW "UNTIL THE LIGHT TAKES US"
GONE AWAY - RHYTHM COLLISION
11-24-09
WHAT A CRAZY WORK DAY! FIRST, ONE OF MY STAFF QUIT...
OF COURSE THERE'S NO HARD FEELINGS, JEN...
THANKS!
...THEN I GOT A BIG RAISE!
HOLY FUCK!! THIS OPENS UP A LOT OF NEW OPPORTUNITIES FOR OL' BEN.
LATER KAREN + I WATCHED UP.
I LIKE WATCHING MORE MOVIES TOGETHER.

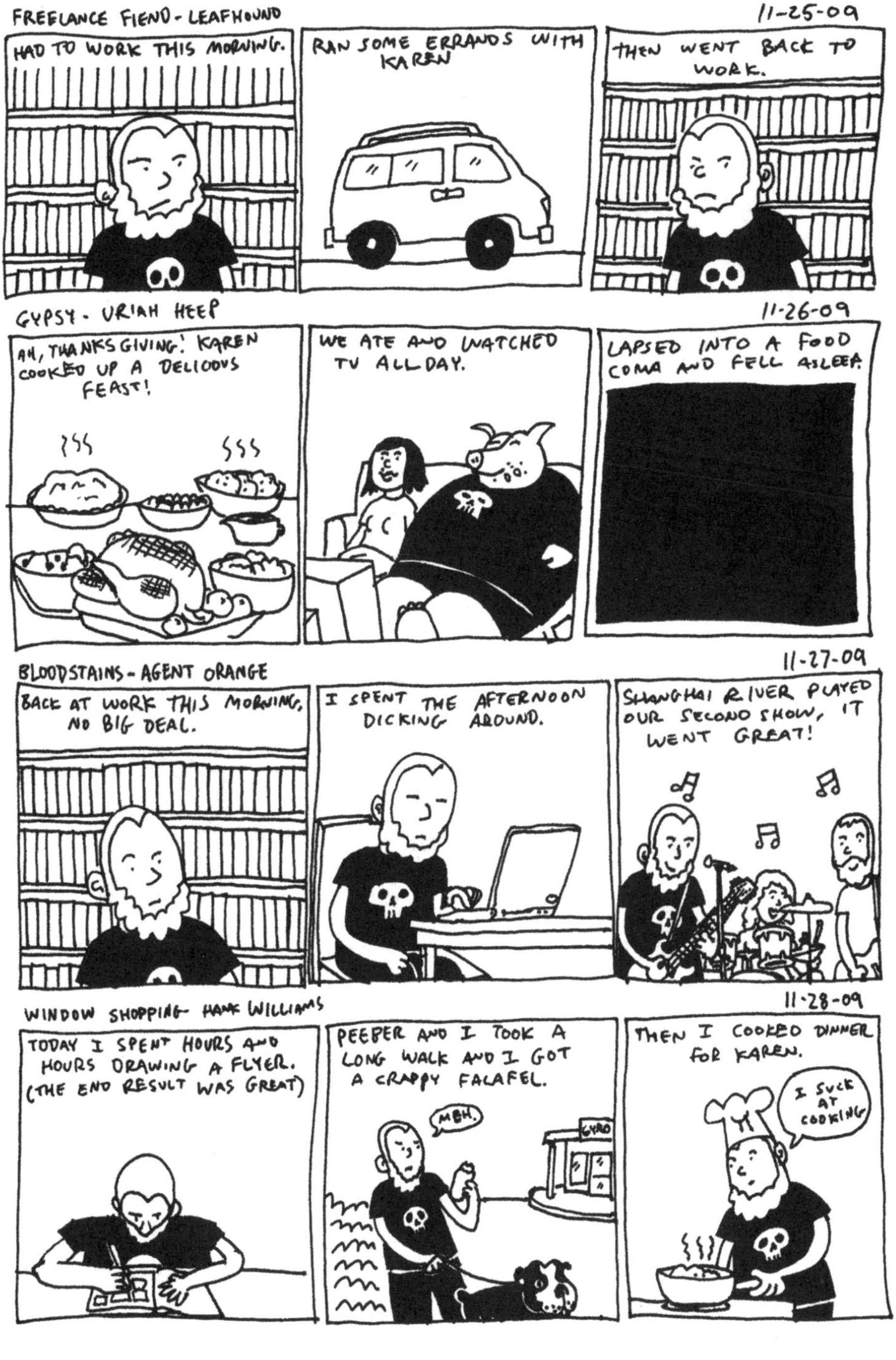
FREELANCE FIEND - LEAFHOUND
11-25-09
HAD TO WORK THIS MORNING.
RAN SOME ERRANDS WITH KAREN
THEN WENT BACK TO WORK.
GYPSY - URIAH HEEP
11-26-09
AH, THANKSGIVING! KAREN COOKED UP A DELICIOUS FEAST!
WE ATE AND WATCHED TV ALL DAY.
LAPSED INTO A FOOD COMA AND FELL ASLEEP.
BLOODSTAINS - AGENT ORANGE
11-27-09
BACK AT WORK THIS MORNING, NO BIG DEAL.
I SPENT THE AFTERNOON DICKING AROUND.
SHANGHAI RIVER PLAYED OUR SECOND SHOW, IT WENT GREAT!
WINDOW SHOPPING - HANK WILLIAMS
11-28-09
TODAY I SPENT HOURS AND HOURS DRAWING A FLYER. (THE END RESULT WAS GREAT)
PEEPER AND I TOOK A LONG WALK AND I GOT A CRAPPY FALAFEL.
MEH.
GYRO
THEN I COOKED DINNER FOR KAREN.
I SUCK AT COOKING

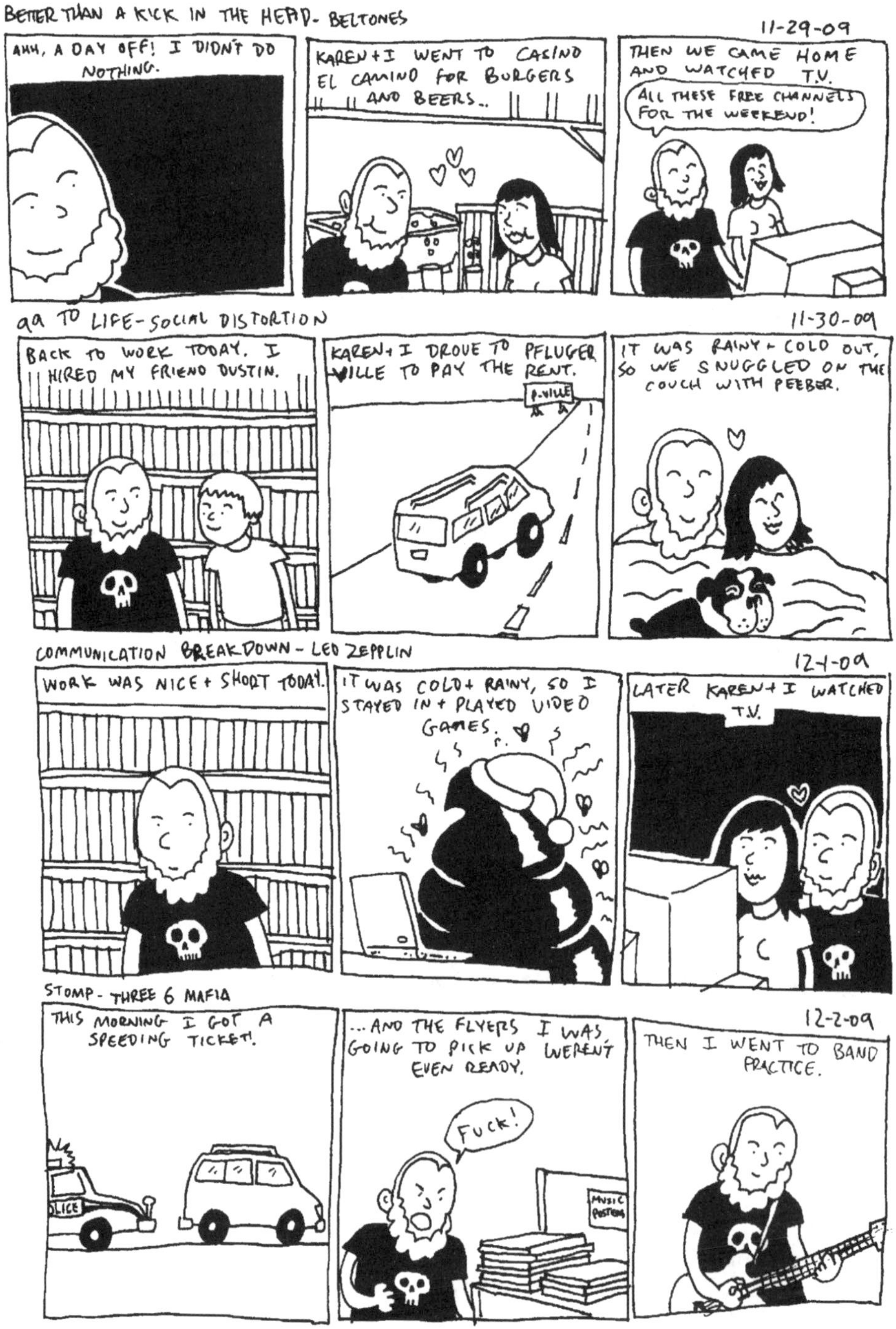
BETTER THAN A KICK IN THE HEAD - BELTONES
11-29-09
AHH, A DAY OFF! I DIDN'T DO NOTHING.
KAREN + I WENT TO CASINO EL CAMINO FOR BURGERS AND BEERS..
THEN WE CAME HOME AND WATCHED T.V.
ALL THESE FREE CHANNELS FOR THE WEEKEND!
99 TO LIFE - SOCIAL DISTORTION
11-30-09
BACK TO WORK TODAY. I HIRED MY FRIEND DUSTIN.
KAREN + I DROVE TO PFLUGERVILLE TO PAY THE RENT.
P-VILLE
IT WAS RAINY + COLD OUT, SO WE SNUGGLED ON THE COUCH WITH PEEBER.
COMMUNICATION BREAKDOWN - LED ZEPPLIN
12-1-09
WORK WAS NICE + SHORT TODAY.
IT WAS COLD + RAINY, SO I STAYED IN + PLAYED VIDEO GAMES.
LATER KAREN + I WATCHED T.V.
STOMP - THREE 6 MAFIA
12-2-09
THIS MORNING I GOT A SPEEDING TICKET!
...AND THE FLYERS I WAS GOING TO PICK UP WEREN'T EVEN READY.
FUCK!
MUSIC POSTERS
THEN I WENT TO BAND PRACTICE.

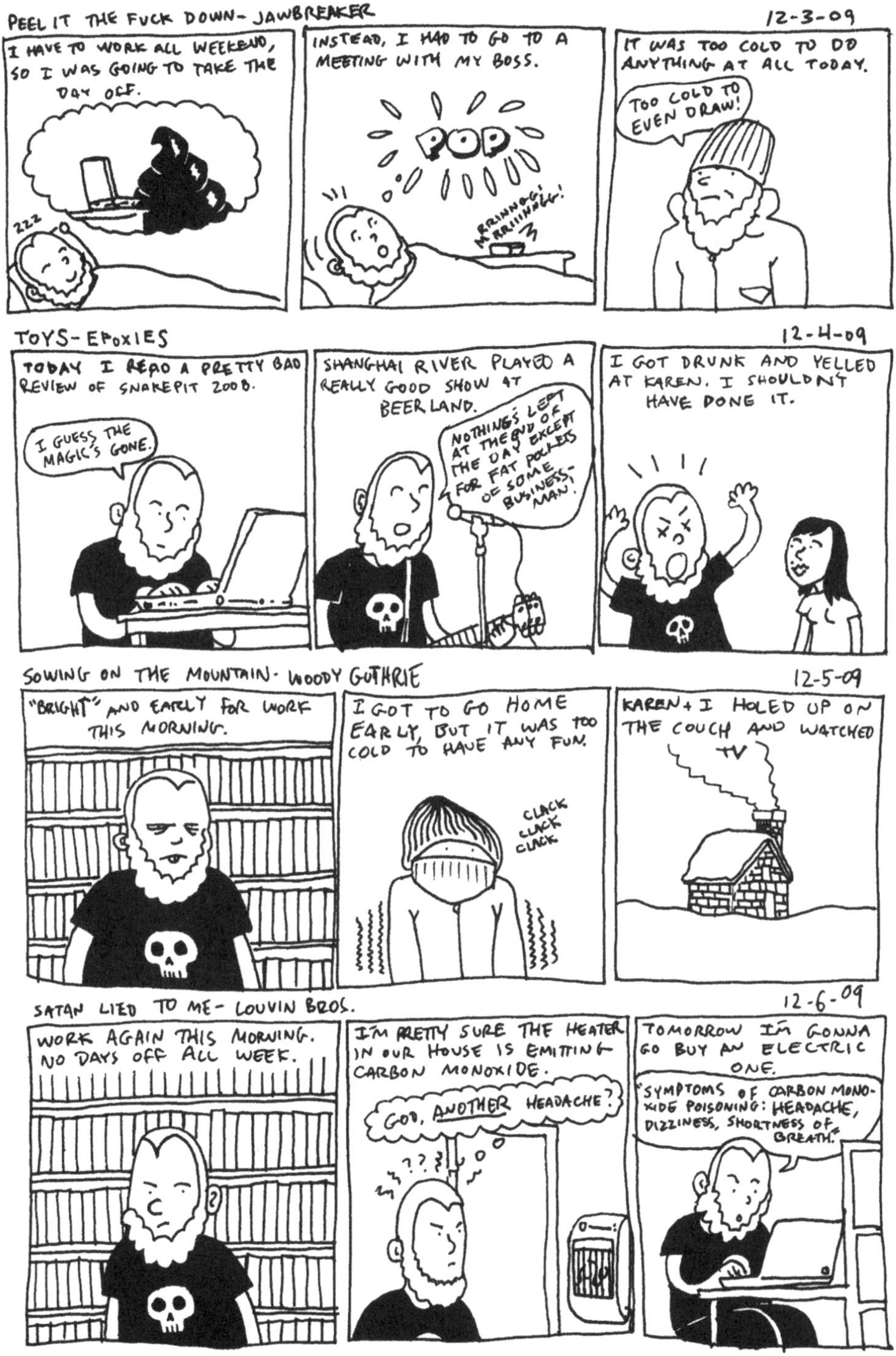
PEEL IT THE FUCK DOWN- JAWBREAKER
12-3-09
I HAVE TO WORK ALL WEEKEND, SO I WAS GOING TO TAKE THE DAY OFF.
ZZZ
INSTEAD, I HAD TO GO TO A MEETING WITH MY BOSS.
POP
RRINNGG! MRRIINNGG!
IT WAS TOO COLD TO DO ANYTHING AT ALL TODAY.
TOO COLD TO EVEN DRAW!
TOYS- EPOXIES
12-4-09
TODAY I READ A PRETTY BAD REVIEW OF SNAKEPIT 2008.
I GUESS THE MAGIC'S GONE.
SHANGHAI RIVER PLAYED A REALLY GOOD SHOW AT BEER LAND.
NOTHING'S LEFT AT THE END OF THE DAY EXCEPT FOR FAT POCKETS OF SOME BUSINESS-MAN!
I GOT DRUNK AND YELLED AT KAREN. I SHOULDN'T HAVE DONE IT.
SOWING ON THE MOUNTAIN- WOODY GUTHRIE
12-5-09
"BRIGHT" AND EARLY FOR WORK THIS MORNING.
I GOT TO GO HOME EARLY, BUT IT WAS TOO COLD TO HAVE ANY FUN.
CLACK CLACK CLACK
KAREN + I HOLED UP ON THE COUCH AND WATCHED TV
SATAN LIED TO ME- LOUVIN BROS.
12-6-09
WORK AGAIN THIS MORNING. NO DAYS OFF ALL WEEK.
I'M PRETTY SURE THE HEATER IN OUR HOUSE IS EMITTING CARBON MONOXIDE.
GOD, ANOTHER HEADACHE?
TOMORROW I'M GONNA GO BUY AN ELECTRIC ONE.
"SYMPTOMS OF CARBON MONOXIDE POISONING: HEADACHE, DIZZINESS, SHORTNESS OF BREATH."

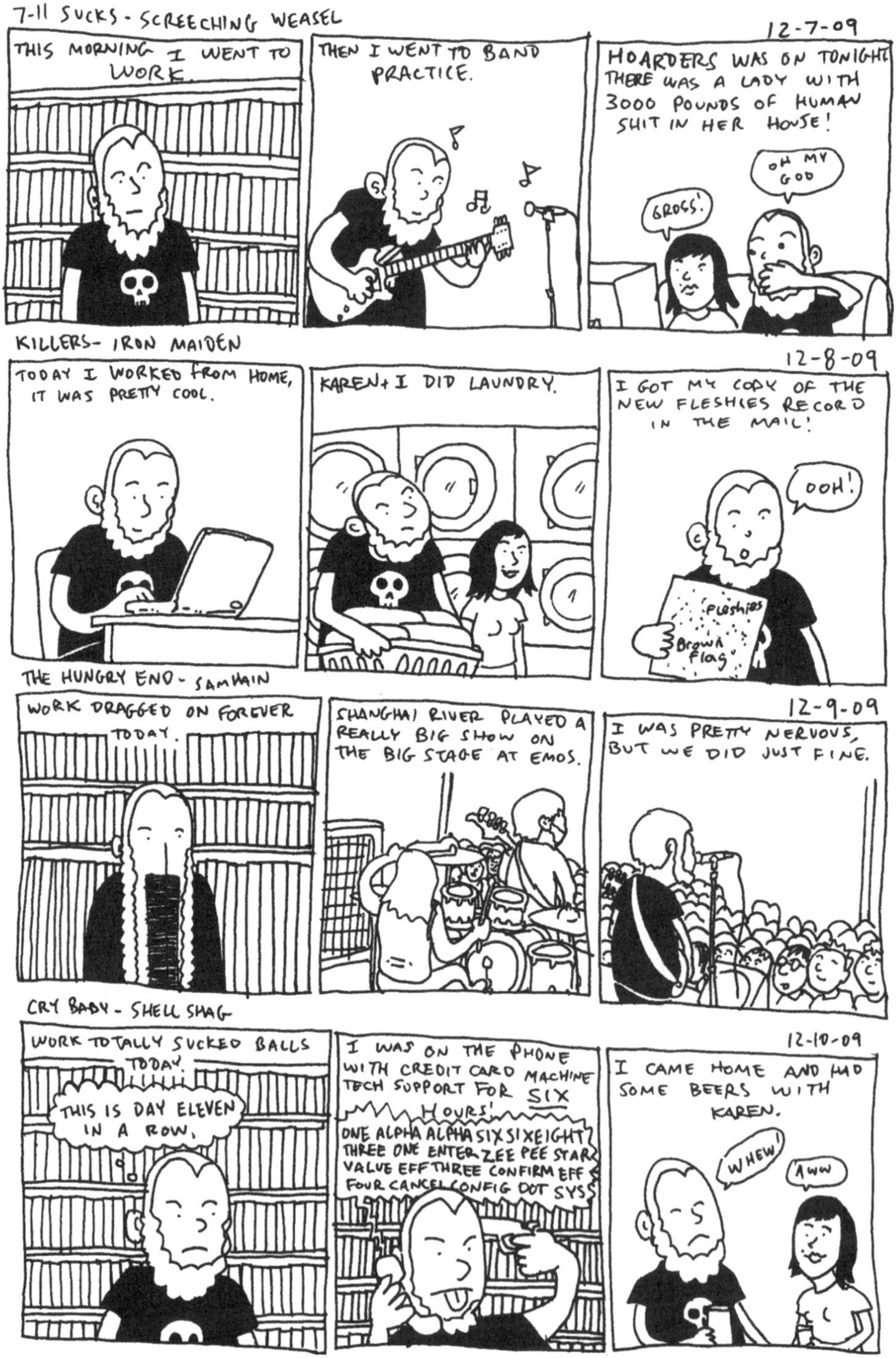
7-11 SUCKS - SCREECHING WEASEL
12-7-09
THIS MORNING I WENT TO WORK.
THEN I WENT TO BAND PRACTICE.
HOARDERS WAS ON TONIGHT. THERE WAS A LADY WITH 3000 POUNDS OF HUMAN SHIT IN HER HOUSE!
GROSS!
OH MY GOD
KILLERS - IRON MAIDEN
12-8-09
TODAY I WORKED FROM HOME, IT WAS PRETTY COOL.
KAREN + I DID LAUNDRY.
I GOT MY COPY OF THE NEW FLESHIES RECORD IN THE MAIL!
OOH!
Fleshies
Brown Flag
THE HUNGRY END - SAMHAIN
12-9-09
WORK DRAGGED ON FOREVER TODAY.
SHANGHAI RIVER PLAYED A REALLY BIG SHOW ON THE BIG STAGE AT EMOS.
I WAS PRETTY NERVOUS, BUT WE DID JUST FINE.
CRY BABY - SHELL SHAG
12-10-09
WORK TOTALLY SUCKED BALLS TODAY.
THIS IS DAY ELEVEN IN A ROW.
I WAS ON THE PHONE WITH CREDIT CARD MACHINE TECH SUPPORT FOR SIX HOURS!
ONE ALPHA ALPHA SIX SIX EIGHT THREE ONE ENTER ZEE PEE STAR VALUE EFF THREE CONFIRM EFF FOUR CANCEL CONFIG DOT SYS
I CAME HOME AND HAD SOME BEERS WITH KAREN.
WHEW!
AWW

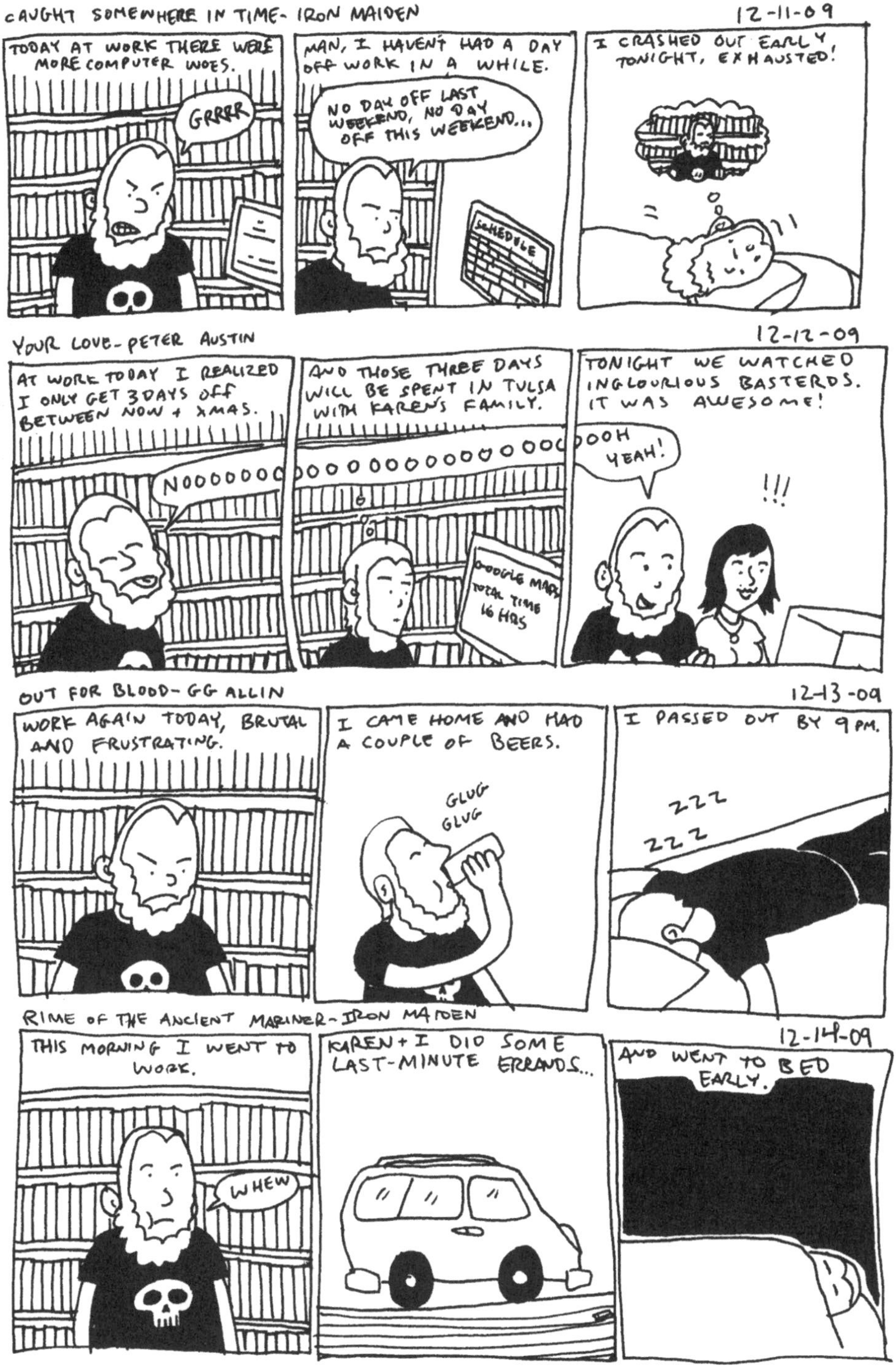
CAUGHT SOMEWHERE IN TIME- IRON MAIDEN
12-11-09
TODAY AT WORK THERE WERE MORE COMPUTER WOES.
GRRRR
MAN, I HAVEN'T HAD A DAY OFF WORK IN A WHILE.
NO DAY OFF LAST WEEKEND, NO DAY OFF THIS WEEKEND...
SCHEDULE
I CRASHED OUT EARLY TONIGHT, EXHAUSTED!
YOUR LOVE- PETER AUSTIN
12-12-09
AT WORK TODAY I REALIZED I ONLY GET 3 DAYS OFF BETWEEN NOW + XMAS.
NOOOOOOOOOOOOOOOOOOOOOOOO
AND THOSE THREE DAYS WILL BE SPENT IN TULSA WITH KAREN'S FAMILY.
GOOGLE MAPS TOTAL TIME 16 HRS
TONIGHT WE WATCHED INGLOURIOUS BASTERDS. IT WAS AWESOME!
OOOH YEAH!
!!!
OUT FOR BLOOD- GG ALLIN
12-13-09
WORK AGAIN TODAY, BRUTAL AND FRUSTRATING.
I CAME HOME AND HAD A COUPLE OF BEERS.
GLUG GLUG
I PASSED OUT BY 9 PM.
ZZZ ZZZ
RIME OF THE ANCIENT MARINER- IRON MAIDEN
12-14-09
THIS MORNING I WENT TO WORK.
WHEW
KAREN + I DID SOME LAST-MINUTE ERRANDS...
AND WENT TO BED EARLY.

MISTY MOUNTAIN ~~HOP~~ - SILVER APPLES

12-15-09

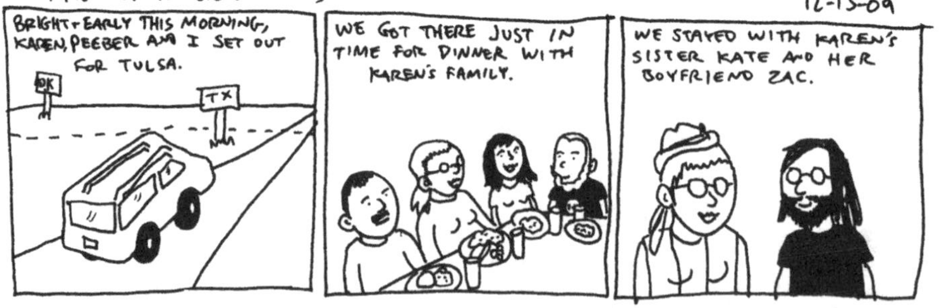

BRIGHT + EARLY THIS MORNING, KAREN, PEEBER AND I SET OUT FOR TULSA.
OK
TX
WE GOT THERE JUST IN TIME FOR DINNER WITH KAREN'S FAMILY.
WE STAYED WITH KAREN'S SISTER KATE AND HER BOYFRIEND ZAC.

FLIPOUT - CRIME

12-16-09

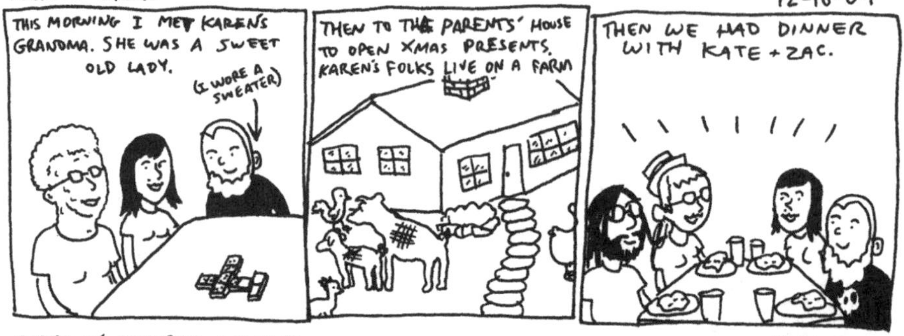

THIS MORNING I MET KAREN'S GRANDMA. SHE WAS A SWEET OLD LADY.
(I WORE A SWEATER)
THEN TO THE PARENTS' HOUSE TO OPEN XMAS PRESENTS. KAREN'S FOLKS LIVE ON A FARM
THEN WE HAD DINNER WITH KATE + ZAC.

BABY LET'S PLAY GOD - BIG BOYS

12-17-09

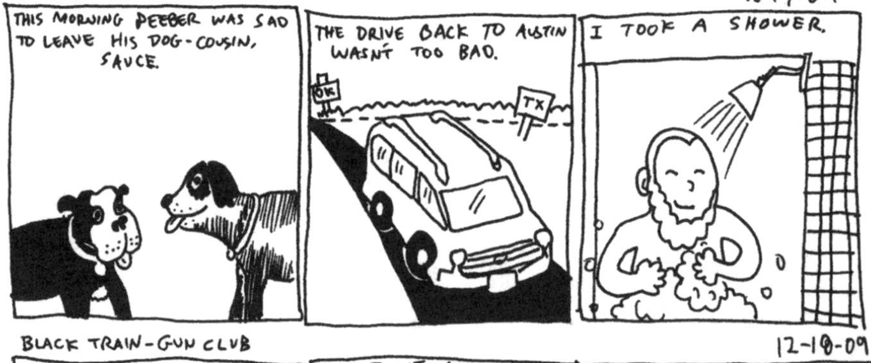

THIS MORNING PEEBER WAS SAD TO LEAVE HIS DOG-COUSIN, SAUCE.
THE DRIVE BACK TO AUSTIN WASN'T TOO BAD.
OK
TX
I TOOK A SHOWER.

BLACK TRAIN - GUN CLUB

12-18-09

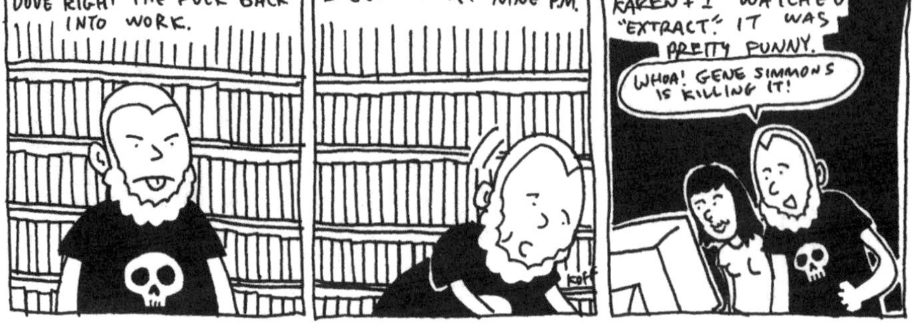

DOVE RIGHT THE FUCK BACK INTO WORK.
I GOT OUT AT NINE P.M.
KAREN + I WATCHED "EXTRACT." IT WAS PRETTY FUNNY.
WHOA! GENE SIMMONS IS KILLING IT!
KOFF

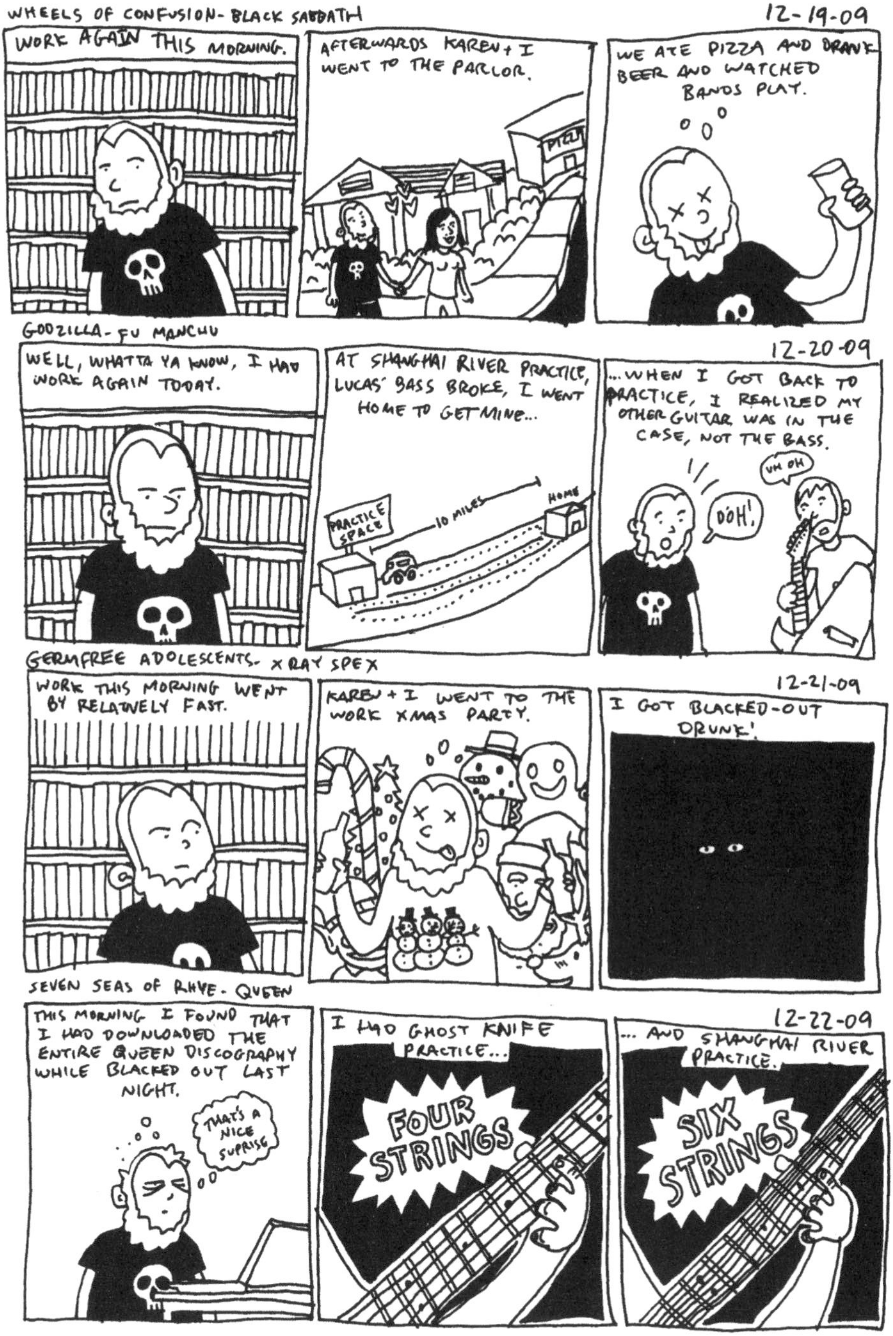
WHEELS OF CONFUSION- BLACK SABBATH
12-19-09
WORK AGAIN THIS MORNING.
AFTERWARDS KAREN + I WENT TO THE PARLOR.
WE ATE PIZZA AND DRANK BEER AND WATCHED BANDS PLAY.
GODZILLA- FU MANCHU
12-20-09
WELL, WHATTA YA KNOW, I HAD WORK AGAIN TODAY.
AT SHANGHAI RIVER PRACTICE, LUCAS' BASS BROKE, I WENT HOME TO GET MINE...
PRACTICE SPACE
10 MILES
HOME
...WHEN I GOT BACK TO PRACTICE, I REALIZED MY OTHER GUITAR WAS IN THE CASE, NOT THE BASS.
UH OH
DOH!
GERMFREE ADOLESCENTS- X RAY SPEX
12-21-09
WORK THIS MORNING WENT BY RELATIVELY FAST.
KAREN + I WENT TO THE WORK XMAS PARTY.
I GOT BLACKED-OUT DRUNK!
SEVEN SEAS OF RHYE- QUEEN
12-22-09
THIS MORNING I FOUND THAT I HAD DOWNLOADED THE ENTIRE QUEEN DISCOGRAPHY WHILE BLACKED OUT LAST NIGHT.
THAT'S A NICE SUPRISE
I HAD GHOST KNIFE PRACTICE...
FOUR STRINGS
... AND SHANGHAI RIVER PRACTICE.
SIX STRINGS

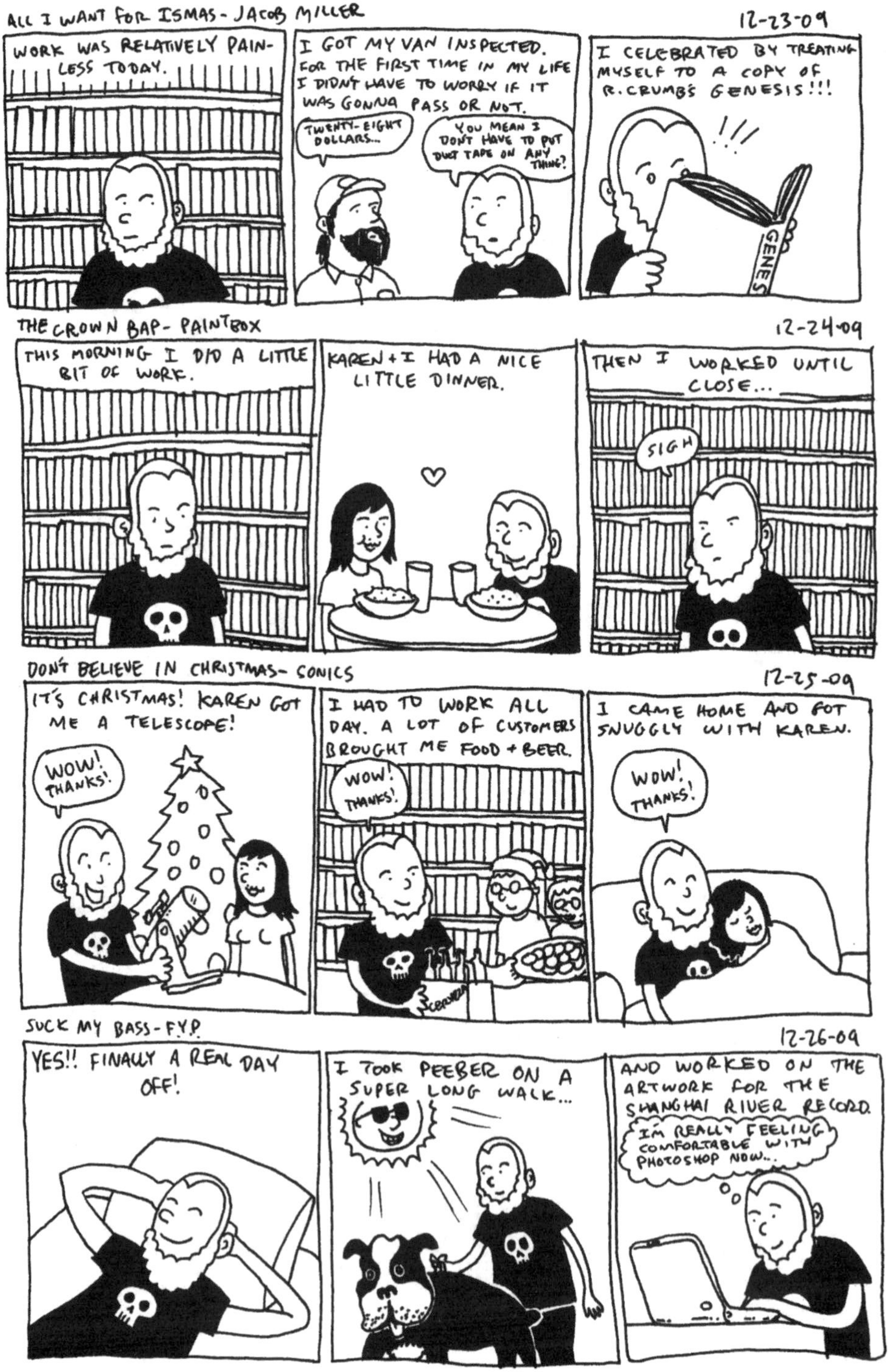
ALL I WANT FOR XMAS - JACOB MILLER
12-23-09
WORK WAS RELATIVELY PAINLESS TODAY.
I GOT MY VAN INSPECTED. FOR THE FIRST TIME IN MY LIFE I DIDN'T HAVE TO WORRY IF IT WAS GONNA PASS OR NOT.
TWENTY-EIGHT DOLLARS...
YOU MEAN I DON'T HAVE TO PUT DUCT TAPE ON ANYTHING?
I CELEBRATED BY TREATING MYSELF TO A COPY OF R. CRUMB'S GENESIS!!!
GENES
THE CROWN BAR - PAINTBOX
12-24-09
THIS MORNING I DID A LITTLE BIT OF WORK.
KAREN + I HAD A NICE LITTLE DINNER.
THEN I WORKED UNTIL CLOSE...
SIGH
DON'T BELIEVE IN CHRISTMAS - SONICS
12-25-09
IT'S CHRISTMAS! KAREN GOT ME A TELESCOPE!
WOW! THANKS!
I HAD TO WORK ALL DAY. A LOT OF CUSTOMERS BROUGHT ME FOOD + BEER.
WOW! THANKS!
I CAME HOME AND GOT SNUGGLY WITH KAREN.
WOW! THANKS!
SUCK MY BASS - F.Y.P.
12-26-09
YES!! FINALLY A REAL DAY OFF!
I TOOK PEEBER ON A SUPER LONG WALK...
AND WORKED ON THE ARTWORK FOR THE SHANGHAI RIVER RECORD.
I'M REALLY FEELING COMFORTABLE WITH PHOTOSHOP NOW...

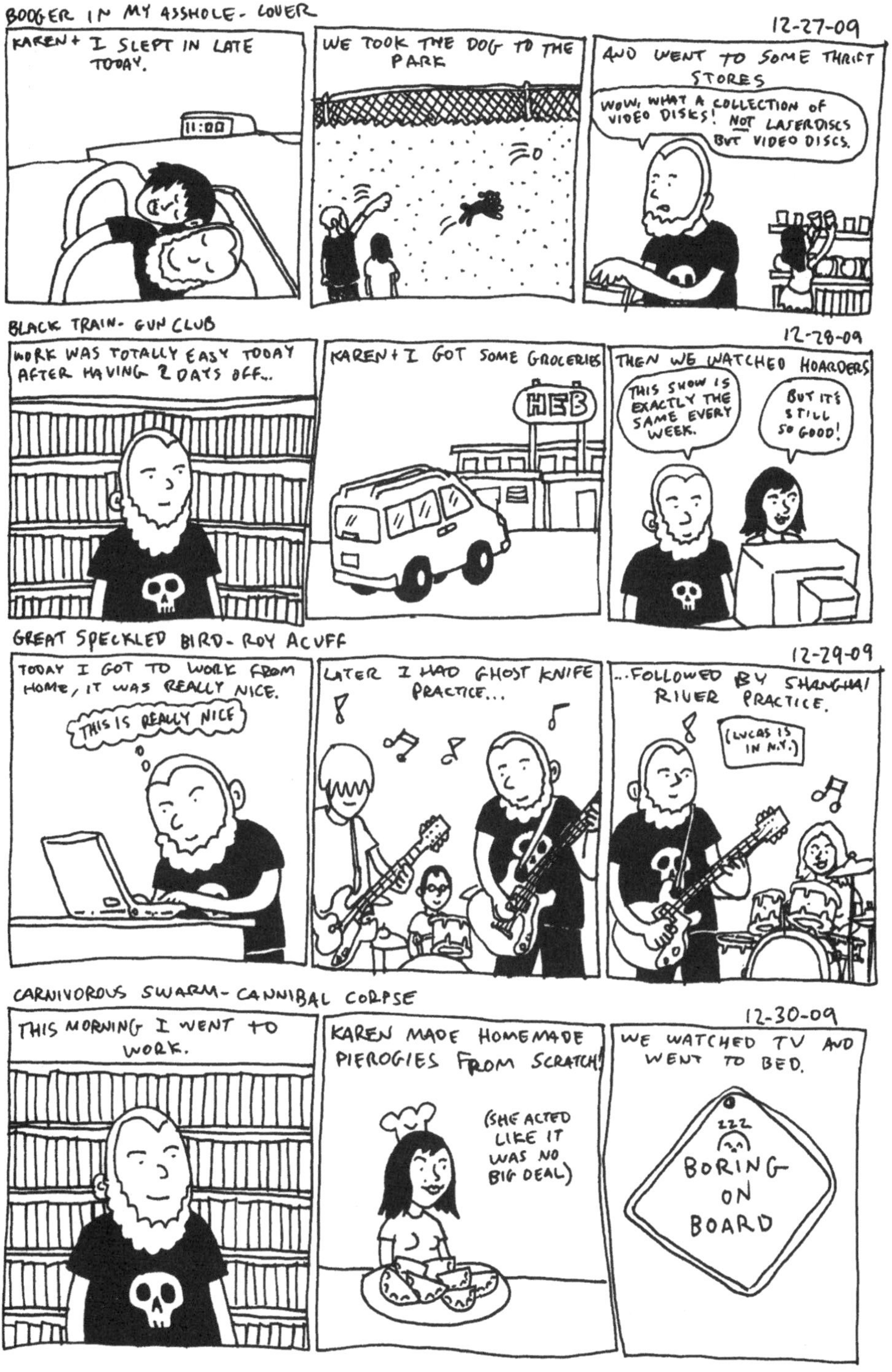
BOOGER IN MY ASSHOLE- LOVER
12-27-09
KAREN + I SLEPT IN LATE TODAY.
11:00
WE TOOK THE DOG TO THE PARK
AND WENT TO SOME THRIFT STORES
WOW, WHAT A COLLECTION OF VIDEO DISKS! NOT LASERDISCS BUT VIDEO DISCS.
BLACK TRAIN- GUN CLUB
12-28-09
WORK WAS TOTALLY EASY TODAY AFTER HAVING 2 DAYS OFF..
KAREN + I GOT SOME GROCERIES
HEB
THEN WE WATCHED HOARDERS
THIS SHOW IS EXACTLY THE SAME EVERY WEEK.
BUT IT'S STILL SO GOOD!
GREAT SPECKLED BIRD- ROY ACUFF
12-29-09
TODAY I GOT TO WORK FROM HOME, IT WAS REALLY NICE.
THIS IS REALLY NICE
LATER I HAD GHOST KNIFE PRACTICE...
...FOLLOWED BY SHANGHAI RIVER PRACTICE.
(LUCAS IS IN N.Y.)
CARNIVOROUS SWARM- CANNIBAL CORPSE
12-30-09
THIS MORNING I WENT TO WORK.
KAREN MADE HOMEMADE PIEROGIES FROM SCRATCH!
(SHE ACTED LIKE IT WAS NO BIG DEAL)
WE WATCHED TV AND WENT TO BED.
ZZZ
BORING ON BOARD

THEY'LL NEVER KEEP US DOWN - HAZEL DICKENS

12-31-09

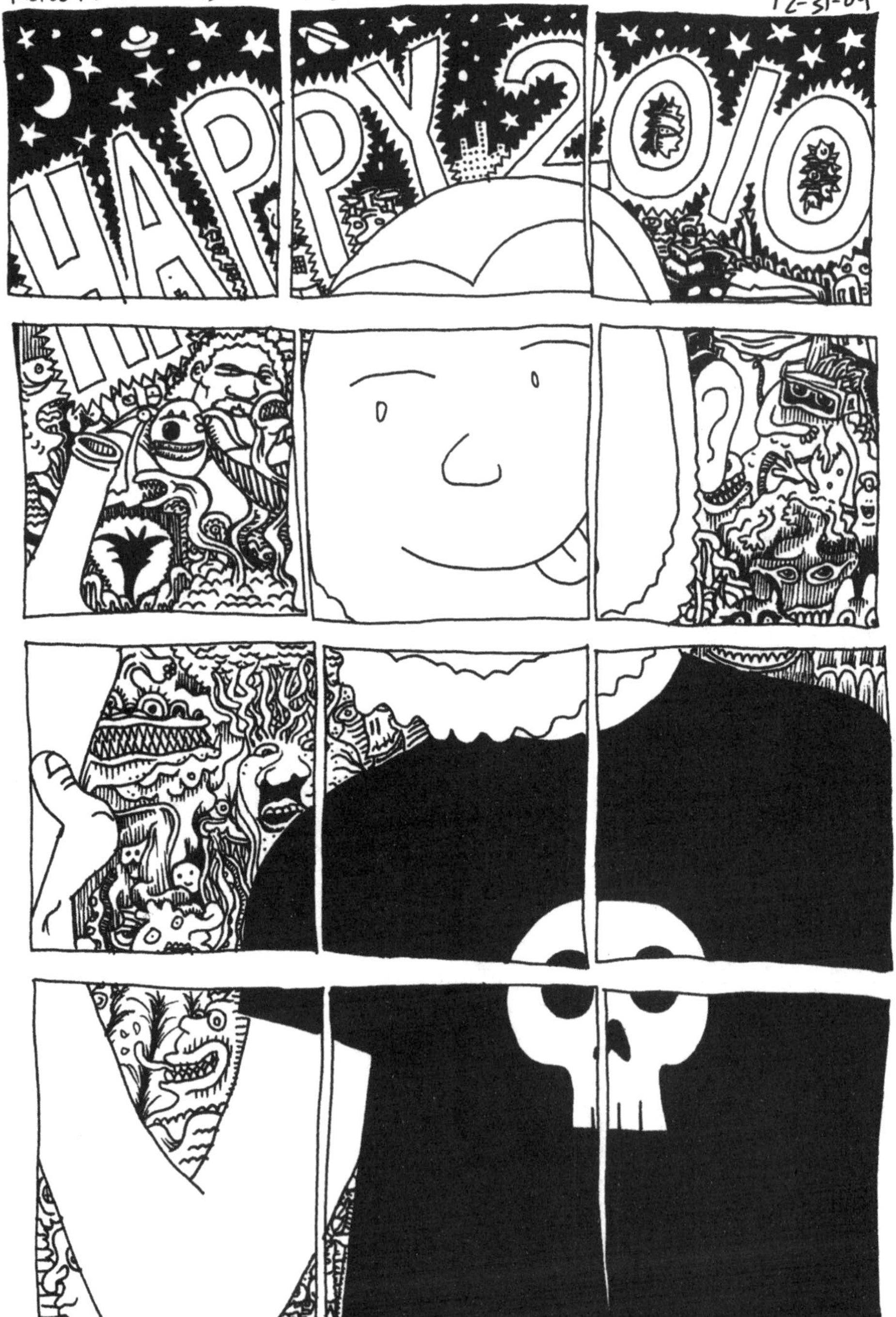
HAPPY 2010

THANKS LIST: J.T.+KAREN YOST AT BIRDCAGE BOTTOM BOOKS, JOE+ MICROCOSM PUBLISHING, TOD+COREY AT YOUNG AMERICAN COMICS (R.I.P.), KAREN+PEEBER FOR LOVE AND SUPPORT, CHRIS+MIKE, LUCAS+AMBER, DAVE DIDONATO, ADAM PASION, KIYOSHI NAKAZAWA, TODD TAYLOR+RAZORCAKE, P.J. FANCHER, SWEET PETE, TIMMY HEFNER, MAX+BEERLAND, JUG +SOUND ON SOUND (R.I.P.), SPOT+TRAILER SPACE, AUSTIN BOOKS, END OF AN EAR, MONKEYWRENCH BOOKS, AND ALL OF MY AWESOME FRIENDS AND FANS ALL OVER THE WORLD! OH, AND OF COURSE, MY MOM! BANDS THAT RULE: SEX ADVICE, WILD AMER- ICA, CRUDDY, THE CASSINGLES, SERIOUS TRACERS, SHELLSHAG, THIS BIKE IS A PIPE BOMB, DUDE JAMS, RATS+BIRDS, SHANG-A-LANG, COME AND TAKE IT, FLESHIES, THE BROKEDOWNS, TOO MANY DAVES, SHARK PANTS, THE ARRIVALS, BAD SPORTS, CAPITALIST KIDS, THE YOUNG, THE ANCHOR, GOD EQUALS GENOCIDE, THE ALTARS, STALLONE, THE LADIES, SEVENTEEN AGAIN. THERE'S A LOT MORE BUT I CAN'T THINK OF THEM RIGHT NOW.

DEDICATED TO THE MEMORY OF LUX INTERIOR.

birdcage bottom
books

Order more comics at www.BirdcageBottomBooks.com